DATE DUE

BRODART   Cat. No. 23-221

Hungarian

University of Washington Press Seattle & London

UBC Press Vancouver

Essays on
Ethnicity,
Identity, and
Culture

Rhapsodies

Richard Teleky

This book is

published with

the assistance of a

grant from the

Donald R. Ellegood

Endowment.

University of Washington Press, P.O. Box 50096,
Seattle, WA 98145
Published simultaneously in Canada by UBC Press,
University of British Columbia, 6344 Memorial Road,
Vancouver, B.C. v6t 1z2

The Library of Congress and the Canadian Cataloging
in Publication Data can be found at the end of the book.

The paper used in this publication meets the minimum
requirements of American National Standard for Information
Sciences—Permanence of Paper for Printed Library
Materials, ANSI z39.48-1984.

Cover and chapter-opening illustration: *Orpheus* by Károly
Ferenczy. The subject of the painting plays a violin—
commonly associated with Hungary—rather than the more
traditional lyre. Courtesy Hungarian National Gallery/Magyar
Nemzeti Galéria

IN MEMORIAM *Mari Poczik Takacs*

Contents

Illustrations

André Kertész, "Underwater Swimmer," 1917 *17*

Courtesy: Jane Corkin Gallery, Toronto, Canada

André Kertész, "Boy Sleeping Over Daily Newspaper in a Coffee Shop," Budapest, 1912 *19*

Courtesy: Jane Corkin Gallery, Toronto, Canada

André Kertész, "Blind Violinist, Abony," 1921 *21*

Courtesy: Jane Corkin Gallery, Toronto, Canada

André Kertész, "Buda (night)," 1914 *23*

Courtesy: Jane Corkin Gallery, Toronto, Canada

André Kertész, "Esztergom (man sweeping)," 1917 *25*

Courtesy: Jane Corkin Gallery, Toronto, Canada

André Kertész, "My Mother's Hands," 1919 *29*

Courtesy: Jane Corkin Gallery, Toronto, Canada

Preface

This is not a book about music, unless you think, as I do, that every language has its own unique music, just as it has its own ways of reasoning, seeing, and being. Yet I've used the word "rhapsodies" for this collection of essays, in part because North American representations of Hungary and Hungarians run in a pattern of free association that begins with Liszt's Hungarian Rhapsodies, and maybe a few by Brahms, moves along from paprika to goulash, and ends with the Gabor sisters. Some people might throw in Béla Bartók, or Georg Lukács, but we're now in specialized company — and still not far away from goulash.

In its original sense, as the *Oxford English Dictionary* explains, a rhapsody was an epic poem, or part of one, suitable for recitation at a single sitting. This usage, dating back to 1542, is accompanied by several related meanings, including "a literary work consisting of miscellaneous or disconnected pieces" and "an exalted or exaggeratedly enthusiastic expression of sentiment or feeling." But "rhapsody," at least, is a straightforward term compared to "Hungarian," and I plan no attempt at a systematic definition or analysis of that loaded word. Instead, this collection of essays about things and people and places that share the attribute of Hungarianness is a record of one person's attempt at understanding.

This book, then, is a combination of essay, lament, celebration, and scholarship that takes its shape from my own exploration of a range of subjects, beginning with my studies (and Edmund Wilson's) of the Hungarian language and ending with a discussion of what I have come to see as the arbitrariness of ethnicity. Along the way, I look at various facets of Hungarian immigrant culture in North America, and representations of Hungarians in the "new world," before turning to a discussion of some Hungarian writers (including my attempts at teaching several of them in my university classes) and recounting — almost inevitably — my first trip to Hungary, and what I found there.

Similar questions are at the core of each essay: how is identity shaped? what part does ethnicity play in it? when do identity and ethnicity forge links with culture? The answers are neither direct nor simple. And certain issues arise again and again — from displacement to nostalgia to anti-Semitism — giving my studies a kind of counterpoint structure. Because the subjects here (language, movies, books and bookstores, photographs, an old church and its archives, political change, North America's lack of knowledge about Central Europe) are important to me, and to the people I know, I think them worth writing about. The people in this book — from dead writers like Dezső Kosztolányi and Gyula Illyés to contemporary Hungarians whose names will be unknown to readers (a private Budapest currency trader, my recently discovered relatives in a small village outside of Győr) — deserve, similarly, their record. Attempting to understand them has provided me with another way of seeing the world. Since the Soviet withdrawal in 1989, Hungary has gained the attention of the West. Yet anyone curious about it should also be interested in the new Hungary's rich old culture, for that is not likely to disappear overnight. Even the most cursory reading of Hungarian history confirms this claim, and by the end of my book I hope that it will have been illuminated. Of course Hungary's immigrants to North America are a part of the story, and my desire to understand the subject I've called Hungarianness extends to them.

While this book touches on several disciplines, such as Hungarian studies, ethnic studies, comparative literature, and popular culture, it is not meant to be a contribution to any single one. My intent is to use approaches associated with a variety of fields to explore a complex of related issues—to be interdisciplinary, in fact. (The essentialist-constructionist debate does not directly concern me here, although I recognize its importance.) Finally, I use various essay forms, from the scholarly article to the personal essay, and even attempt a synthesis of the two, as well as one dictionary-essay that owes its form to Ambrose Bierce and Roland Barthes.

The decline in Hungarian studies in North American universities has intensified since Steven Bela Vardy published his survey "Hungarian Studies at American and Canadian Universities" in 1975 in the *Canadian-American Review of Hungarian Studies* (vol. 2, no. 2). And it will continue to decline unless the third- and fourth-generation children of Hungarian immigrant families begin to learn the language of their forebears—an unlikely prospect, I realize. According to statistics from the 1990 U.S. census, the decade between 1980 and 1990 saw a percentage drop of 17.9 in the number of American residents over the age of five who spoke Hungarian in their homes (180,000 in 1980; 148,000 in 1990). At the same time, the figure for people speaking languages other than English increased 38 percent. While knowledge of a language does not automatically lead to a study of its culture, it might increase the possibility. Certainly the future of Hungarian studies in North America will depend mainly on people who have learned Hungarian as adults, as I did. They will no longer be part of the line of distinguished Hungarian-born scholars who shaped Hungarian studies in North American universities since 1904, when the first Hungarian program was initiated. But I believe they still have important contributions to make.

I would like to thank two colleagues from my Oxford University Press days—Sally Livingston and William Toye—who read the essays in this collection when they were first written and offered invaluable editorial comment. Various anonymous editors and readers have also made comments before many of these essays were published, and I'm grateful for their assistance. At the University of Washington Press, my manuscript received support and care from Michael Duckworth and Julidta Tarver, and meticulous copyediting from Leila Charbonneau. While writing this book I was fortunate to be able to consult the staffs of several university and public libraries, and I want to thank especially Evelyn M. Ward, head of the Literature Department of the Cleveland Public Library. I am also grateful to the Toronto Arts Council for its support of this project.

As well, I want to thank the following people whose interest in Hungarian studies, and special knowledge of various facets of that subject, have been of great help, and who have read portions of my manuscript at different times in its evolution: Professors Oliver A. I. Botar, Louis Elteto, Marlene Kadar, and Steven Tötösy de Zepetnek; and Dr. Magda Csécsy Sömjén, the extraordinary linguist who taught me Hungarian over her dining-room table, and to whom I owe a special debt. Daughter of the distinguished Hungarian political writer Imre Csécsy, Magda embodies everything that, intuitively, I hoped to find in the study of a new language. My parents, Louise and Paul Teleky, were eager to help me practice my new Hungarian during visits to their home, and their enthusiasm was much appreciated, as are their many wonderful stories and years of encouragement. Finally, Professors Lee Rainey, Rosemary Sullivan, and James B. M. Schick offered valuable comments about matters that were not related to Hungarian scholarship, as did my good friends (and sometimes critics) Larry Fineberg, Gail Geltner, and Teresa Stratas. The errors and limitations of this book remain my own.

Richard Teleky
October 1996

A Note on Hungarian Names

The use of accents for Hungarian names, particularly the names of Hungarians living outside Hungary, can be problematic. There are four categories: Hungarian names as they appear in Hungary, with accents; the names of Hungarians outside of Hungary who continue to use accents (for example, André Kertész); the names of Hungarians outside the country who drop all diacritical marks (the historians John Lukacs and Stephen Bela Vardy, or Zsa Zsa Gabor); and, most difficult to call, names that sometimes appear with accents and sometimes not (for example, the historian István Deák). I will take my cue from the people themselves. This may account for seeming inconsistencies, but normalizing all names by either adding or dropping all accents would be incorrect.

Hungarian Rhapsodies

Playtime Adult Language Learning, Edmund Wilson, and Me

On difficult days I sometimes tell friends that I'd like to live in a small, clean hut somewhere in Hungary, surrounded by apricot trees. I would tend a few goats and contemplate nature. We laugh. One friend has always wanted to be a bell-ringer in a Tibetan monastery, another would like to herd llamas in Peru.

In the summer of 1960, Edmund Wilson, then sixty-five, decided to learn Hungarian. He was living in an ancestral limestone house in Talcottville, northwest of Utica in upstate New York, where he had spent most summers since the early 1950s. He knew of only one Hungarian in the area, a young woman named Mary Pcolar, who worked in a local pharmacy. She was, he found, literate in Hungarian as well as in English. I learned this from *Upstate: Records and Recollections of Northern New York*, the diary-notebook Wilson kept about his forebears, the house, and his day-to-day life there until 1970. On first reading it a decade and a half ago I was puzzled by Wilson's decision. Since the book begins with an account of his distinguished Yankee family, and the grounds of their home with its old peony beds, his Hungarian plan struck an odd note. Hungarian is the language of my background, although at the time I discovered *Upstate* I could barely speak more than a few words of greeting. Wilson, of course, was well known for his linguistic prowess. But if Hungarian seemed a peculiar choice, the decision to teach oneself a language seemed even odder, the kind of thing people did in books, and a special kind of person at that: someone with world enough and time. Wilson already knew six languages. Why another?

Like most North Americans, I had my first experience of a foreign language in high school. I remember the worn French primer, my name added to the last page under a list of students who had previously used it; study halls where I memorized French conjugations, surprised at my mistakes; those initial, stumbling efforts at pronunciation in a roomful of adolescents all hoping someone else would be called on; and, inevitably, our teachers—always women, usually spinsters—who oversaw this rite.

Miss Emma Campbell was a small, dark woman with thinning black hair everyone thought dyed, and rimless glasses. But she had an intense and animated face, apparently finding a mission in our initiation to the gender differences that made French nouns so peculiar. (Hungarian has no grammatical gender, but that's another story.) One day Miss Campbell entered the room to see a swastika chalked on the blackboard. Crossing to it, her expression resolute, she lifted an eraser. "This has caused enough trouble," she said softly as the graffiti vanished. She then faced the class and began describing an orphanage in France that she visited every summer, a place for children who had lost their parents during the Second World War. That swastika (along with other crimes of history) was transformed by midwestern know-how: Miss Campbell helped our class arrange a bake sale to raise money for the orphans.

Next came Miss Coral McMillin, a robin-plump woman in her late fifties who always wore dresses with matching jackets and a single strand of large, even pearls. For several years she took us deeper into the language, and I still can't look at the summer constellations without recalling a story in Alphonse Daudet's *Lettres de mon moulin* where a lonely shepherd takes comfort in the stars. Here we moved from the rites of language to the rites of culture; all those conjugations began to cohere into something. One Christmas, to our surprise, Miss McMillin settled at the old upright piano in the back of the classroom and led us through several French songs, starting with "Dominique," which had just swept the country. Then she offered to sing for us, and her thin but serviceable soprano began "La vie en rose." My seat was in the back of the room, and I watched her, transfixed, as she accompanied herself. Her eyes glistened, and the fragile melody—made sadder by her quaver—filled the room with melancholy. What lost love came to her mind as she sang, what pain did she conceal? (I was reading *The Charterhouse of Parma*, in translation.)

By the time I started university, where languages could be studied systematically, French no longer seemed a mystery even when it was a pleasure, and I was on the road of American language training. It didn't take long to see that French wasn't for men, since the ratio of women to men in French class was three to one. German, Latin, Greek—here the balance evened out. But these were languages in the service of something else: requirements for advanced degrees. French, in comparison, seemed frivolous. Today I know only a few university graduates—or academics—who have ever used the languages they piled up, and fewer who read in them for pleasure. They may secretly vow to perfect a favorite one again, some day, but apart from attempts (soon abandoned) to follow local newspapers during European travels, languages studied as academic requirements remain a thing of the past, along with old yearbooks. And yet a belief in their value remains. They are a rite of civilization, of class and mobility—like music lessons.

In the tradition of nineteenth-century amateurs (now called "men of letters") from Carlyle to Thoreau, Edmund Wilson was an amateur in the best sense: he wanted to understand—to make sense of—anything that held his attention. Yet I can't help wondering if he would have decided to learn Hungarian at an earlier point in his life. Perhaps timing is all. In the summer of 1960, Wilson received a volume of his plays translated into Hungarian — hardly reason enough to struggle with a notoriously difficult language, even for a writer with a considerable ego. But he had time on his hands and no intention of spending it gardening. (The Talcottville house might seem a city dweller's dream, but Wilson's diary shows him largely oblivious to its pastoral charms.) This is not unimportant. There has to be some reason to begin the study of a new language, even if one has a natural aptitude for it, and then to keep up the rote drill required.

In his life away from Talcottville, Wilson knew several Hungarian intellectuals who had settled in the United States — among them István Deák, a professor of European history at Columbia University, and Zoltán Haraszti, the former librarian of the Rare Books Department of the Boston Public Library. He and Haraszti often met in Cambridge to discuss Hungarian writers; Wilson is vague about this process and about how much Hungarian he knew, but he may have brought some acquaintance with the language to his sessions with Mary Pcolar. That her language skills were not the only thing that impressed him is clear from his description of her as "a very handsome girl in whom the Mongolian stock is evident: high cheekbones, slightly slanting gray eyes, set rather wide apart, a figure erect and well built."[1] Alone, in the country, he was drawn to her, although she was married with three children and an unlikely candidate for romance. Aware of Wilson's reputation as a ladies' man, Mary Pcolar still agreed to teach him Hungarian if he would teach her French.

A friendship developed between the two, and Wilson often accompanied Mary and her husband to the movies. His attachment to her did not go unnoticed by his family, who sent him this April Fool telegram: "We request the honor of your presence at banquet and would like you to judge beauty contest of New England chapter of Magyar women."[2] Mary, who confessed to Wilson that she had little time for herself and felt overwhelmed by tending to the needs of others, had a temperament suited to him. He accepted the fact that she had been born in the United States and had learned her parents' language as children of immigrants often do — randomly, without careful study. This meant that Mary knew Hungarian but could not always explain the grammatical conventions that interested Wilson. Yet her amateur status appealed to him, and they consulted grammar books together.

I mention this in some detail because any decision to learn a new language carries with it the inevitable problem of finding a teacher—the right teacher. Fortunately, the city I live in has a large Hungarian community; most of the residents arrived after the abortive revolution of 1956. Along Bloor Street West, within walking distance of the University of Toronto, they supplied "ethnic" charm with their restaurants, feeding several generations of students on cheap schnitzels. Although gentrification now rules this stretch of Bloor, the Hungarian presence hasn't entirely disappeared. Today the children of these immigrants often enroll in Introductory Hungarian courses offered at night by the university or local high schools. My own attempts to learn Hungarian over the past decade have always been defeated by such classes. Each time I've registered in a course, with the assurance that it would be *introductory*, I was soon lost in a room of young people who already had more than a rudimentary knowledge of the language. Occasionally another student would be in my position—usually a young woman who had married into a Hungarian family—and we would soon visit the registrar's office for a refund of our tuition. Almost giving up the idea, I decided to try to find a private tutor, someone who knew the language and could also teach it. When I did, in time, find such a person, it felt like a moral imperative to begin my studies. But the question that dogged me, since I have no particular flair for learning languages, was why bother now?

My mother had saved a box full of letters written by my greatgrandfather to his daughters, who came to America in 1909, and for some years I had been curious about them. Without romanticizing another time, it seemed important to understand alternatives to my own. Even as a child I felt more connected to the Hungarian manner and temperament of my own background than to the contemporary North American culture that seemed to be relentlessly swallowing up all differences not compatible with its icons and dreams—from Elvis Presley to the perfect suburban lawn. I still feel this process at work, though the dreams have changed to designer boutiques and plentiful, inexpensive guns. I'm also sure that as a child I sensed that Hungarianness was something foreign to the fifties in North America—something unwelcome, wrong. Perhaps this is why I showed little interest in learning Hungarian.

But a box of old letters wasn't reason enough to study Hungarian as an adult. And since my mother had written out translations of the most interesting ones, there was no need to trouble with the originals. I think my resolve to learn the language formed when I read several histories of Hungarian literature, and found that important writers had been neglected in the English-speaking world simply because they hadn't been translated. A *New Yorker* profile of turn-of-the-century novelist Gyula Krúdy, by the Hungarian-born historian John Lukacs, fed my desire. In Lukacs's hands Krúdy's bohemian life in the twilight world of old Buda became an invitation. I looked for books by Krúdy in translation but found only one of his stories in an anthology of Hungarian fiction, published in Budapest for export sale. Along with writers such as Endre Ady, Zsigmond Móricz, and Margit Kaffka—also largely untranslated— Krúdy seemed to hold a key to something I wanted to understand, without knowing what it was.

Most of the time we're in control of our work, and any challenges tend to be predictable ones. We're trained for them, we get the lay of the land, we adjust. A new language won't cooperate with the need to be in control; part of the nature of its newness is that we aren't, and can't be. Of course it will have familiar elements, the parts of speech we once parsed in grammar classes. Yet this is really a matter of faith until we have sufficient grasp of the language. The inevitable response to this unfamiliarity—that all one needs is a large enough vocabulary—leads only to more words. Why? Because learning a language is learning a new way of thinking, and that's more than a matter of vocabulary, or word order, or linguistic conventions. Not that they don't have a place in approaching a new language—they do. The best grammar review of one's own language is the attempt to learn another.

Hungarian is not an Indo-European language, but a member of the Finno-Ugric language group. Finnish, along with Estonian, forms one branch, and the Ugrian languages—of which Hungarian is the most important—make up the other, which includes several minor languages still spoken in the northern areas of the former Soviet Union. The first Hungarians probably lived on the southern slopes of the Ural Mountains, and moved westward across the Russian steppes during the fifth century. Linguistic evidence suggests that they came into contact with Turkic and Iranian groups before finally conquering the Carpathian basin, where the nomadic tribes settled in the ninth century. The name of this people and language, in their own tongue, is *Magyar*. (The English word "Hungarian" is derived from the German, which has roots in the medieval Latin "Hungarus.") To my ear the language has a rich, rough, primitive sound, in part caused by the stress pattern of pronouncing individual words with an emphasis on the first syllable, although this emphasis is modified in speaking a phrase. You can hear this distinctively Hungarian rhythm in the music of Bartók and Kodály. Other tonal elements include the unusual combination of consonants such as *cs* (pronounced ch, as in church), *ny* (gn, as in cognac), *sz* (s, as in sun), *zs* (s, as in pleasure), and *gy* (d, as in duke), along with varied vowel sounds. (In Hungarian, accent marks do not indicate stress but rather a change in the sound of the letter itself.)

When I first began memorizing the conjugations of Hungarian verbs, I felt overwhelmed by one of the main peculiarities of the language: each verb has two different sets of conjugations, depending on whether or not it has a specific direct object. In other words the conjugation is determined not by the subject alone, but also by the object and by whether the object is specific or general. (Some verbs are only intransitive, with one conjugation.) The problem, as Edmund Wilson succinctly noted, is that "the Hungarian idea of what is specific and what is general does not quite correspond with ours."[3] I began writing out lists of verbs, in my old study-hall fashion, thinking that I would solve the conjugation problem by learning the endings of new verbs, expanding my vocabulary at the same time. It seemed a good idea until I came up against further peculiarities. There are not only a seemingly endless number of irregular verbs, but verb endings change in relation to the *sound* of the root of the verb, whether it has a dark (back) sound or a light (front) sound. My Hungarian teacher took one look at the page of conjugations I'd carefully written out and said that I was trying to learn by a paradigm, and not globally, not idiomatically, which is the way she teaches. I had to learn to give up my desire to control in order to master even the simplest sentence.

This is where it helps to have a sympathetic teacher. Magda, in her late sixties, has the broad, high cheekbones I associate with Hungarians of a Calvinist background (like my father's family), a generous smile, and lively eyes full of well-wishing. As I came to know her I wasn't entirely surprised to learn that she had been married only five years before, when she moved to Canada from Nice. A gifted linguist who knows ten languages, and often uses examples from literature or opera libretti to illustrate a point, she has taught Hungarian and French at several universities in Europe, and, more recently, in Toronto. (During our lessons she often falls into French, and the directions on the exercises she gives me are also in French, adding another dimension that has charmed me.) When I mentioned István Deák and other Hungarian names in connection with Edmund Wilson, Magda began to reminisce about Deák's sister, a girlhood friend. This can all be pretty imposing as I stumble along, forgetting verb endings, but Magda is one of the most encouraging teachers I've ever known.

Still, language drill has to be done alone. My frustration came into focus one evening while I visited friends whose son, a month short of his second birthday, had yet to begin talking. We assured ourselves that Marc would speak when he was ready to, for it was clear that he listened, understood us, and could make many of his desires known, although he sometimes turned a splendid shade of red when language—or his lack of it—failed him. Alone, with his toys, Marc yattered away happily in a system of his own. (Many of the numerous books about language development have discussed the difference between first- and second-language learning, which I'm not equating; there are, however, common elements.) At least, I told my friends, Marc wouldn't have to learn two conjugations for every verb. Yet Hungarian children pick these up naturally, and will use the correct one, even if they can't explain why. Being surrounded by a language makes a big difference, but any adult learning a foreign language in his own culture can't create another environment. Then what to do? Watching Marc play I saw that my own solution corresponded to something he did naturally. I had to learn to play with the language, and to value the play for itself. This is one of the best surprises learning a language can offer.

I began by labeling unlined file cards with a Hungarian word on one side and the English equivalent on the other, making flash cards that could be shuffled to add a random element to my language practice. In no time I was approaching this growing pile with the enthusiasm I've seen on the faces of people who love crossword puzzles. In addition to the file cards, I purchased a small, portable tape recorder so that I could use it anywhere, as the mood struck. My tendency is to stay close to the written word, and I knew I had to overcome it, or at least break the habit for a while, in order to deal with the sounds that are uniquely Hungarian. At this stage I wasn't concerned about perfecting an accent, but I did want to be able to make myself understood. Magda had tape-recorded the lessons she'd written out for me, leaving enough time after each sentence for me to repeat it. Unfortunately the tape recorder seemed like an enemy, showing up my mistakes, my faltering attempts to speed up recitations without forgetting how Hungarian vowels are pronounced. As I sat down to practice aloud, I felt like a child with unwanted homework.

Once you break through that space of resistance to studying a new language, which is a recurring experience, the pleasure in the work — the work as play — is great. But the resistance keeps returning. By the end of the day I was usually so filled with the details of my job, with other people's words, that I had little energy for turning my attention to anything else. The first step was to acknowledge this resistance, so that I could find a way to enjoy the act of practicing conjugations. As I learned to do this more successfully I came away from my practicing with a heightened awareness.

Sitting down to my Hungarian time, I now enjoy the sensuous aspect of learning the language. Flash cards for review are crisply white and unlined so that each word floats on its own, and I can take pleasure in its foreignness, its shape, sound, and meaning. (One friend claims that I like foreign movies because they have subtitles and I love reading.) However, it's a big step from words to sentences, to remembering the right word without cards. If I think of this at the start of a practice session, it's easy to be discouraged. Instead, as I move a card from the top of the pile to the bottom, I enjoy the sensation. Perhaps I'll make several piles, one for words vaguely recognized, another for those known well, a third for the ones I haven't yet learned to spell. A child intently playing with blocks? The comparison is not unfair. In this transition from the workday to language time, I'm overcoming resistance. Why should this be so difficult? Perhaps for the reason that our culture prefers shopping and romance (which inevitably leads back to shopping) to learning, for learning something new can be a radical experience, even dangerous, when it makes you question the assumptions of your world.

After the flash cards comes the tape recorder—first with a written text, then without. As sentence patterns start to take shape, words connect with each other. The problems they pose—all those suffixes and prefixes that dominate Hungarian, an agglutinated language where the suffix is all—keep my attention on edge. After using the recorder I turn to my notebooks, and this revives memories of elementary school. There are three of them, each with a different-colored cover. One is for notes made during lessons, another for exercises and questions that come up as I study, and the third for English translations of the texts that my teacher has written out. Three may seem unnecessary, but there is satisfaction in moving from one to the other. These stacks of paper become the physical equivalent of my Hungarian time: along with books of translations, dictionaries, grammars, histories, and biographies, they are my Hungarian things. Contrary to the impression language courses give, language learning is not simply cerebral.

The sounds of Hungarian have always been comforting to me. My grandparents, who lived in the top half of our duplex, spoke it with my parents whenever they wanted to discuss something I shouldn't overhear, or late at night when they talked of the "old country." So Hungarian naturally became associated with mystery and adult secrets. Since then I've seen virtually all the Hungarian movies that make it to North America, and the sounds of the language still hold mystery. As I gained some familiarity with words, with those sounds, phrases my grandmother once used began coming up like fragments remembered from a dream. Often I had no idea what they meant. *Mit csinálsz* was one, and Magda smiled when I told her that Grandma used to say it often when she cared for me while my mother worked. "Write it phonetically," Magda suggested. *Mit,* I knew, came from *mi* (what) with the *t* ending of the accusative. *Csinálsz* had the *sz* verb ending of the second person familiar, and in this case the ending of the indefinite tense. With the root of the verb—*csinál*—now isolated, I combined "what" and "you" in a good guess: "What are you doing?" There are other such phrases, and some of them I'll never repeat to Magda—my grandparents had a volatile marriage.

After attending a symphony concert one Saturday night, I anticipated trying out my newly acquired past tense on Magda. I meant to say, "Szombaton hallottam egy koncertet" ("Saturday I heard a concert"), but I was unsure of the word *koncert,* because Hungarian has very few crossover words. I quickly thought of the word *muzsikát,* a crossover I was certain of, but out came *macskát* in its place. Magda looked surprised. I'd said, "Saturday I heard a cat." I'm slowly getting used to this sort to thing, and to the fact that it will be a while before I'm reading the writers I want to. With books by Margit Kaffka and Zsigmond Móricz on my shelves, right now I'm making do with Éva Janikovszky's *Ha én felnőtt volnék* (If I Were Grown-up)—one of the classics of Hungarian children's literature. "Minden gyerek tudja, még a legkisebb is, hogy rossznak lenni sokkal mulatságosabb, mint jónak lenni,"[4] it begins, as I read the first page aloud to practice my pronunciation. Or: "Every child knows—even the youngest one—that it's more amusing to be bad than good."

What I could never have guessed from the start is the bonus of learning a new language: it allows you to block out the world. Because a language demands time, it demands allegiance, but it returns the compliment. No matter how often we remind ourselves that language shapes us—the way we see, what we feel, what we expect of life, and of ourselves—there's nothing like a foreign word for a familiar one to bring us up short. String together enough of them and you suddenly face the arbitrariness of your own culture, and your place in it. The desire for escape (my imaginary hut, blooming apricot trees, and gamboling goats) is as old as the first written books we have. That language can help us do this should come as no surprise, although a regular diet of newspapers and magazines, and memos and reports, not to mention whatever books we do read, goes a long way toward anaesthetizing us. Sometimes we need to escape from our own words.

Of course I'm describing my own experience, and can't assume that others will share my enthusiasm for a new language. This may be why Edmund Wilson's experience interests me — I feel a kind of comradeship.

Wilson died in 1972, and Mary Pcolar in 1986. Her son Edward, who still lives in upstate New York, remembers Wilson, as well as his mother's claim that Wilson knew no Hungarian when they met. She took pride in the fact that eventually it was one of the seven languages in which he was fluent.[5] While Wilson's fluency with languages has sometimes been questioned — particularly by Vladimir Nabokov, who criticized his Russian, and by Mary McCarthy, Wilson's second wife, who observed that he could read but not speak foreign languages[6] — fluency isn't the point here. What matters to me is Wilson's interest in languages, and the effort he made to learn and appreciate them.

Upstate was published the year before Wilson died and remains his last word on learning Hungarian, or any new language. I can only conjecture about its meaning to him, although he does make connections between the brooding landscape of Hungary's greatest modern poet, Endre Ady, and his own: "I purposely had Mary read with me Ady's wonderful winter poem, so full of the terror and mystery of a wild Hungarian forest, *Az Eltévedt Lovas*, which reminded me rather of upstate New York. I did not mention this, but when we afterwards drove to Glenfield, she spoke of the resemblance herself, as we approached the Adirondacks, in the bleak and misty landscape beneath a completely ashen sky."[7]

A language can lead to other places — to another culture, its sounds, its history, its writers, its heart. Unlike my small, clean hut, it is not merely a temporary escape, a holiday, but a place to live in. How odd that we're content to spend our lives with school learn-

ing, almost frozen in time. A new language is about all of life —
youth and joy and love, and death and change. No wonder that
at sixty-five Edmund Wilson was ready to start another. Learning
Hungarian took him back into his own world, which he saw anew.
I would like it to do the same for me.

"*What the Moment Told Me*"

The Photographs of

André Kertész

In 1912, the year that André Kertész began working as a clerk in the Budapest stock exchange, he bought his first camera: an ICA box using 4.5 × 6 cm plates. He was eighteen years old and ready to teach himself the mysteries of light. Over the next thirteen years, before moving to Paris, he made hundreds of photographic images of Hungary. A soulful young man dozing in a Budapest coffee shop; a blind violinist fiddling in the middle of an unpaved street; two lovers embracing on a park bench; soldiers lined up for the latrine; a snow-covered street in Esztergom—these are only a few of the most familiar. Almost seventy years later Kertész collected 143 of these images for his elegiac book *Hungarian Memories*. Most frequently remembered for surrealist photographs of contorted women, or contemplative images of his adopted New York City, Kertész had preserved the underside of *belle-époque* Hungary in some of the finest photographs of the twentieth century.

Avoiding the wealthy and the middle class, Kertész preferred to focus on the less privileged, in a seemingly haphazard manner that belied his instinctive sense of composition. As a historical record, his photographs are invaluable to the study of a vanished world—they preserve its texture, its density. Although Susan Sontag, in *On Photography*, wisely questioned the relation of photographic images to reality, it is possible to "read" photographs of the past in their own context, a process that Sontag tends to disregard. The context of Kertész's photographs, naturally, has many facets, from the fiction of Zsigmond Móricz and the poetry of Endre Ady to music and painting, as well as the history of the last years of the Dual Monarchy. While Kertész's photographs can be looked at in isolation, or in terms of the development of modern photography (and his contribution to it), an appreciation of them is enriched by their context. Kertész was a pioneer, but he did not work alone.[1]

Yet even "context" is not enough to explain the difference between Kertész's Hungarian photographs and his work outside of his native country. As soon as one looks at the sweep of his work, a gradual shift in tone and a darkening sensibility become apparent. Kertész's Hungarian photographs exude a warmth, an immediacy and freshness that gradually disappear from his work as more formalist concerns begin to dominate it. While his early subject matter inevitably gave way to new surroundings (first Paris and then New York, where he spent the last forty-nine years of his life), the difference is more than a matter of subjects, although they are part of it. Something else seems to be happening, as if, cut off from his roots, from his origins, Kertész can record only an alien world that the immigrant observes but does not fully inhabit. He seems to be retreating into formalism, yet an air of melancholy emerges, his emotions gradually withdrawing from the photographic image.

Kertész's long career has often been seen as part of the development of modernism. While the connection is an obvious one,

it can be made a good deal more specific. That is, I think that
the psychological burden and freedom of emigrating made Kertész
particularly open to modernist conventions and had a profound
effect on his work. Twice an immigrant, Kertész was a person twice
removed from his homeland. His Hungarian photographs take on
a different resonance when this is remembered.

Kertész's impulse to preserve a dying way of life was not unlike that of his compatriots Béla Bartók and Zoltán Kodály, who
recorded the folk music of the remote rural regions where old traditions persisted. And like his musical counterparts, Kertész re-
lied on a relatively new technology. In his case it was the camera.
This desire to preserve the past reflects a cultural movement in
Hungary interested in expressing what was distinctly "Magyar" — a
movement launched by the celebrations of 1896 to commemorate
the first thousand years of Hungarian history.

Andor Kertész was born in 1894 into an assimilated Jewish
middle-class family in Budapest. At six, he saw "an illustrated
magazine" and decided he wanted "to do the same with a camera as it had with drawings." [2] Purchasing his first small camera
after receiving his baccalaureate, he used it as "a little notebook, a
sketchbook. I photographed things that surrounded me — human
things, animals, my house, the shadows, peasants, the life around
me. I always photographed what the moment told me." The glut of
photographic images of the past century has made subjects such
as these so familiar that it is easy to forget that Kertész was one
of the first to record them. What may now look like stock images
were once radically new. Self-taught, Kertész had to improvise a
darkroom in his parents' house and do his printing at night, while
the family slept. He reserved weekends for his camera, clerking at
the stock exchange throughout the week.

During World War I, Kertész served in the Austro-Hungarian
army, taking along his cumbersome camera (now a Goertz Tenax
with 4.5 × 6 cm plates) and photographing comrades whenever
he had the chance. At the front line he took informal, candid
photographs, unlike official photographers for the War Department, "who always came with a huge camera on a tripod after the
battle was over to make a scenic photograph that would show the
destruction." [3] Kertész preferred intimate moments — his latrine

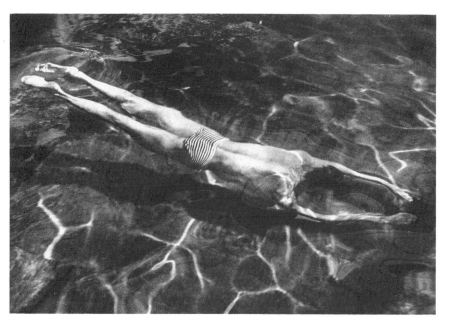

© André Kertész, "Underwater Swimmer," 1917.
Courtesy: Jane Corkin Gallery, Toronto, Canada.

companions, a young soldier writing a letter home, another flir-
tatiously touching the hip of a babushkaed peasant woman. After
being wounded in 1916 he printed some of his pictures, and his
regiment planned to collect them into a small book and give the
proceeds to the Red Cross.[4] (The project never materialized because most of the negatives were destroyed.) He had to spend
almost nine months in the hospital, where he went swimming in
the pool daily. Here he discovered the distortions caused by looking through water and began to incorporate this effect in a series of
photographs of male swimmers. When friends asked why he took
such photographs, he replied, "Why only girl friends? This also
exists."[5] These first body distortions, made in 1917, foreshadow his
more famous surrealist female nudes of 1933. Once recovered, he
rejoined active service and traveled throughout Central Europe,
making photographs along the way. Some of his war photographs
appeared in *Borsszem Jankó*, in 1916, and in *Érdekes Ujság*, in 1917.

After the war Kertész returned to work at the Budapest stock
exchange and continued to make his visual record of Hungary.
Yet rather than emphasizing urban images, he often visited the

country. "I grew up in Budapest, but I always felt very close to the countryside,"[6] he wrote in the caption for a photograph of a peasant family in Sziget-becse holding violins and double bass upright—a string trio preparing to play. "I never had to go very far for subjects—they were always on my doorstep. But I can't analyze it. People ask me how I did it. I don't know; the event dictated it."[7]

The event dictated it. Appealingly romantic, the claim is not entirely true. Kertész went in search of his subjects, although there was nothing mannered about the way he photographed them. Even when taking pictures in Budapest, he tended to concentrate on peasants, blocking and isolating their figures so that the sophisticated city seemed remote, even nonexistent. "Waiting for the Ship, Budapest, 1919," for example, shows three peasant women huddled on the docks, talking, with two large and seemingly empty straw baskets before them. They could just as well have been from any of the villages Kertész visited.

Kertész's Hungarian subjects rarely spill beyond their frames. "Boy Sleeping Over Daily Newspaper in a Coffee Shop, Budapest" (1912) is more than the photographic record of a handsome young man leaning on his right hand, his eyes shut, his mouth open; the image is a psychological statement about someone in suspension, as if Kertész were anticipating the dream space of Surrealism. The young man is lost in a state somewhere between a finite and an infinite landscape, neither a dream nor a nightmare, but another world—sleep space. The power of the image comes partly from Kertész's ability to photograph two kinds of space. First, the formal composition of the photograph—its spatial arrangement—isolates the figure in an X shape almost in the center of a square, and the coffee shop is suggested mainly by the trapezoid of newspaper spread out before him and the triangle of newspapers hanging on a wall rack behind and above him, as if to balance the white-and-gray trapezoid that may have put him to sleep in the first place. Second, the spatial duality established by the subject's face, in half shadow, suggests the sleep space beyond the world of waking, a space within another space. A trace of eros marks the young man's features, along with a languid melancholy that seems tinged with Kertész's good humor—the young man will, of course, awake and return to the cares of the day. Given that Kertész was only eigh-

© André Kertész, "Boy Sleeping Over Daily Newspaper in a
Coffee Shop, Budapest," 1912.
Courtesy: Jane Corkin Gallery, Toronto, Canada.

teen when he took this photograph, it can be seen as a self-portrait
of sorts. But like any serious portraitist he probed the character of
his subject: the young man is gentle, dreamy, almost vulnerable,
with the unselfconsciousness of youth.

Unselfconsciousness is a feature of Kertész's Hungarian work, and frequently of the people he chose to photograph—beggars, Gypsy children, a blind fiddler. Unhappy with his office job, Kertész may have identified with these marginal figures and their sense of dislocation. His family did not encourage his desire for a career in photography, fearing that he would end up like numerous Budapest photographers making studio portraits; this was, after all, a time when photography had a lower status than the other visual arts. Instead, his mother encouraged his interest in beekeeping, for Kertész had loved the countryside since childhood, when his family spent summers in Sziget-becse, on the *puszta*, and at Tiszaszalka on the Tisza River. In July 1921, Kertész spent six weeks in a village near Buda, learning about beekeeping. Fortunately he never pursued the subject, but it was during this time that he took his photograph of the blind violinist, one of the masterworks of European photography.

At first glance "Abony" (July 19, 1921)—which Kertész described as "A blind musician not a Gypsy, who wandered from village to village with his boy. He made a living playing for alms"[8]— seems to be a sociological comment. But closer examination shows that this is much more than photojournalism. The photograph is a statement about making art. The face of the violinist suggests that his music has transported him beyond the unpaved street where he plays to himself, transcending his ordinary world yet still a part of it. This reflection on the process of creation observes the boundary between art and life (the violinist's child companion is clearly on the lookout for alms) while the musician inhabits another world. Here again, space is relative, not absolute. In this early study Kertész managed to make the invisible visible—the artist's need to create, and the space that creation makes. He photographed the violinist's essence. Years later Kertész wrote of this subject: "Look at the expression on his face. It was absolutely fantastic. If he had been born in Berlin, London, or Paris, he might have become a first-rate musician."[9] There is something almost consoling about this image, as is true of all great works of art. One critic, Sandra S. Phillips, has remarked that the figure has "the timeless authority of Homer."[10] (It is no accident that Kertész felt drawn to another blind musician later in his life, in New York.)

Kertész had not yet given himself up to the experiments that

© André Kertész, "Blind Violinist, Abony," 1921.
Courtesy: Jane Corkin Gallery, Toronto, Canada.

would follow in Paris, where painting and photography seemed to merge. In Hungary he insisted on the strict separation of the two, affirming the integrity of photojournalism. Yet he was not interested in mimesis, but rather in exploring the external world through the camera. Like all early modernists, he had to recognize the separation between external reality and the work of art, even as he presented the anecdotal with a modernist's sense of fragmentation. His own emotions, his own responses, were always central to his photography. "My work," he wrote, "is inspired by my life. I express myself through my photographs. Everything that surrounds me provokes my feeling."[11] An instinctive artist (perhaps a function of being self-taught), Kertész emphasized that he found his subjects: "I always photographed what the moment told me." Yet he lived in search of the moment, and organized his weekend travels in aid of the search. "You do not have to imagine things; reality gives you all you need." His angle on "reality," however, was unique, and Kertész knew it: "It has been said that my photos 'seem to come more out of a dream than out of reality.' I have an inexplicable association with the things I see. This is the reality."[12] Loath to give away his secrets, Kertész understood that his work was based on an "inexplicable association." When he did speculate on the nature of this association, he recognized the unusual character of his Hungarian work: "The only one I knew to make pictures like mine was a kind of calendar photographer. He arranged his scenes. But I captured mine. My youth in Hungary is full of sweet and warm memories. I have kept the memory alive in my photographs. I am a sentimentalist—born that way, happy that way. Maybe out of place in today's reality."[13] A sentimentalist, but never a sentimental artist, Kertész was able to photograph an added dimension of the world around him because he felt that dimension, one world contained within another. His work is visually exciting precisely because he knew how to reveal the unseen.

An art of contingencies, photography requires a habit of readiness. Photographers must always be watching for the moment when light and subject meet; they have to act in a matter of seconds, making a decision based on an emotional response. In photography, Kertész has written, "two seconds are a thousand years."[14] For a good photograph to result, all elements must cohere, yet this is far from a matter of mere coincidence: Kertész was always mindful of what he was looking for. "Of course a picture can lie," he wrote, "but only if you yourself are not honest or if you don't have enough control over your subject. Then it is the camera working, not you." In Hungary he trained himself to be in control of his camera.

© André Kertész, "Buda (night)," 1914.
Courtesy: Jane Corkin Gallery, Toronto, Canada.

Unlike the Hungarian pictorialists whose work filled popular magazines, or the "calendar photographer" he remembered, Kertész insisted on the real rather than the staged. Yet it is clear from his early photographs that he was not beyond staging moments. In one night scene, "Buda (night), 1914," a solitary man stands before a pool of light on a cobblestone street, an image that evokes the lonely world of Gyula Krúdy's short stories. In fact Kertész used one of his brothers for a model, and he had to stand still for eight to ten minutes—"the film wasn't so sensitive then," Kertész recalled.[15] Is this realism? Maybe. The photograph is not spontaneous, yet it appears to be completely natural, as if Kertész had taken a snapshot. Other images from these years are also obviously posed (for example, "Nude in Abony, July 23, 1921" and "Sziget Becse, September 26, 1926," a portrait of a peasant woman breast-feeding her baby) and seem rather stiff. Perhaps part of the success of Kertész's sleeping youth or blind fiddler comes from the fact that these subjects were unaware they were being photographed. Of course this gave Kertész more freedom. He may have chosen marginal people as his favored subjects, seeing in them his own feelings about the world, but he did not meet them on equal ground: the camera that stood between them conferred power on him whether he wanted it or not. His subtle use of this power, and his refusal to exploit it, account for the charm of his early work.

In 1923 Kertész sent four pictures to a photo exhibition in Budapest, and learned that the jury wanted to give him the silver medal. Asked to print in bromoil, a process that made photographs look like drawings, Kertész refused, and the offer of a medal was withdrawn. "That was all right with me," he remembered years later. "I have always known that photography can only be photography and is not meant to imitate painting."[16] At first this may seem surprising for a young man who dreamed of living in Paris, then the center of modern art. Kertész, however, always insisted on the integrity of photography, and remained years ahead of his time in his perception of the value of his art.

Kertész's Hungarian work seems untouched by the avant-garde art that developed alongside of it. The fin de siècle had seen a great flowering of art and architecture in Budapest, but no one would guess this from most of Kertész's photographs. The Nagybánya painters and, later, painters like the Eight, were in their prime, exhibiting regularly in Budapest, where a genuine Hungarian avant-garde style was developing. And Kertész would have read the modernists Ady and Móricz in the pages of *Érdekes Ujság*, which continued to publish his own work. Yet as Oliver A. I. Botar has pointed out, Kertész's circle of friends included Vilmos Aba-Novák and István Szőnyi, painters of the Szolnok School who were

© André Kertész, "Esztergom (man sweeping)," 1917.
Courtesy: Jane Corkin Gallery, Toronto, Canada.

"committed to painting Hungarian landscapes, townscapes, and rural genre scenes."[17] Kertész remained separate from the avant-garde, struggling by himself to photograph his world as directly as possible while learning the technical secrets of his various cameras. Remembering this time years later, he said, "We had an absolutely special spirit in Hungary, especially in Budapest."[18] The words suggest that Kertész knew he belonged to a larger movement, although he had been content to embody it in his own way.

After wearing down his mother's objections, Kertész finally applied for a visa to live in France, and left Budapest for Paris in 1925. At once he joined the Hungarian community there and was probably glad for their help, since he knew little French. He gravitated to the Café du Dôme in the heart of Montparnasse, to the Hungarian table with architect Ernő Goldfinger, painters and sculptors such as Lajos Tihanyi, József Csáky (whose Cubist sculptures he particularly admired), Dénes Forstner, and Etienne (István)

Beőthy, the writer Sándor Kemeri, Noémie Ferenczy, ceramicist Margit Kovács, and photographer Ilka Révai. He also befriended a Transylvanian Hungarian named Gyula Halász and showed him how to take photographs as a way to make money, sharing his knowledge of night photography, a subject that Halász, later known as Brassaï, came to be associated with.

As his circle of friends grew to include Mondrian, Leger, and László Moholy-Nagy, Kertész saw the most avant-garde art of the day. These were the years of his surrealist experiments with distortion, which had their roots in his swimming-pool photographs made during the war. The model in his famous "Satiric Dancer, Paris, 1926" was a young Hungarian woman named Magda Forstner, and the photograph was taken in the studio of his sculptor friend Beőthy. Did Kertész feel particularly free to experiment because he shared a common language with his model? We'll probably never know, but the question is still worth asking. It is not a large leap from Magda Forstner to the photographs Kertész took in the early 1930s with distorting mirrors he bought in a flea market. Sandra S. Phillips, however, has shown that Kertész's move to abstraction was not unlike Moholy-Nagy's, which also occurred only after he left Hungary.[19]

One can merely speculate about why such changes took place. The heady combination of personal freedom in a new city, which happened to be the world's art capital, along with Kertész's own intense, melancholy, but outgoing nature, must have made him particularly open to an atmosphere of experimentation. It was during a visit to Mondrian's studio in 1926 that Kertész took his well-known photograph of a table with a vase and artificial flower near the stairwell. Regarding Mondrian, he wrote: "I went to his studio and instinctively tried to capture in my photographs the spirit of his paintings. He simplified, simplified, simplified. The studio with its symmetry dictated the composition."[20]

During these years Kertész's many photographs of friends—both portraits and casual gatherings—are a link to the faces that stare out from his Hungarian photographs. Budapest beggars have been replaced with the *clochards* of Paris, but these images are more picturesque than similar ones taken back home, as if Kertész's mind and heart were elsewhere. Yet he recorded friends and colleagues with the same kind of sympathy and spontaneity that he once brought to peasant women and Gypsies. Like immigrants before him, Kertész took the measure of his new surroundings and saw what they asked of him. He could be entirely modern too. In 1936, Kertész and his Hungarian wife of three years, Elizabeth Sali (born Erzsébet Salomon), moved to New York City, where he planned to spend a year photographing the United States. Initially she did not want to make the trip, and even joked, "I'll divorce you."[21] What followed is an almost familiar story of European émigrés in America during the years before the Second World War. Offered a contract with a prominent picture agency, Keystone Studios, by fellow Hungarian Erney (Ernő) Prince, Kertész settled into the Beaux Arts Hotel, the first of his Manhattan addresses. These were difficult years for him. Yet it is easy to forget that photography as an art was new to the museum world in the 1930s. In 1936, when Kertész was en route to America, Beaumont Newhall, the photography curator at the Museum of Modern Art, was preparing the museum's first photography exhibition, "Photography 1839–1937." Five images by Kertész were used (including a nude study cropped by Newhall to eliminate the model's pubic hair).

In Budapest his photographs had received almost immediate recognition, but in New York Kertész had to struggle as a freelance photojournalist whose work seemed largely irrelevant to American taste. His photographs were exhibited in several galleries and even published in *Look*, where they were credited to Prince. "My sort of photography was not understood," he later recalled. "I made an interesting New York book. I took the layout to a publisher. 'You are too human, Kertész, sorry,' was the answer, 'make it more brutal.'" At *Life* magazine he was told: "You are talking too much with your pictures. We only need documents." Kertész felt cheated, "I was trapped."[22]

Because of the war he was forced to remain in America. Classified as an enemy alien, he was even prohibited from taking photographs outdoors. Eventually his photographs were published in magazines such as *Collier's, Harper's Bazaar, Town and Country,* and *Vogue,* but he never found easy acceptance. After becoming an American citizen in 1944, he began working for Condé Nast Publications, and signed an exclusive contract with them in 1949, supplying mainly interior photographs for *Town and Country*. In 1946 the Art Institute of Chicago mounted a one-man show of Kertész's photographs, but he had to wait another sixteen years for his next solo exhibition.

Although Kertész referred to himself as a "sentimentalist," he did not try to recreate a bit of old Hungary in America. He was already a seasoned immigrant. Unlike his first years in Paris, where he had belonged to a vital Hungarian community, his early years in New York were devoted to the business of doing business. In studying his work it is important to give some thought to the subjects he *didn't* photograph. There are no Hungarian restaurants, pastry shops, butcher shops, churches, clubs, dances, or community activities, often the solace of the new immigrant. Certainly in the years before and after the Second World War there were plenty of these in New York for anyone inclined to photograph them. And as Weston J. Naef has noted: "The Americanization of Kertész was proceeding in a way not unlike that of other aspiring immigrants. He did not, for example, choose to live in New York's Hungarian enclave, situated on Manhattan's commercial Lexington Avenue between 68th and 78th streets."[23] Of course Kertész's family had a history of assimilation in Hungary, maintaining little of their Jewish identity, and perhaps he had learned the lesson well. In New York he devoted his free time—and his free emotions—to his own photography. It is fair to say that he had assimilated himself into the international style of modernism. His world had no need of picturesque immigrants, so neither did he.

After settling in New York, it seems that Kertész lost interest in faces, or found none that moved him as much as the Hungarian faces of his youth. His work became increasingly abstract, his camera angles more unusual. Of course people weren't Kertész's only subject in Hungary. He had also made images of cobblestone streets and dirt roads; rain on the streets, mirror-like puddles, and piles of snow; clouds and shadows. The camera's lens was Kertész's eye on patterns in nature, patterns that reflected the clean geometry of modernism. Now there are few faces to equal those in his early photographs: the artist's brother, Jenő, swimming; children in Esztergom; a Gypsy girl modeling her embroidered scarf; a small-town judge, teacher, minister, and notary; and even an aston-

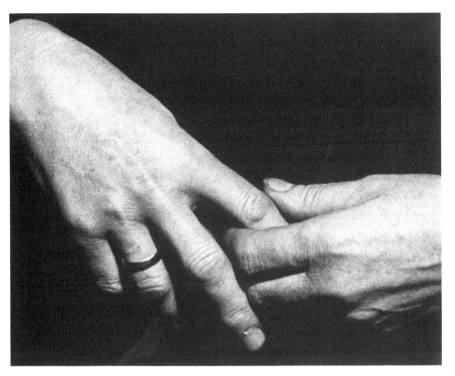

© André Kertész, "My Mother's Hands," 1919.
Courtesy: Jane Corkin Gallery, Toronto, Canada.

ishingly tender photograph of his mother's hands, taken in 1919, when she was sixty, about which Kertész wrote for a caption, "I have the same hands today."[24]

America provided few human subjects that stood out in their own right. People merged into their landscapes as the documentary aspect of Kertész's photography completely transformed itself — a considerable achievement because photography nearly always hints at some link with its realist, documentary origins. The power relation between Kertész and his subjects had also changed from his early excursions to the Hungarian countryside. Kertész was now the marginal figure, the immigrant trying to "make it," and he had to be aware of this on the streets of New York.

Kertész continued to take photographs "for myself,"[25] including a series focusing on Washington Square, the park below his apartment building, which he added to over several decades. His isolation was deeply felt, and one photograph from the late 1950s,

"Sixth Avenue, New York City, 1959," suggests the depth of it. On a busy street corner a blind accordionist looks out blankly while a dwarf, who works as a circus clown, drops a coin into the cup held by the musician's female companion. Inevitably, the image evokes Kertész's earlier blind violinist. The effect, however, eerily prefigures the work of Diane Arbus: the artist is not transcendent here, but sadly marginal. Kertész wrote of this image: "You have different feelings with each happening—good ones and bad ones: a killer can be an artistic person; wars are fought in beautiful landscapes. But I cannot analyze my work. People often ask, 'How can you do this photograph?' I do not know, the moment came. I know beforehand how it will come out. There are few surprises. You don't see; you *feel* the things."[26] Like Mondrian, he had taught himself how to simplify.

In 1962, at the age of sixty-eight, Kertész was finally recognized as one of the pioneer photographers of the century by a one-man exhibition at Long Island University of New York. Retrospectives followed immediately at the Venice Biennale (1963), the Bibliothèque Nationale in Paris (1963), and the Museum of Modern Art in New York (1964). It was as if the art world had suddenly happened on a major figure, just as Kertész claimed to find his subjects.

The attention gave Kertész freedom and a degree of security he had not known before, and he was able to terminate his contract with Condé Nast. He continued to take photographs in New York, but also in Europe and Japan. And he gave interviews, discussing his work with a new generation fascinated by it. In 1982, three years before his death, his collection *Hungarian Memories* was published. It was the most lavish of the books that Kertész undertook, and shows his deep attachment to his early Hungarian work. Yet he did not call the book *Hungarian Images*, or something similar, but rather *Hungarian Memories*. The choice is significant because the word "memories" highlights the personal aspect of Kertész's work as well as the distance he felt from his youth. "Memories" also suggests nostalgia, even a bittersweet mood. Hungary now belonged to the past. It should be no surprise that at the end of his life Kertész photographed a small glass bust of a woman that reminded him of his deceased wife, as it reflected the light of the cityscape outside his living-room window. Displacement and alienation had always drawn his eye, and now he became one with them, recording pure light as precisely as possible. The external world no longer captured his attention: pattern was all, and the form and content of photography united.

The Archives
of St. Elizabeth
# of Hungary

Like an abandoned fortress, the old sandstone church stood surrounded by urban blight. Since life and history seemed to have stopped here, it was difficult to imagine this neighborhood as the once-thriving center of any community. Block after block of empty buildings had been boarded up against the weather and transients.

Anyone who has glimpsed the aging immigrant churches of America from freeways bypassing them may share my curiosity about their fate. Although it's been twenty-five years since I lived in Cleveland, Ohio, I visit it frequently, and I've often wondered what happened to St. Elizabeth's, which is off any route I drive from one part of town to another.[1] During a recent trip I decided to find out. After telephoning the church's rectory and making an appointment to visit the next morning, I felt troubled by my plan, which seemed an invasion of sorts. I wanted to resist the attractions of nostalgia, and the lulling of conscience—and perception—that accompanies it. Yet I wasn't clear about what I hoped to find, or why I needed to see the church again. I felt mainly the sad passing of generations. And I wanted to talk with grandparents long dead.

After morning mass, four of us gathered in the basement kitchen of the church. I leaned against a counter beside Endre Ritly, my guide and companion for the day, while Father Antal and Margaret Ratkovsky stood at the stove, toasting bagels in a large cast-iron frying pan over one of twelve burners. This kitchen once easily fed hundreds, and still does on the few occasions when members of St. Elizabeth's return for celebrations or communal meals.

"I'm Father's nutritionist," Margaret Ratkovsky said with a smile as she pointed to the package of Philadelphia *light* Cream Cheese she'd brought to spread on the bagels. Everyone drank instant Nescafé.

Margaret has been a member of St. Elizabeth's parish since 1933. Fifty-eight years later, she says there were too many changes to remember. She has outlasted most of the priests, and seen the congregation decline from its largest membership of over 4,000 in the 1940s to the present figure of around 800, who contribute about 450 weekly envelopes in support of the church's work.

Father András Antal—who stands about five feet three inches tall, has a pleasant round face, thinning brown hair, and lively eyes—arrived from Hungary three years ago. Previously he headed a parish for ethnic Hungarians in an area of Romania that was once part of Hungary, before the Treaty of Trianon carved up its borders after World War I. The often brutal Romanian treatment of its Hungarian minority of two million had made life increasingly difficult. One day, when Father Antal returned to Romania from a visit home, a border guard spat in his face. Hungarian Catholic priests in Romania have been beaten and even killed by the Ro-

manian security service, the Securitate, so perhaps Father Antal
got off lightly. But this episode may have made him open to the
offer of a Hungarian American parish in Cleveland.

"I've put Father on a diet," Margaret continued as she spread
cream cheese—no butter—on the bagels. "He's gained weight
since coming to us."

Father Antal smiled awkwardly. His command of English is still
primitive, although he studies the language at a local community
college.

"Your English is better than my Hungarian," I offered, embarrassed at the way we were discussing him. But everyone knew that
Margaret's comments were well intended.

Saint Elizabeth (1207–31), the daughter of King Andrew II of
Hungary, was known for her acts of charity. While still a child
she was married to the young prince of Thuringia. After he joined
Frederick II on a Crusade and died of the plague, she was driven
from the court by her brother-in-law. Elizabeth entered a Francis-
can cloister in Marburg, Germany, working in its hospital and
helping the poor. Her spiritual confessor, Conrad of Marburg, a
prominent inquisitor of heretics, treated Elizabeth with a rigor
that bordered on the sadistic, yet she did not return to Hungary.
She died at the age of twenty-four and was canonized five years
later. Elizabeth is associated with a number of miracles familiar to
every Catholic Hungarian child, but it was not the miracles alone
that made her an appropriate patron for this church in Cleveland.
Founded in 1892, it was the first Hungarian Catholic church in the
United States.[2] As the premier Hungarian saint, Elizabeth was the
inevitable choice. But her life has a deeper resonance here: this
church served a people who had also lived, for various reasons, far
from their homeland.

Listed on the National Register of Historic Places by the Department of the Interior, and designated a Historic Site by the
State of Ohio, St. Elizabeth's was built in 1922, of Indiana sandstone, in the modified Romanesque-Baroque style popular at the
time. It replaced an older brick church that sat 800 worshipers.
The new church, accommodating 1,400, embodied an important
moment in the life of Cleveland's Hungarian community.

When the first Hungarian immigrants arrived in the 1880s, they settled around the southeastern edge of the city, at East 79th Street and Woodland Avenue, near the factories where they worked.[3] Moving eastward, into inexpensive houses, they eventually formed the Buckeye Road community, and by the First World War it was claimed that, after Budapest, Cleveland had the largest Hungarian population of any city in the world. Yet not everyone came with the intention of putting down roots. Many of the men who found jobs in Cleveland's steel mills returned home each spring to work the fields until harvest, and then they crossed the ocean again like migrating birds. By the end of the war this pattern was changing, however, for many Hungarians had married and started families and were no longer eager to return to a Hungary they didn't know; instead, they decided to remain in America.[4] Always frugal, they had saved money for houses, and could also afford a splendid new church, which cost $360,000 to build.[5] Gradually the statues of saints were added.

After our bagels with Father Antal, Endre and I went outside to look at St. Elizabeth's handsome bell towers, which rise to the roofline where they become square belfries topped with octagonal cupolas. On this cold March morning the powerful church facade still dominates the street. Endre was glad to let me examine details, asking questions as they struck my fancy. A handsome man in his mid-sixties, with silvery hair and black eyebrows over his blue eyes, he had worked as a research photographer at the Cleveland Clinic before retiring early, several years ago. Now an active member of the parish, he was drawn to St. Elizabeth's by its complex heritage as an important part of the history of Hungarian immigration to the United States.

Everyone I met at St. Elizabeth's had a story, and I particularly liked Endre's, because it included several generations of Hungarian immigrants. Although his grandparents came to the United States in the large wave of immigrants before the First World War, their son, Endre's father, remained in Hungary to complete his high school education before joining them. But the war changed his plans. Unable to leave Hungary, he eventually married and raised his own family there. Endre himself spent years as a Soviet prisoner of war before escaping Hungary following the revolution of 1956. After years of living in France he settled in Cleveland, took any job available (he had been a librarian in Budapest), and finally landed at the Clinic in 1962.

Endre had been asked by Father Antal to organize the archives of the church. "It's a treasure for researchers," he said, "and someone has to save it — not for today, but for tomorrow." Endre warned me that his work was still in the early stages. The parish does not have money for the task, so he had built the bookshelves himself and kept an eye out for sales on used filing cabinets or inexpensive office supplies. He had attended lectures at universities in Ohio and Indiana on preserving old paper, and written widely for advice from various archives on how to make photocopies of old, folded documents. Because he reads Hungarian, German, and Latin, as well as English and French, he can make sense of the church papers, which have been taken to the vacant third floor of the rectory. (At the turn of the century correspondence between priests and bishops was often in Latin, and the first priests of St. Elizabeth's were fluent in Hungarian, Latin, and German. Endre ventured to say that there may have been "an element of show" in using Latin for correspondence; however, it was once the official language of Hungary — the country had been reluctant to make the German of the Habsburgs its official language — and Hungarian priests were fluent in it.)

With regret, Endre explained that after Father Antal's predecessor died, the elderly parishioners who cleaned the church and rectory had a field day, discarding several large bins of old papers and hundreds of books (probably in German). He was aghast when he learned of the loss, especially because no one knows its extent. I couldn't help wondering what value boxes of yellowing baptismal certificates might have. His desire to preserve them seemed almost quixotic.

Although Endre was anxious to show me the third floor, where the archives were, I wanted to visit the church first. My grandparents had worshiped here, my mother was confirmed here, and this church has always had a special meaning for me that couldn't be explained by the beauty of its graceful domed ceiling or its fine stained-glass windows. Yet the quiet was unsettling. The empty church seemed isolated, even forlorn, locked during the day to any casual passerby who might want to step in for a few minutes and enjoy its peaceful cool light. Except for a few signs in Hungarian, there was little that didn't appear to be standard issue for any immigrant Catholic church in the 1920s: the white marble communion rail, the carved wooden stations of the cross, the scenes from the Bible on the stained-glass windows, all testaments to the past. I entered the nave and for a moment the church seemed to close in on me, as if something of the prayerful longings once whispered here still hung in the air. I was an intruder.

In the vestibule, like a crowded corner from the set of a biblical movie, stood half a dozen almost life-size plaster statues of saints, collected from Catholic churches that had been redecorated — and modernized — in the spirit of Vatican II. Standing there, I wondered why I'd never insisted that my grandmother visit Hungary again, the home she hadn't seen since 1909. And why hadn't I offered to go with her?

We left the church through the basement, its walls lined with old photographs of priests, of classes from St. Elizabeth's grade school from the twenties to the forties, of fall harvest festivals in the thirties. The oldest photograph, taken in 1902, was of Father Charles Boehm (né Károly Böhm, 1853–1932), the founding pastor. I had to resist getting lost in the photographs as Endre pointed out a broken player piano, with forty rolls, that he wanted to see repaired. Nearby, a large glass cabinet held the early banners of the church, their bright colors barely faded. Sewn with gold and silver braid, and embroidered with Hungarian words, these were the banners I had missed in the church. (At the end of the hallway a door led into a museum run by the Cleveland Hungarian Heritage Society, but the door was locked and the museum open only after mass on the first Sunday of the month.)

Entering the rectory from the back door, we were greeted with the wild barking of Father Antal's dog, an eleven-month-old Rhodesian Ridgeback called Betyár, Hungarian for "outlaw." Resembling a cross between a Great Dane and a whippet, with a ridge of dark hair down his back, he should have been running across the African plain, a golden streak of light.

The rectory was much larger than I had guessed from the street, and handsomely furnished in the style of a Central European embassy of the 1930s, or a Hollywood movie set for one. As many as four priests—and their staff—once lived here. After admiring the dining room, with its long, polished table that seats twelve, we stopped in the rectory office. While Endre photocopied some papers for me, I leafed through the prayer books lining one wall and found several cards commemorating the first mass celebrated by various priests. Through the grill-covered windows I could see a state liquor store across the street. The rectory had its first and only break-in two years ago, and Endre told me that upper Buckeye, which is more heavily populated, is more dangerous.

Soon we were joined by Joseph Toth, another retired parishioner who has moved to the suburbs but spends several days a week at St. Elizabeth's, helping Father Antal with the church's books, interpreting for him, and even sweeping the floors if necessary. During the week, when usually five people attend morning mass, Joseph often kids Father Antal: "I'd better get out there or I won't get a seat."

"What about the local community?" I asked. According to Joseph, St. Elizabeth's, an ethnic parish, has little involvement with the local community, which is black and largely Baptist. The school that St. Elizabeth's once ran, with student enrollments as high as 1,000 before World War II, closed in 1964.

Finally we mounted the newly carpeted front-hall stairs to the third floor, and stepped back in time. The walls were covered with faded wallpaper—bouquets of white and pink carnations on a tan ground—that must have been fifty years old. A musty smell seemed to emanate from them, the inviting scent of an attic filled with treasures. Old wooden furniture covered in cracked dark leather—which would fetch a high price if restored—was pushed up against the walls and piled with books and boxes. Everywhere, more books and boxes. On one wall near a closet door hung a wooden plaque with the painted inscription: "It is a blessing to be Hungarian."

The space for the archives ran the full width of the rectory, and the uncovered windows let in what light this day had to offer. The two main front rooms were connected by a large walk-in closet, where Endre had built bookshelves to help organize the collection. He has classified the titles by language, separating religious books from others. He took one off the shelf and showed me a postcard that had been left inside. "You see, I have to go through all the books and take out the postcards, or letters, or sometimes even papers with notes by a priest for his Sunday sermon, and then record where I found them—it's important for the chronology."

Along one wall there was the complete Hungarian census from 1890 (where I found my grandmother's village), a series of books from the 1920s dealing with Trianon called *The Hungarian Peace Negotiations*, the *Proceedings of the First World Congress of Hungarians* (1929) in Budapest, and numerous books on this subject in English, Hungarian, French, and German. There were also French maps of Hungary's economic structure in 1920, after two-thirds of its prewar territory had been ceded to Czechoslovakia, Romania, and Yugoslavia; and Sir Robert Donald's famous study *The Tragedy of Trianon: Hungary's Appeal to Humanity*, with an introduction by Viscount Rothermere urging a review of the treaty. (Trianon was, unfortunately, reviewed by Hitler in 1938, and no government has wanted to touch it since then.)[6]

When I asked why this collection had been acquired, Endre explained that St. Elizabeth's, and other Hungarian American parishes, had been actively involved in Hungary's political fate, especially around the time of Trianon, and had even fought for a review of it. "There is probably no place outside of Hungary with such a complete collection of books about Trianon," he said and added that the earliest Hungarian Catholic parishes in the United States maintained close ties with the Catholic Church in Hungary and often disagreed with the American Catholic Church, partly because the American hierarchy was dominated by Irish Catholics. After years of Anglican oppression, Irish Catholicism had developed a spirit different from that of its Hungarian counterpart, which had no such tradition of religious suppression, and an Irish style had been transported to America. (The American Catholic Church is commonly thought of in terms of its Irish version— Cardinal Spellman and the Kennedy family, and novels by writers like Mary Gordon and John Gregory Dunne; or the Italian variety, after the flamboyant Mafia Catholicism of Francis Ford Coppola's movies. But there are other ways of being Catholic.)[7]

As Endre talked I glanced at the yearbooks of the parish, sample textbooks from Hungarian publishers, numerous dictionaries (German/Hungarian from 1882, Romanian/German from 1890, etc.), and, closer to the present, a collection of the writings of Bishop Sheen. Then Endre pointed out some of the personal belongings left behind by various priests. I was drawn to an unopened trunk once owned by a priest who liked traveling. Near it were boxes of old lantern slides that he had collected, some taken by him, and others—of Hungary—bought from Hungarian suppliers. I could have spent an afternoon poring over them, but Endre wanted to show me his prizes.

In the second room, where he had put several old metal file cabinets, we faced the bulk of the church's papers. There were boxes of baptismal certificates, boxes of marriage certificates, letters and diaries, lists of parishioners in St. Elizabeth's health-care association from the 1890s (along with its account books), a copy of the Liturgical Desk Calendar for 1964 (I flipped through it and noticed that in March the priest had gone to Key West), tickets from old social activities (the price on one, for the St. Elizabeth's Ladies Social Club 20th Anniversary in 1944, was $1.50), tickets for card parties—the detritus of a parish's daily life. Endre had not yet decided on a system of classification for all this. Should it be chronological by year, or by era of priests? He was certain, however, that it would need to be elaborately cross-referenced if it was to be useful to scholars. Only then would they be able to determine, for example, how many marriages took place during a certain year, and thus chart shifts in the immigrant community from transient workers who intended to return to their homeland to new American citizens who had made lives for themselves far from the old country—as they were beginning to think of it.

Until recently one of the conventions of American history has been the idea of the melting pot, which had been fueled by the various pressures on immigrant groups to assimilate. This was especially true after the First World War, when restrictive quotas were placed on immigrants from Europe.[8] An archive like that of St. Elizabeth's could shed light on the melting-pot phenomenon, and how—or if—it worked, for the activities of the church helped maintain the "ethnic" identity of its parishioners.[9] On the surface, assimilation was the order of the day; but deeper loyalties, fears, and anxieties kept the Hungarians keenly interested in the affairs of their homeland. Hence the concern at St. Elizabeth's about Trianon. If immigration from Hungary (among other countries) had not been so severely limited after 1920, the course of the community's history might have been quite different. By the time the next large wave of Hungarian immigrants reached Cleveland, after the 1956 revolution, it was too late to revitalize an aging community that was ready for the suburbs, along with other upwardly mobile Americans. The melting pot became a partial reality more by erosion than by choice.

The newest filing cabinet held the papers of the priests of St. Elizabeth's. Endre was particularly interested in those of its founder, Father Boehm, and unfolded his high school diploma, from the Diocese of Esztergom, dated 13 July 1872.[10] I immediately remembered a family story about him. My grandmother had been religious in her fashion and regularly attended mass, but she'd somehow neglected to have my mother baptized. As time passed it became too awkward to mention, so she put it out of mind. When my mother was preparing for First Communion, Grandmother — who worked a long day at Stone Knitting Mill — suggested that she stop after school on the way home and ask a priest to baptize her. The priest turned out to be Father Boehm, and Mother still recalls the look of shock on his face at her request. "You go home and tell your mother to come and see me," he commanded. A stiff communion portrait proves that they resolved the problem, but what I like best about this story is the way it counters the stereotype of immigrant women as timid souls who allowed priests to run their lives.

All of Boehm's school papers were in Latin — including letters from the rector of the University of Vienna, where he had completed his studies for the priesthood. Boehm arrived in Cleveland in 1892 and established St. Elizabeth's — built the church, founded its school, and organized the associations that would secure the welfare of his parish. He was also committed to serving Hungarians who lived far from a church, and in 1893 founded a weekly bulletin, *The American Messenger of St. Elizabeth of Hungary* (*Magyarországi Szent Erzsébet Amerikai Hirnöke*), which he edited and published. This was an uncommon practice for its time, and the first edition must have brought great comfort to lonely immigrants, as it opened with a stately call to faith: "Listen to me! For I speak to you in your beloved mother tongue" ("Keresztény hívő lelkek!

Édes anyátok nyelvén szólok hozzátok; hallgassatok hát meg!").[11]
After fifteen years at St. Elizabeth's, Boehm devoted himself to
missionary work, traveling to the coal-mining areas of Pennsylvania and West Virginia, and throughout the eastern United States
and Canada, ministering to the needs of Hungarian communities
wherever he found them. In 1923, after the new church was built,
he returned to St. Elizabeth's and was given the title of monsignor
by the Vatican.

At first I had wondered why Endre spoke so enthusiastically
about Father Boehm. How different could he have been from other
priests who came to America in the nineteenth century? The missionary style of that time is so unfashionable today, so unmodern
(let alone postmodern), that its complexities are hard to appreciate. At the same time, it is close enough to us that we cannot dismiss it as quaint. And, as anachronistic as the sentiment is, Father
Boehm appears to have been a truly good man.

Not all the large ethnic parishes in America's cities have preserved such records as St. Elizabeth's, which are invaluable for
anyone interested in social history, ethnic studies, and religious
and ecclesiastic history, as well as local and regional history. Yet
when the function of a building or institution changes, and it is
preserved—even in part—for historical reasons, we see it differ-
ently. This happens all the time in museums, where objects that
were once part of someone's daily life subtly take on the quality
of an artifact. And this is happening at St. Elizabeth's too. I don't
want to suggest that the meaning of a church is measured by the
size of its congregation, yet I can't help wondering what St. Elizabeth's future will be—especially as the parish continues to age. No
longer a neighborhood church, it has to rely on citywide worshipers of Hungarian background to come from the suburbs for mass.
It has lost the vital neighborhood link that made it a place to be
preserved.

Ironically, with each step beyond my family's immediate connection to St. Elizabeth's, I felt closer to my grandparents, as if
I saw the workings of their world more clearly. Later I enjoyed
hearing my mother recall Father Boehm's deep, almost sepul-
chral voice, and also the handsome young assistant pastor, Father
Martin, on whom all the girls had a crush. But the connection I

sought had less to do with anecdotes than with imagining the inner lives of my grandparents' generation. It was about the historical imagination, about trying not to see the past only in terms of the present. Because it isn't enough for a building to be included in the National Register of Historic Places—that's only the beginning.

It was nearly two in the afternoon when we left the third floor and joined Father Antal, who had invited us to share his lunch. While I sat at the table, with its checkered cloth and three jars of instant coffee as a centerpiece, Betyár put his large head in my lap. Since coming to America, Father Antal had taught himself to cook, and Endre and Joseph were giving him advice about using the microwave to heat up some leftovers from the night before— cabbage mixed with noodles. It was a childhood favorite of mine, and I felt very safe.

By the end of my visit I thought that I understood Endre Ritly a little better. He had the desire to preserve the history of St. Elizabeth's, so the job was his. If he didn't, who would? People might come along, but he was there now. And this made sense to me, because I had begun to ask myself a similar question about St. Elizabeth's: if I didn't write about it, who would? That job, apparently, was mine.

Without
Words
Hungarians in
North American
Fiction

In her novel *The New Yorkers*, Hortense Calisher includes a young male character, Edwin Halecsy, who comes from
an ethnic background he cannot identify. One night in a Manhattan restaurant where his mother works as a scrubwoman, he learns
from a stranger that the mysterious language he speaks is Hungarian. Now Edwin has the first clue in his quest for self-discovery.
For years his mother has been estranged from her sisters, and once
Edwin identifies their language he can search for them. He finds
the name of his mother tongue and his family at the same time.

Calisher's image is powerful because it links a number of issues in the immigrant experience. But she is not writing a novel about immigrant life, although Edwin's Horatio Alger adventure takes him into a world of wealth and privilege that he has to reconcile with his past. Calisher's focus is elsewhere, and Edwin's Hungarian background is not a central part of *The New Yorkers*. He might just as easily have been Czech or Bulgarian, but he isn't either of these—he's Hungarian. It may seem stubborn to emphasize this fact, yet it does matter. Edwin Halecsy's story is a paradigm for the place of Hungarians in the fiction of North America.

Finding words for the stories one wants to tell is the essence of a writer's life. But words do not exist as absolutes; they are part of the narratives that people tell themselves—the discourse of a lived life. In this sense, the first language of an immigrant writer or character, and that language's narratives, are crucial. What is individual and unique, rather than general or stereotypical, reveals itself in language, whose nature goes against the idea that there could ever be a single truth. The attitudes that immigrant writers (and characters) have toward language can shed light on the conflicts they feel while also refocusing our attention on the way writers of a dominant culture create figures from other groups or minorities.

Novelist Mary Gordon, in her essay "Getting Here from There: A Writer's Reflections on a Religious Past," discusses the effect her family's Irish roots had on the development of her sense of herself as a writer—the "artistic ego,"[1] as she calls it. For Gordon, Irish Catholic Americans are part of a tradition "committed to the idea of keeping silence," and this made it difficult for them to embrace language and storytelling. She laments the lack of "Irishness" in American letters, in spite of such figures as Eugene O'Neill, Mary McCarthy, William Kennedy, and John Gregory Dunne. The situation that Gordon delineates is not unlike the one Gay Talese describes in his essay "Where Are the Italian-American Novelists?" As a young man, unable to find novels by Italian Americans, Talese felt drawn to Jewish and Irish American writers—especially John O'Hara, "in whose outsider's voice I heard echoes of my own."[2] Talese asks how it was possible that an ethnic group of "20 million Americans with Italian roots," a group that produced important painters and film directors, "was so *underrepresented* in the ranks of well-known American writers." He can't answer the question, but it is worth asking.

Talese and Gordon raise important issues about the contribution their ethnic groups have (and have not) made to the literature of North America, and by extending their exploration I would like to consider here some images and stereotypes of Hungarians in North American literature. (I use the term "North American" to suggest that a distinction between the United States and Canada is virtually nonexistent with respect to the place of Hungarians in the writings of both countries.) Language regularly plays a significant role for Hungarians who appear in North American fiction — ranging from the work of writers not of Hungarian descent, such as John O'Hara, Hortense Calisher, Margaret Atwood, and Michael Ondaatje, to that of writers with Hungarian origins, including John Marlyn and Stephen Vizinczey.

This is not the place for a detailed account of North American writers of Hungarian descent, or for a survey of the history of Hungarian immigration to North America. Nor am I including in my discussion any works published by immigrants in Hungarian (mostly poetry), since these are not part of the English-language tradition of North American writing and have rarely been translated. But in discussing various writers, it will be helpful to take note of the historical and social context of their work.

The major period of Hungarian emigration to the United States — the early 1900s — was seen as a national tragedy by Hungary's greatest twentieth-century poet, Endre Ady.[3] (Emigration averaged 170,000 per year and reached over 200,000 in 1907.)[4] Ady called the exodus a "fugitive revolution" and lamented the loss of Hungarians who were "swallowed up by America" while those who remained at home found themselves increasingly "swallowed up by Europe."[5] This is worth noting because it suggests another perspective on the immigrant experience — the awareness, by those who do not emigrate, of the impact that emigration has on their nation and culture. Ady's image of an entire people being "swallowed up" or eaten — absorbed — suggests a human mouth that eats and speaks. Food and language, after all, are both kinds of nourishment.

The Hungarians who emigrated before the First World War kept their mother tongue alive, as most immigrant groups did. They founded and joined ethnic organizations, published their own newspapers, built churches (which often sponsored social clubs and language classes), and ensured, through their communities, that their children had opportunities for bilingual education. But these immigrants generally came from peasant backgrounds, and few would have had more than a sixth-grade education. Not many would have read even the popular nineteenth-century novelist Mór Jókai, let alone Hungary's more difficult authors. And, of course, they left their homeland just as a new generation of fiction writers—Gyula Krúdy, Zsigmond Móricz, Margit Kaffka, and Desző Kosztolányi—were writing many of the greatest works of the Hungarian narrative tradition. Primarily concerned with making a living, such immigrants would not have been likely to encourage their children to pursue literary careers. Educated in English, the second generation would not see itself reflected in the literature of North America.

The next substantial number of Hungarian immigrants, who arrived after the revolution of 1956, discovered established communities with many social services. Apart from work, the older newcomers could choose to lead their lives mainly in Hungarian. Many of this new wave of immigrants came from urban, educated, middle-class backgrounds. While some would have been familiar with Hungary's writers, they had to fight the stigma of being political refugees and struggle to find work suited to their education or professional training. Only in the last twenty years or so has the idea of multiculturalism gained currency in public debate. In the meantime, the younger generation of Hungarians had found assimilation fairly easy compared to many other ethnic groups. They had been truly "swallowed up," and in the process many discarded their native tongue.

Hungarian immigrants who came to the United States before the First World War, in the years Ady called a "fugitive revolution," often appear as minor figures in John O'Hara's early stories set in the Pennsylvania coal-mining country. The autobiographical story "The Doctor's Son," one of O'Hara's finest, recounts the effects of the 1918 influenza epidemic on the life of Jim Malloy, the son of an exhausted local doctor. Jim agrees to drive young Doctor Myers on his father's rounds, to visit various "patches," or small mining villages. Although the patches are home to many immigrant groups, including Irish, Slavs, and Germans, "The Doctor's Son" focuses on Hungarian immigrants — referred to as "Hunkies." Despite this term, the story is not disparaging, and O'Hara treats his immigrants with respect.

During one of the car trips, Doctor Myers meets a group of sick women at Kelly's saloon. Jim describes the scene:

> I was standing there when the first of the Hunkie women had her turn. She was a worried-looking woman who even I could see was pregnant and had been many times before, judging by her breasts. She had on a white knitted cap and a black silk shirtwaist — nothing underneath — and a nondescript skirt. She was wearing a man's overcoat and a pair of Pacs, which are short rubber boots that men wear in the mines. When Doctor Myers spoke to her she became voluble in her own tongue.[6]

The doctor offers to visit the woman's house to see her sick child, but one of the Irish women in the group objects. Kelly cuts her off at once: "A fine way you do be talkin' wid the poor dumb Hunkie not knowing how to talk good enough to say what's the matter wid her gang. So keep your two cents out of this, Mamie Brannigan, and get back in line."[7] O'Hara is too much of a naturalist (and social historian) to ignore the tensions between different ethnic groups, and this passage — almost a casual aside — suggests the bitterness that can erupt in any competitive atmosphere. Mamie's knowledge of English gives her a sense of status; she knows the pecking order in the world of immigrant workers and wants to affirm her place in it.

Kelly offers brandy to the doctor and the troubled woman before they leave. Jim reports that "the Hunkie woman raised her glass and said something that sounded more like a prayer than a toast." Once outside, she climbed into the doctor's car "timidly" and later seemed "happier and encouraged, and prattled away as we followed her into the house." The rooms reveal a life of grim poverty. Doctor Myers speaks to the sick child, "but the girl apparently made no sense even in the Hunkie language." She dies almost immediately, of diphtheria. While the doctor turns his attention to the other children, Jim watches the grieving mother: "The woman had the dead girl in her arms. She did not need the English language to know that the child was dead. She was rocking her back and forth and kissing her and looking up at us with fat streams of tears running from her eyes."[8] This portion of the story devoted to the Hungarian woman (roughly a fifth of it) shows how O'Hara brought immigrant life into American fiction. Although it is currently out of fashion, O'Hara's best work has an energy and compassion sometimes missing in the fiction praised today. I make this point because "The Doctor's Son," written in 1931 and later published in the collection of the same name (1935), presents less stereotypical Hungarian figures than we find in more recent fiction.

O'Hara's Jim Malloy remains an outsider to the world of immigrant miners. His main interest in the story is his love for the daughter of David Evans, the district superintendent of Collieryville's largest mining corporation. Yet Jim doesn't look away from the suffering of the "Hunkie" woman, or dismiss her as foreign and therefore beyond sympathy. At the moment he watches her cradle her dead child, he drops the term "Hunkie" and calls her only "the woman." Suffering has moved her beyond ethnic labels, at least for a time. Jim comes to understand that illness and death are the great levelers. At the end of the story, when David Evans dies of the flu, Jim recalls "the bottle that he had shared with Steve and the other Hunkies" and realizes that the epidemic has spread from one community to another with an ease that mocks class distinctions.[9] While the immigrant experience is never O'Hara's focus, in his fiction Hungarians — "Hunkies" — start to become visible.

Along with Mordecai Richler and Adele Wiseman, John Marlyn belonged to the pioneering generation of writers who brought the immigrant experience to Canadian fiction. His novel *Under the Ribs of Death* (1957), set in Winnipeg's North End during the years leading to the Depression, tells the story of Sandor Hunyadi, a Hungarian immigrant who settles in Winnipeg with his parents, as Marlyn did himself. In the first chapter, Marlyn sketches the isolation felt by a sensitive immigrant child who already knows that words have power. For example, Sandor is ashamed of the Hungarian boarders who rent rooms in his family's house: "They were all foreigners, everyone of them, and as though that were not bad enough they were actually proud of their foreign, outlandish ways. Not one of them had yet made a serious effort to learn English."[10] Sandor himself has no interest in anything but being accepted as a Canadian. Although he isn't sure what that entails, he knows that it means rejecting ethnicity, or any ethnicity other than the culture associated with the British Isles. The boarders, representing the antithesis of everything he aspires to be, serve as a rebuke to his pretensions. Like anyone fearing immigrants, he thinks of them as selfish and ungrateful:

> Probably wishing they were still in the old country, he thought, where the sun was always supposed to be brighter, where everyone laughed and sang all day, and where even a crust of bread tasted better. Well, why didn't they go back there, then?[11]

Sandor wants to forget that he, too, is an immigrant—the other.

His plight has a context in language. He is being educated in an English-language school that espouses the narrative of English-speaking peoples, and of course there is no place for his ethnicity in that narrative. His own language has no meaning for him; he can barely remember it. Thinking of the boarders again, Sandor reveals the frustration of someone who lacks a genuine language:

> They were speaking Hungarian, of which he remembered scarcely enough to ask for a crust of bread. When they had arrived in Winnipeg it was to find that for every Hungarian there were twenty Austrians or Germans, so that over the years the Hungarian language was heard less and less at home and German, the second language of their mother-country, more and more. English began to alternate with German when Sandor was present, and it was only on rare occasions now, or when they had something to keep from him, that they spoke Hungarian.[12]

Sorting out the language ties in this passage is a complicated matter. German is not exactly the second language of Hungary, which was still part of the Austro-Hungarian empire when Marlyn was born there in 1912, and his hero would have come to Canada at roughly the same time that Marlyn did. German, however, was

commonly spoken in the western area of Hungary known as Transdanubia (even today German is often used there by merchants).
More important, Sandor thinks that speaking a foreign language
is a shameful thing. He fails to understand that *not* speaking one
is also dangerous for an immigrant. Since he lacks his mother
tongue, he also lacks its stories—its narrative. Inevitably, Sandor,
who lives in English, wants to be part of the dominant culture. Its
language validates his experiences, his life.

Of course Sandor also longs to change his name—a metamorphosis that will finally, he hopes, make him belong.[13] Describing
an after-school fight to his father, he is filled with shame and self-
loathing:

> "Everywhere I go," he cried, "people laugh when they hear me
> say our name. They say 'how do you spell it?' The lady in the
> library made fun of me in fronta all the people yesterday when
> I took your book back and she hadda make out a new card. And
> the school nurse . . . everybody . . . even the postman laughs. If
> we changed our name I wouldn't hafta fight no more, Pa. We'd
> be like other people, like everybody else. But we gotta change
> it soon before too many people find out."[14]

Sandor learns to feel ashamed of his background in schools and
libraries—places of books and learning. If even those associated
with the best his new home offers regard him with contempt,
how can he not internalize their image of him? Eventually Sandor
changes his name to Alex Hunter. "Hunter" is not a translation
of the Hungarian name "Hunyadi" (*vadász* is the Hungarian word
for "hunter"), but it does share its first syllable with "Hunyadi,"
"Hungarian," and "Hun." Symbolically too, the new name con-
veys Sandor/Alex's situation: he is always on the prowl, hunting
for something.

Father Hunyadi may have admirable values, but he is not a
prophet:

> "You are ashamed of the wrong things, Sandor," he said. "It is
> shameful to be a money-chaser, to be dishonest, and to remain
> ignorant when the opportunity for learning is so great here. But

to be ashamed of your name because you are Hungarian and are poor! When you grow up you will laugh to think that such things ever troubled you. . . . Do you understand, Sandor?"[15]

Sandor's tragedy, and the tragedy of many children of immigrants, is that growing up does not always bring this realization. The end of the novel finds him caught in the grip of the Depression— sharing the plight of his country. As he sits watching his baby son, his eyes fill with tears but there is a smile on his face. This ending refuses to resolve the issues Marlyn has raised. In fact the entire book explores the conflicts contained in the passages I've cited from its first chapter. Sandor knows that his father is right, but he also knows that Canada has no place for either of them. Life, he hopes, will be different for his son.

The issue of claiming an ethnic heritage also drives much of Hortense Calisher's fiction. Born a year before Marlyn, she was the child of a German Jewish immigrant mother and a Southerner who had moved to New York City. The Mannixes in *The New Yorkers*, a prominent, philanthropic Jewish family living on the upper East Side, draw Edwin Halecsy into their world, taking pity on the sad child. Judge David Mannix, the family patriarch, has a grim secret: at the age of twelve his daughter Ruth found her mother in the arms of a lover and shot her fatally. Ruth, who has blocked the episode from her memory, meets Edwin at the home of his aunts, who are seamstresses. "Our nephew," they say, introducing him, "we found each other only a few weeks ago."[16]

The teenagers are drawn to each other and Ruth confides in Edwin: " 'We're Jews.' She said it proudly, the way all Jews did, the ones he knew. 'I know a lot of Jews,' he said."[17] Ruth invites him back to her house for ice cream, and naturally he accepts. He is impressed by the lavish brownstone:

> When he didn't come right in after her, the girl reached out, one hand still on the doorknob, and gave him a patting push inward, with the other. She hadn't seemed to mind the corruption of his clothing, from whose dim, anciently inhabited checkers whatever soul he had shrank with recluse instinct, saying mutely and with all a foundling's urge, "I'm Hungarian."[18]

Edwin's mute "I'm Hungarian" apologizes for everything he isn't —comfortable and assimilated. Not daring to say the words, he internalizes his shame. Like Marlyn's Sandor, he knows himself to be an outsider, without understanding the burden of a fragmented personality.

Little more is mentioned about Edwin's Hungarian background, except that he dislikes the Mannixes' maid, resenting her gaze: "Her flat-set eyes—Polack, Hungarian?—scanned his Charlie Chaplin trousers."[19] Calisher turns instead to the issue that interested her from the start—what it means to be Jewish in modern America. In the cosmopolitan world of the Mannixes, people are gauged by appearances. But Edwin remains apart. Although he matures, and grows closer to the Judge, he still stands out: "In physique nothing much, his face and manner had already had a duality; it was never quite possible to tell from either what Edwin *was*."[20] Exactly what Edwin is—and his sense of himself—vanish from the novel. He becomes a factotum, absent even when present. Not exactly assimilated, he has gained as much acceptance as his life will allow. The novel ends in 1955, a year before the Hungarian uprising, which probably wouldn't have mattered to Edwin or the other characters in *The New Yorkers*.

Marlyn was forty-five when *Under the Ribs of Death* was published, and twenty-four years passed before his second novel, *Putzi, I Love You, You Little Square*, appeared. Putzi, a precocious talking fetus on the verge of being born, worries about his mother, Ellen, a virgin who has not yet chosen a husband from several suitors. Also set in Winnipeg's Hungarian community, the novel is peopled with characters named Molnar, Bodnar, Kovacs, Gabor, and Barta, and various dead husbands with names like Istvan. The older generations make casual references to their background, but mainly as complaints or outbursts of frustration. Ellen's Aunt Jessie remarks to Alvin, one of Ellen's suitors:

"You think maybe I didn't hear you that night you called me a Hungarian Aunt Jemima and said my life style was out of style. I found out quick enough what you meant. You want people like me to drop dead because old ladies aren't in fashion anymore.

You believe we haven't got the right to live because we're not like you. So maybe we'd rather be dead."[21]

The combination of "Aunt Jemima" and "Hungarian" mixes the two stereotypes of the genial old black cook and the elderly babushkaed immigrant. Aunt Jessie realizes that her ethnicity seems dated, but she challenges Alvin's assumptions, which equate ethnicity with death. Stereotypes, she knows, are a kind of death for anyone forced to wear them.

Generational conflict dominates this short comic novel, but Marlyn presents it almost genially. Aunt Jessie accepts the talking fetus without a second thought: " 'Maybe you talk Hungarian too?' Jessie asked, addressing herself to Ellen's abdomen. 'Anyway, say something already to your Auntie Jessie my little angel.' "[22] Putzi ignores her, preoccupied as he is in finding the right father for himself. But when he does talk, Putzi speaks eloquently, mixing quotations from British poetry with modern colloquialisms. The chorus of immigrant women who watch Ellen select her husband, wondering if she will pick one of their sons, speak in a broken English that shows Marlyn's pleasure in fractured language. Mrs. Ungar, the mother of one of Ellen's suitors, asks:

"And what's wrong with Mrs. Epstein? Half the ladies on the street she learned how to talk English. You should hear what happened to poor Mrs. Basco and Mrs. Gabor after Mr. Wunderlich learned them how to talk English. Better you should try to talk to a dog."[23]

Even Marlyn's characters are amused by broken English. Such passages add to the novel's humor and give it a kind of ethnic local color, but they reduce ethnicity to background noise. Often a defense against feelings of marginality, immigrant humor is a complex subject. Marlyn uses it to convey the tensions between generations who don't understand each other. But his humor is not at the expense of the women who provide it; unlike their children, they at least know what they want. No one in the novel ever speaks a word of Hungarian.

Near the end of the novel Putzi realizes that his incessant nagging has tormented his mother:

But I never realized I was such an impulsive character. It must be all that black coffee you drink and all that goulash you eat. Or maybe it's just my ardent Hungarian nature. Of course, that's it. Ah, what a lover I shall be with that fire raging in my veins and that Hungarian rhapsody throbbing in my loins.[24]

The speech is a high comic moment, especially because the novel never addresses the issue of Hungarianness. Ethnicity seems to be something "out of style," as Jessie noted earlier. And Putzi is, in fact, biologically fatherless. (Ellen had been participating in a university-sponsored experiment on memory formation but she accidentally took pills for another experiment with laboratory animals.) Putzi inherits his mother's ethnic background, but the laconic Ellen displays none of the qualities that Putzi associates with an "ardent Hungarian nature." *His* ardent nature may just as likely come from the goulash Ellen eats as from any genetic link between mother and child. Ellen sensibly responds to his discovery with "Putzi—not now, please." She is about to give birth, and Putzi can only hope that Ellen will go along with his choice of the kind Dr. Julian Donat—definitely not Hungarian—as husband/father.

These books by Calisher and Marlyn were written after the Second World War, and long after a number of immigrant groups had been treated in North American fiction. Calisher belongs to the generation of Jewish American writers who came into prominence in the 1960s, and Marlyn is generally included under the umbrella of Canadian ethnic writing rather than associated with his specific group. Their novels, of course, don't add up to a tradition, or anything that can be regarded as one. This is the central problem in dealing with Hungarians and North American fiction. My discussion is inevitably limited to the few books we have that include Hungarian characters and concerns. They may seem like a random sampling, perhaps one difficulty in attempting to analyze the absence of something. Yet it is fair to suggest, as Mary Gordon and Gay Talese have, that a lack of tradition also deserves attention. One may even speculate that this absence has affected the ability of Hungarian North American writers to see themselves, and their displacement, as a subject for fiction, limiting their ability to achieve a voice.[25]

There are, of course, practical problems in writing novels, and George Bisztray addressed the issue in a 1979 survey of fifteen Hungarian Canadian writers by asking the question, "Why are there so few Hungarian-Canadian novels?" Inquiring about all aspects of their writing and publishing experience, he discovered a pattern in their responses: "Some find the reason in a lack of time, others in the difficulties of publishing a novel, still others in lack of talent and experience. In numerous answers, the astonishing argument occurs that one cannot write a novel outside of the sphere of one's native tongue."[26]

The first four reasons—lack of time, publishing problems, lack of talent, little experience—face all writers whether or not they are immigrants. These are common explanations, or rationalizations, for not writing. But they also pose genuine obstacles. More interesting is the last reason, as well as Bisztray's astonishment at it. When he offers his own answer to the question, he reiterates elements that the writers themselves had emphasized, but he does not specifically include language in his own list: "Aesthetically, the writing of novels demands more epic distance and intellectualism, or at least 'wisdom,' and less emotionalism and subjectivism than the writing of poetry. Since these prerequisites do not characterize the frustrating period of acculturation," he continues, "the process of immigration inhibits the writing of creative prose for a while." He goes on to say: "A novel requires more time, determination, and existential security to write than poetry; it costs more to produce; has less chance of publication, and, finally, is definitely a risky market item."[27] This is good common sense, yet Bisztray's use of the phrase "for a while" suggests that he does not wholeheartedly accept the conclusions his writers put forth. If "for a while" really operated, one would expect to see more novels by Hungarian North Americans.

Some writers, however, are not defeated by the bleak situation that faces first novelists. In 1965, Stephen Vizinczey, a young Hungarian immigrant living in Toronto, published his novel, *In Praise of Older Women*. The book became a cause célèbre and has gone through thirty-six printings in English alone. Born in Hungary in 1933, Vizinczey fought in the 1956 revolution and escaped to Canada, much like his novel's hero, András Vajda. *In Praise of*

Older Women is Vajda's account of his amorous and political adventures. Addressed "To Young Men Without Lovers," it tells the story of a philosophy professor at the University of Michigan, in Ann Arbor, who escaped from Hungary at the age of twenty-three and found himself at sea in North American culture, a culture that "glorifies the young; on the lost continent of old Europe it was the affair of the young man and his older mistress that had the glamour of perfection."[28] In the last twenty pages of the novel (a tenth of its length) Vizinczey deals with András's experiences in North America, specifically Toronto, where he attends university and receives a doctorate.

The most verbal of characters, András is hell-bent on surviving well. After arriving in Toronto, he meets an Austrian cab driver who warns him that the city is "peopled with different spirits than the ones I knew back home." Although András has little money at first, he can bypass many of the experiences that overwhelm immigrants because he knows English. Language is never a problem for him, and he finds work as a lecturer at the University of Toronto. However, the language of love, North American style, will be another matter. András quickly becomes "Andrew" and learns that Canadian women will add a new "type" to his dictionary of the female personality—"grown women as teenage girls." Almost instinctively he knows that he has to keep his distance "from women who adored Comrade Stalin or gypsy music," and he misses the sophisticated European women who once kept him company.[29]

András/Andrew is the immigrant as picaro, a sort of Hungarian Tom Jones. He sees that he has come to a city in a moment of great change—"whole streets of old houses were renovated and transformed into exotic boutiques, art galleries, bookshops and outdoor cafes"—and if the streets are smaller than those in Budapest, and named after developers instead of writers and musicians, András will accept them as they are, sensing that he has walked into "the phenomenon which became known as the North American Sexual Revolution." Yet András's sense of self is frequently deflated by the attitudes of the women he meets, and he eagerly moves to Ann Arbor and a new life, becoming, in retrospect, "a typical small-town American, who often misses the big-city life of Toronto."[30] Assimilation is total: András ends up missing Toronto, not Budapest. In 1966, Vizinczey left Canada for London, and his subsequent novels do not deal with Hungarian immigrants or issues.

Two recent examples of the North American cultural context in which Hungarians remain faceless will give an idea of the background contemporary fiction writers may have absorbed. In March 1993, Frank Rich of the *New York Times* reviewed the musical based on Neil Simon's film *The Goodbye Girl*. He wrote, in passing: "Fearful of being politically incorrect, Mr. Simon has pointlessly changed the hilarious gay director of 'Richard III' in the film to a Hungarian in the musical."[31] I am not faulting playwright Simon for being "politically incorrect" about Hungarians, but his alteration does suggest that in North America Hungarians are easy butts of humor. One reason for this may be that in our fiction they are "underrepresented," to borrow Gay Talese's word. Several years ago, during an interview about multiculturalism and the arts, novelist Robertson Davies remarked: "To mention only one group that has contributed very greatly to the intelligent appreciation of the arts in Canada, there are the Hungarians. Because of the Revolution, an enormous number of them came here, upper-middle-class people of education and culture at home, and they brought culture with them."[32] Davies saw fit to mention Hungarians only as art consumers, not art makers. He would, of course, know John Marlyn's novels, as well as Vizinczey's. Although Davies might amend his remark, and Simon is not a fiction writer, both suggest how stereotypes of Hungarians can flourish even today.

The title story of Margaret Atwood's *Wilderness Tips* includes a character named George, "whose name is not really George."[33] A variant on the sophisticated continental, he left Hungary after the 1956 uprising. "He spent the forties rooting through garbage heaps and begging," Atwood notes, taking no further interest in his childhood. After settling in Toronto, like Vizinczey's András, George meets Prue, one of three sisters who change his life, at a party "thrown by a real-estate developer with Eastern European connections." The detail of the real-estate developer adds a hint of sleaze — one wouldn't meet someone like George at a small party given by friends. George's description verges on parody: "At that time he was young, thin as a snake, with a dangerous-looking scar over one eye and a few bizarre stories." With its echoes of Holly-

wood villains from some sinister Central Europe of the imagination, this passage marks George as the other, and fundamentally
inhuman. Of course he has "unorthodox business practices."[34]

The story "Wilderness Tips" explores the world of an old Ontario family at their summer home, Wacousta Lodge, and George's
attachment to the family. Married to Portia, and now running to
fat, he remains an outsider: "George, who has seen many people
taken out and shot, though not for driving motorboats, smiles, and
helps himself to a sardine. He once shot three men himself, though
only two of them were strictly necessary." No doubt these killings
are among the "few bizarre stories" Atwood has alluded to, reducing George's history to farce. The phrase "though only two of
them were strictly necessary" marks George as a character without claims to sympathy. Speaking to his mother-in-law, he draws
close, "bending his scar and his glinting marauder's eyes towards
her in the light from the kerosene lamp." He exploits the role of
the continental charmer: "A hint of opposition and he'd thicken
his accent and refer darkly to Communist atrocities."[35] Atwood
can't resist taking potshots at George's foreignness. Her three sisters may be lost souls, even fatally weak, but they're still human —
and Canadian. George is an ethnic cartoon.

One day George picks up an old book, from 1905, called *Wilderness Tips*. We already know that he speaks five languages, yet the
title confuses him. Surely such a linguist wouldn't stumble over
a common word like "tips," confusing it with asparagus, advice
about stepping into a canoe, and homemakers' columns in women's
magazines. But Atwood wants to exploit her story's title and is will-
ing to do so at George's expense. She makes George look like a
"dumb Hunkie," to use the words of one of O'Hara's characters.
But while the prejudices of O'Hara's characters are not his own
feelings, George is the puppet of Atwood's condescending humor.

By reducing George's connection with humanity to a kind of
ethnic shtick and making a joke of his ethnicity, the story loses its
moral center, and any potential for social criticism. I'm not suggesting that Atwood should have presented George as an immigrant hero. Some immigrants have been opportunists and poseurs.
But George comes from a genre different from that of the story's
naturalistic Canadian characters. At one point, Portia's brother

imagines George as an invader driving past a subdivision of new houses with "little pointed roofs—like tents, like an invasion. The tents of the Goths and the Vandals. The tents of the Huns and the Magyars. The tents of George."[36] There is little difference between this view of George and the character Atwood has created. Nothing is gained in the story by making him Hungarian. Atwood takes a free narrative ride on George's ethnicity, but he is neither a foil to the self-absorption of her Ontario family nor a believable character in his own right. George merely adds a frisson of sinister foreignness, and that is his function. Atwood is too clever a writer to make "George" a black Jamaican, a Soviet Jew, or a Vietnamese businessman. He is Hungarian because his Hungarianness provides a safe target.

Unlike Atwood, whose humor often requires exotic stereotypes of one kind or another, Michael Ondaatje is a writer who has always been drawn to exotic people and places. His novel *The English Patient* is no exception. In it, four people meet during the last months of the Second World War at a deserted Italian villa: the unnamed English patient, whose body has been severely burned; Hana, his troubled Canadian nurse; Caravaggio, a professional thief and war hero; and Kip (Kirpal Singh), a young Sikh bomb expert. It takes more than half of the novel for readers to learn that the eponymous English patient is, in fact, a Hungarian count named Ladislaus de Almásy—yet another version of the sophisticated continental.[37]

Almásy claims to be English in the first pages of the book, and nothing about him makes Hana suspect otherwise. His memories range from English country gardens to brutal experiences in the desert. There are no clues to the English patient's background. He refuses to give his name, but he does offer a serial number that proves he worked for the Allies. He speaks English without an accent, knows British poetry, appears to love his country. Hana notices that he also speaks German, but that fact means little to her. More than a third of the way through the novel, Caravaggio suggests that the patient may not be what he seems: "We don't even know if he's English. He's probably not."[38] Eventually Caravaggio exposes him, and recounts Almásy's history as an aristocratic adventurer whose love of the desert led him to help the Germans by guiding one of their spies to Cairo under Rommel's orders.

Nothing we learn about Almásy gives him the identity of a Hungarian. His ethnicity is without meaning—merely a word, like the Hungarian background of Marlyn's Sandor or Calisher's Edwin—although it gives Almásy less trouble than them since he isn't treated as an immigrant. When he talks with Caravaggio about their experiences in the Middle East, the thief explains that people thought him "a mystery, a vacuum," [39] and Almásy seems to understand and offers the reasons for his involvement with the Germans. Though he joined the wrong side during the war, by the novel's end Caravaggio and Hana accept him as one of their own, and want to protect him.

In one of the climactic scenes, Kip accuses the English patient of cultural imperialism: "I grew up with traditions from my country, but later, more often, from *your* country. Your fragile white island that with customs and manners and books and prefects and reason somehow converted the rest of the world." [40] There are several ironies at play here. Kip doesn't yet know the English patient's identity, so he can't realize that his accusation is unjust, at least on a literal level. The reader knows, but it makes little difference because we know nothing of Almásy's Hungarian origins—only that he appears to be an Anglophile. Yet a few pages later, after bombs have been dropped on Hiroshima and Nagasaki (we hear nothing of Dresden), and Kip finds out that the English patient isn't English, he exclaims: "American, French, I don't care. When you start bombing the brown races of the world, you're an Englishman." [41] Since Kip becomes the novel's conscience, it would seem that Ondaatje supports his refusal to make distinctions along the lines of nationality. Almásy's ethnicity doesn't matter, if one accepts the logic of *The English Patient*, because he is a white man, and all white men are the same. This may explain why Ondaatje conceals the identity of his English patient for much of his novel. Certainly the distinction doesn't matter to Almásy. But why is "the English patient" a Hungarian count rather than a Polish one? Or Danish? Or Russian? The question may seem strange, yet I think it is worth asking. Ondaatje undoubtedly had his own reasons. Almásy, however, belongs to the picture of Hungarians that North American writers have developed. For the most part his background is meaningless, making him a cipher that can be used to present or examine notions of foreignness. In this sense Almásy is the typical Hungarian of North American fiction—absent even when present. His ethnicity interests no one, neither his creator nor himself.

Mary Gordon and Gay Talese have offered a range of practical reasons for the lack of Irish and Italian American novelists, from religion to educational opportunities to the financial pressures on immigrant children to assimilate. True as these are—for Hungarian North Americans as well—I think that the issue of language must be emphasized, and broadened to include the absence of a narrative tradition. Without one, Hungarian North Americans are—in the truest sense—without words. They see no reflection of themselves in North American fiction, or only a few mirror tricks suggesting, momentarily, that they are about to come into being, like ghostly images. Books, after all, lead to other books. The writers I have discussed offer barely a sketch of what might be included in fiction about the Hungarian North American experience, and they show how little we know of it.

At a time when "multiculturalism" tends to refer to non-European ethnicities, it seems unlikely that Hungarian American subjects will come to the fore or be fashionable. A moment in time was lost after the 1956 uprising, and I suspect that it will not return. At least we can acknowledge the loss, or wonder what might have been.

The Empty Box
Hollywood Ethnicity
and Joe Eszterhas

Fifty years ago movie insiders could joke that it wasn't necessary to be Hungarian to work in Hollywood, but it helped. The list of eminent Hungarians includes Adolph Zukor, founder and president of Paramount Pictures, and William Fox, founder of Fox Pictures; directors like Michael Curtiz, Charles Vidor, George Cukor, and for a time, Alexander Korda; actors Arisztid Ort (Béla Lugosi) and László Steiner (Leslie Howard); and the composer Miklós Rózsa. These were cosmopolitan Europeans, known for their charm and style, yet many of the films they made are thought of as quintessentially American: *Casablanca* and *Yankee Doodle Dandy* and *White Christmas* by Curtiz, or *Gilda* by Charles Vidor. Today's most prominent Hollywood Hungarian (or Hungarian American, to be exact) is Joe Eszterhas, the screenwriter responsible for Sylvester Stallone's *F.I.S.T.* (1978), the two mega-hits *Flashdance* (1983) and *Jagged Edge* (1985), and some notable subsequent bombs, including *Betrayed* (1988) and *The Music Box* (1989). Having tried for "serious" art, Eszterhas returned to his origins—B movies—with a 1992 film, *Basic Instinct*, about lesbian and bisexual killers, widely mentioned in the press because of protests from California's gay media watch.

With a screenplay by Eszterhas, Costa-Gavras as director, and a cast that included Jessica Lange and the distinguished German actor Armin Mueller-Stahl, *The Music Box* held promise. In the Hollywood manner of blending politics with melodrama, it is based loosely on the true story of John Demjanjuk, the Ukrainian-born Cleveland autoworker who had been extradited to Israel, where he was tried for war crimes as the notorious Ivan the Terrible of Treblinka. *The Music Box* adds a twist to the facts, when Mike (Miska) Laszlo, a retired steel-mill worker who settled in Chicago in the early 1950s, is charged in the mid-1980s with lying on his application for American citizenship to conceal war crimes in Hungary. Mike turns to his daughter, Ann, a prominent criminal lawyer, for help. As she prepares her father's defense, believing in his innocence completely, Ann begins to feel uneasy, at first fighting her doubts; eventually she has to learn the truth at all costs.

Yet the film's ostensible subjects—filial love and the Holocaust—aren't the real center of activity on the screen. At the core of *The Music Box* is a curious ambivalence that amounts to ethnic self-hatred. In a work that tries to deal with Hungarian Jews and Gentiles from the vantage point of late twentieth-century North America, which hasn't (yet) suffered the kind of horrors of anti-Semitism that fed Nazism and made the Holocaust, anything obviously foreign, or un-American, appears to be threatening and even wrong. Ethnic self-hate is a curious phenomenon that occurs when individuals in a minority group accept the values of the dominant culture—and its view of them—as they try to assimilate, separating themselves from all that is "other" in their background, often without even being aware of what they are doing or the price of this rejection. It is not an uncommon phenomenon in Hollywood, where films dealing with ethnic subjects usually give reason for pause. Francis Ford Coppola's *Godfather* films are the most obvious example, promoting stylish cartoon stereotypes of Italians that amount to ethnic slurs. What's amazing is that such popular movies, made by an Italian American, are rarely seen for what they are as long as people have a good time and the wine — and blood — flow generously.

Eszterhas grew up in Cleveland, Ohio, which once claimed the largest concentration of Hungarians outside of Budapest. In 1980, for a series called Ethnic Heritage Studies published by Cleveland State University, he wrote the introduction for a volume by Susan Papp, dealing with the city's Hungarians. He was then living in San Rafael, California — the kid from the old neighborhood who had made good, like his film counterpart, Ann. Eszterhas recalled the world of Cleveland's west side in the 1950s with a mixture of affection and distance. The son of an immigrant writer and newspaper editor, he had spoken Hungarian with his parents, and described his father as a man who "lived in a completely Hungarian world, set in this strange, sharply-contoured American context, while my world teeter-tottered between the two."[1] In their small, walk-up apartment (Eszterhas has a penchant for words like "walk-up," as if they have a special pathos) a collection of colorful immigrants talked of books and music and poverty ("they were poor, naturally; we were all poor"). One particular friend of the family even confessed that he sometimes ate cat food, because it was cheap and filled with minerals, and tasty enough when sprinkled with paprika. What kept these people alive was "a passionate love for the old country, for Hungary." Although Eszterhas used Chicago as the setting for *The Music Box* rather than Cleveland — Chicago has a sexier national profile — his childhood memories still might have informed it. Instead, he betrays his heritage with stereotype piled on stereotype. The danger is that people might believe him.

Hungary's treatment of its Jews should be a difficult subject for many contemporary North Americans to comprehend, because it is so easy to pass judgment, to sound superior in discussing it. Yet any attempt to differentiate between the various Central European powers in their treatment of Jews during the Second World War is liable to sound heartless or hairsplitting—or both. If I say that, unlike the Poles, Hungarians did not begin rounding up Jews for Hitler's Final Solution until 1944, it may even sound as if I'm excusing anti-Semitism. There has to be a way of examining the subject without resorting to historical simplification. And for this reason Eszterhas may have been right to confront it through a surrogate North American like Ann, who can stand in for our first-hand ignorance of the crimes of the Holocaust. He must have been aware of how the Holocaust defies most attempts to deal with it in film, of how easily it becomes a subject for exploitation. There are exceptions, but the Holocaust produces such an array of emotions that a great part of the screenwriter's work seems already done simply by deciding to write about it.

Melodrama and politics can make an effective combination in film, especially when the balance doesn't tip to one side. Graham Greene's screenplay for *The Third Man* is a prime example. We are genuinely surprised at the course events take because they seem to happen the way life does, unpredictably and yet almost inevitably. The unpredictable is not the way of *The Music Box*. Instead, Eszterhas gives us a history lesson in lengthy courtroom scenes that detail the horrors of the Holocaust, Budapest style. As witness after witness claims to recognize her father, Ann struggles to believe in his innocence. The only thing Eszterhas withholds is the fact of Mike's guilt or innocence, but any audience can see where this movie is heading.

The 1950s community recalled during the course of *The Music Box* bears no resemblance to Eszterhas's portrait of the Hungarian community in his introduction to Susan Papp's book. Although he wrote of artists and writers who had to take menial jobs to support themselves, "suffering the exhaustion of eight and ten hour shifts"[2] before returning to their paintings and novels, in his screenplay all postwar Hungarians seem to have been anti-Semites and Nazi-sympathizers (often ex-members of the Arrow Cross, the Hungarian fascist party that allied itself with the Nazis) or Holocaust victims. No one with the humane values Eszterhas once celebrated belongs to his fictional Chicago, nor is there a word about the many Hungarians who resisted the Nazi regime. Eszterhas's film characters are endowed only with a passion about "the old country."

Mike, the accused, had inadvertently drawn FBI attention to himself five years earlier by disrupting the performance of a Hungarian national dance troupe to protest the country's Communist policies. This establishes his volatile yet serious character, and he claims that the Hungarian government is helping to prosecute him as punishment. The film's other Hungarians are either troubled but noble victims who testify to Nazi atrocities, dupes of the Communist system who will testify to anything, or stereotypical neighborhood women like Mrs. Kiss, who makes donuts for church suppers and occasionally sleeps with Mike. It comes as no surprise that an old-country acquaintance, Tibor Zoldan, an Arrow Cross cohort, had been blackmailing Mike about his past. When Ann finally visits Budapest, the Hungarians she meets are equally one-dimensional. Tibor Zoldan's sister, who suffers a bad case of historical amnesia, proudly shows Ann a photograph of her brother, years younger, in his wartime uniform. After this encounter Ann realizes that her father had indeed played a part in the Holocaust, and grasps her stomach as if she's about to vomit. Hungary has literally made her sick.

The film is punctuated with discussions about the nature of being an American. Mike's first cry of defense to his daughter sets the tone: "I worked in the mill, I raised my kids, it's my country, I been here thirty-seven years, and now they want to take my citizenship away."[3] Later, when Ann and Mike meet the opposing counsel, Jack Burke, Mike says, "I'm a citizen, I'm a good American," but Burke refuses to shake his hand and replies to Mike's protest of innocence: "If you're a good American, Mr. Laszlo, this country's in big trouble." And when Burke runs into Ann later on, he tells her: "You know, it's a perfect camouflage. Raise a couple of all-American kids and you avoid even a shadow of suspicion. You know, you're his perfect alibi."

As the details about Miska's treatment of Jews come to light,

Ann, who often seems to be learning about the Holocaust for the first time, has this exchange with her father:

> *Ann:* "It makes me sick, Papa. They took those people—women and children—and they lined them up on the riverbank . . ."
> *Mike:* "That's why I came to America."
> *Ann:* "It made me ashamed of being Hungarian."
> *Mike:* "You're an American. We are American. You're lucky to be young in America, not in Europe."

But how Hungarian is Ann? Her background seems to mean little to her. Having invited Burke to a pretrial dinner at a restaurant, she answers his question about the wine they are drinking, Egri Bikaver (Hungary's famous red wine), by saying: "It's called bull's blood. It kind of sneaks up on you and clobbers you. It's a Hungarian trait." As Burke later tells her, in words that sound as though they come from a plaque on the Statue of Liberty, the American traits are fairness and justice: "Our country has always tried to be a haven for those who have been persecuted, and after the war we let in thousands of its victims, but unfortunately we also let in some of the executioners. The war was almost over. We were in Germany and the Russians were crossing the Hungarian border. But the Hungarians were still killing their Jews. They turned the fucking romantic Danube into their own shade of blue." Ann replies angrily: "Some Hungarians. Not my father." If at that point she knows any more of the "details," she doesn't bother telling Burke.

As a screenwriter Eszterhas has a limited bag of tricks, and the discovery of hidden evidence is his favorite. In *Jagged Edge* the heroine finds a battered typewriter in the back of a closet; in *Betrayed* she finds a collection of guns under a floorboard in her bedroom; and in *The Music Box* she travels to Budapest, where she is given a pawn ticket which claims a music box that holds incriminating photographs of her father killing Jews. By this point *The Music Box* has turned into a monster movie. The subtleties of Hannah Arendt's theory of the banality of evil, argued in *Eichmann in Jerusalem*, are not for Eszterhas (or Hollywood). As Arendt explained how cultivated men could order the extermination of

Jews in the afternoon, and later that evening listen to Mozart while they played with their children, she developed one of the conventions of modern historiography. But Eszterhas isn't buying it. (In his opening speech at Mike's trial, prosecutor Burke remarks: "We are not speaking here of the banality of evil, of an anonymous bureaucrat sitting in an office giving orders, or a gendarme executing them. We are speaking of a man who committed these crimes with his own hand, we are speaking of evil incarnate.") When the film reaches its confrontation between Ann and her father, Mike cannot remain the feisty old man we've come to like. Instead he attacks Ann, his deadly cold eyes full of hate: "What happened to you? What did the Communists do to you?" Ann lowers her head.

The physical details of the film are impressively realistic, yet Jessica Lange's unfashionable hairstyle and wardrobe (which many critics considered particularly appropriate, as if it were natural to assume that the daughter of Hungarian immigrants would look different from other Americans, and be somehow less stylish) reveal only a surface ethnicity, which Lange wears like a costume. We only learn that she speaks Hungarian because she needs to serve the plot by having a conversation in Budapest that will lead her to the fatal pawn ticket. Since Ann doesn't dish up pots of goulash, we're saved from the crudest kind of ethnic stereotyping; but stereotypes have many faces. The small silver crucifix she sometimes wears (she's a *good* woman) is telling. Ann, however, knows the value of appearances, and warns her brother not to show up in court in his worker's clothes. Lange actually manages to deliver that line with conviction, which is a testament to something — that blind faith will get Ann through? And this relentless seriousness almost works in her favor. You have to like Ann: the movie might have been called *The Good Daughter*.

While her feelings about her background are fuzzy, Ann's ambivalence is suggested in the opening scene as she dances a stiff *csárdás* at a church party, and we hear that the community considers her a success, unlike her brother, who having failed to assimilate has remained "ethnic." Later we learn that she was once married to the son of a wealthy Chicago lawyer with prominent political connections. That her father-in-law is a right-winger in a *realpolitik* manner goes without saying — this film was directed by Costa-Gavras—and of course his last name, Talbot, reeks of the Establishment. So Ann traded the shabby but neat little house of her childhood, of the old neighborhood, for the big time. In the pretrial dinner with Jack Burke (another *non*ethnic name), he asks, "How does a Laszlo become a Talbot?" as if there was something extraordinary about the child of immigrant parents marrying outside her ethnic background in the 1970s. Ann replies with good humor: "I didn't want to stay a Laszlo." Why she divorced we never learn, so I can't fairly speculate that she felt uncomfortable in the world of WASP power and privilege. But Ann does go on to say: "There's a big move from Daymon Avenue to Lake Forest. I guess I never quite got there." Yet we have already seen that she is on easy terms with her father-in-law, and not unwilling to let him pull a few strings in Washington to help her clear Mike.

Eszterhas may have no use for Hannah Arendt, but are we to assume that Ann also lives in an intellectual vacuum? As Lange plays her, she is much more than a clever lady lawyer, the plot convention of so many Hollywood films. Lange's weary eyes look as if they *had* spent hours poring over volumes of small print. Like Eszterhas, Ann "teeter-tottered" between two worlds. In an early scene, when she tells her father that she has decided to represent him, the two are standing on a darkened stairwell outside her son's bedroom. A shadow covers half of her face, and Lange tilts her head so that for a moment she is entirely in the dark, and then back in the light as she says, "Papa, it'll be okay, Papa."

One of the dominant visual images in the film is water. During the trial scenes we hear that the notorious Miska took his victims to the banks of the Danube, where they were killed. One witness actually says, "River red, ice on side of river red, bodies on side of river blue, blue Danube was red." Later, during Ann's first trip to Budapest, where she exposes a surprise witness as a possible Communist dupe, Jack Burke urges her to visit the riverbank. Ann resists at first, but finally she looks into the reddish-brown swirling water as she prepares to accept her father's guilt. Earlier she had stood on the patio outside her living room, looking across a calm blue lake, and said to her black assistant, Georgine: "He is not a monster. I'm his daughter. I know him better than anyone." After she accepts the monster that he is ("I never want to see you again,

Papa. You don't exist") and sends Jack Burke the photographs that prove her father's guilt ("I went down to the riverbank," her letter begins), she takes her son out onto the patio, beside the same calm and very blue American lake, and, as the film ends, tells him the truth about Grandpa.

But what will Mikey understand? He will grow up like the other Americans in the film, believing that any foreigner is capable of the most heinous crimes. (Both Ann's ex-husband and ex-father-in-law casually ask if Miska did it, assuming the worst.) The immigrant world of Mike's church is a dying one, and Ann has already removed herself from it. In the opening dance sequence Mikey watches his mother and grandfather, and when asked to join in says, "I don't know how, Ma, I don't know how." Of course he won't learn, because this film never seriously questions the values of the dominant culture. In one of the silliest (yet most revealing) scenes, Ann explains to several colleagues that she intends to prepare her father's defense at Harry Talbot's office so that her own law firm won't suffer a loss of clients. One black colleague replies, "Why don't you get somebody else to represent your father? Get that guy from Cleveland, he handled that Dem . . . that Dem . . . that Demjock guy, whatever his name was," stuttering and stumbling over "Demjanjuk" until Ann and her fellow lawyers burst into amiable laughter, like guffawing actors in a TV beer commercial. The moment leaves a nasty impression of the easy contempt felt for anyone with an unfamiliar or difficult name—a contempt the film as a whole endorses. Such details are telling: they make up the melting-pot ethos in action. While *The Music Box* clearly wants to be politically correct—it is a daughter, not a son, who defends Mike; and her closest colleagues are black—it never faces the us/them split at its core.

In an interview with Paul Chutkow for the *New York Times*, on the eve of the opening of *The Music Box*, Eszterhas said: "I think some Hungarians will take umbrage at the film. But there is no doubt of it historically."[4] While no reasonable person denies the horrors of the Holocaust, there is something simpleminded about the way Eszterhas has used them in the film. "For my generation of Hungarian kids," he told Chutkow, "for kids with sensibility and sensitivity, the question 'What did you do in the war, Daddy?'

was potentially the worst possible personal nightmare." The self-congratulatory phrase "for kids with sensibility and sensitivity" is revealing, though one might dismiss it as pre-premiere jitters. One might—if the tone of Eszterhas's interview wasn't so self-serving. At sixteen, he admits to having spent a summer reading about the Holocaust: "I also put my parents through a grilling in terms of 'What did you see? What did you do?'" Are these the people Eszterhas professed to admire in his introduction to Susan Papp's book? They must have passed the "grilling," but what about other Hungarians? Are they all Nazis villains, as his film suggests? "In terms of my ancestry and history," Eszterhas continued, "I felt a kind of personally purgative, cathartic thing writing it. To be honest, and not to be dramatic about it, I'm very American, and I'm much more American than I'm Hungarian. But I'm Hungarian-born and in terms of making peace with your roots, this was something I felt I had to do." This is his bottom line: "I'm very American." On the side of the Statue of Liberty, like his prosecutor Jack Burke, Eszterhas may feel something "purgative, cathartic" about *The Music Box* as he tries to distance himself from his Hungarian background, but he still hasn't come near the case of ethnic self-hate that he seems on the verge of acknowledging in this interview. It's not surprising that he returned to a Hungarian theme in interviews about *Basic Instinct*. For *Premiere* he recalled an anecdote about his well-publicized feud with agent Michael Ovitz: "They say that if a Hungarian walks into a room and there are hundreds of people in that room and one person in that room has an ingrown toenail, the Hungarian will go right up to that person and start hopping up and down on that toe. Clearly that's what I've done." The cheap joke, apparently, pleases him: "There's one thing I can't deny, and that's that I'm Hungarian."[5]

The us/them split of ethnic self-hate is a genuine subject for films. An alternative (or antidote) to *The Music Box*, Jim Jarmusch's film *Stranger Than Paradise* (1984) presents a young woman, played by Hungarian actress Eszter Balint, visiting the United States for the first time, as a contrast to deadpan, burned-out, contemporary Americans. Yet she turns out to be as deadpan as they are. Hungary doesn't register on America, and America doesn't register on Hungary.

When everyone ends up in Cleveland in the bleakest winter, Jarmusch introduces what is often the most stereotypical of characters—the ethnic grandmother. This tight-lipped old woman enjoys beating her nephew and his friend at cards, but like everyone else in the film's alienated comic universe, she shows emotion only after achieving a small triumph, crying with glee, "I am da vinner!"[6] A whole character lives in her cry—years of hope and disappointment, of time passing and a tired, aging body—and when she finally explodes at her departing guests, in a mixture of Hungarian and foul-mouthed English, her frustration is palpable. Jarmusch never condescends to it, or reduces her to local color. While there's a world between his freewheeling road film and Eszterhas's glossy melodrama, it would be too easy to dismiss the comparison by referring to the intent or the economics of each film. That world of difference, after all, has to do with truth. And it is, finally, the falseness of *The Music Box* that defeats it. Since Eszterhas was one of the film's executive producers, his values and conception are probably more fully realized than most screenwriters dare dream. The film is his.

A Short Dictionary of Hungarian Stereotypes and Kitsch

BLUE DANUBE

The Danube is probably familiar to more people as a waltz than as the river that cuts through Budapest to produce the well-known postcard image of Hungary's capital. Unlike the waltz, the river now has a dull brownish cast, largely from the pollution of its upstream countries, Germany and Austria. But more than a century has passed since Johann Strauss II wrote *An der schönen blauen Donau*, op. 314, in 1867. Although it is associated mainly with Central Europe, the Danube is in fact the second longest river of the continent, after the Volga. Formed by two headstreams in the

Black Forest, it flows west to east to the Black Sea. In the past few years the Danube has been much in the news because of territorial conflicts between Hungary and the newly formed Slovakia regarding a Slovakian plan to build a diversion canal from the Danube for a dam and hydroelectric facility north of Budapest. Of considerable economic importance, the river is an environmental tragedy in the making. Claudio Magris, in his magesterial social history cum travelogue, *Danube*, had this to say: "The Danube is German-Magyar-Slavic-Romanic-Jewish Central Europe, polemically opposed to the Germanic *Reich;* it is a 'hinternational' ecumene, for which in Prague Johannes Urzidil praised it; it is a hinterworld 'behind the nations'."[1] Hungarians know it as the Duna.

CAROUSEL

The difference between American and Hungarian kitsch is clear when one compares the Rodgers and Hammerstein musical *Carousel* with the play on which it is based, Ferenc Molnár's *Liliom* (1909). The story of a tough but charming bouncer in a Budapest amusement park who physically abuses his wife, Juli, *Liliom* is taken from one of Molnár's short stories. The original play ends unhappily, like a waltz in a minor key, after Liliom kills himself to avoid capture by local police. When Rodgers and Hammerstein were urged to do an adaptation after their success with *Oklahoma!* they resisted the idea, fearing that the ending wouldn't work in a musical. Although the play had been popular on Broadway when first performed by the Theatre Guild, and again in revival in 1940, the Hungarian setting was deemed a drawback. By moving the locale to New England, and letting Liliom — now Billy Bigelow — die accidentally, several problems were resolved. There was, however, still the problem of the final scene, where Liliom returns from heaven to visit his daughter. After she refuses the offer of a star, he slaps her across the face, only to be led away, grimly, to hell. What worked in Budapest in 1909 was simply out of the question for American audiences in 1945. Billy's daughter has to be inspired by the almost-encounter with her ghost-father, who leaves the star behind to comfort his wife, Julie, as he returns to heaven, apparently successful in his ventures. The difference between these two endings is a difference in sensibilities that seem unlikely to meet.

Although Rodgers and Hammerstein had solved the problems of adaption for an American market, one problem remained: Ferenc Molnár himself.

Notoriously difficult, Molnár (1878–1952) had even refused Giacomo Puccini's request to adapt *Liliom* as an opera. After lengthy negotiations, Molnár agreed to the musical, but he had no idea what to expect. He first saw a run-through of *Carousel* several weeks into production. Rodgers and Hammerstein were naturally worried about how he might react to their revised ending, but they needn't have feared. After the rehearsal, Molnár was in tears. "What you have done is so beautiful!" he exclaimed, going on to add, "And you know what I like best? The ending."[2]

CONTINENTAL LOVER, HUNGARIAN STYLE

A stock figure in British and American popular culture, with roots in Gothic fiction, the continental lover needs little introduction. In his Hungarian manifestation, however, he also draws on the tradition of late nineteenth-century erotic literature in which Hungary often appeared as a setting. Western enough to be familiar, but Eastern enough to be exotic, Hungary produced a line of continental lovers usually associated with Gypsy music.

The eponymous hero of *Teleny* (1892), an erotic novel now attributed to Oscar Wilde, is a handsome young Hungarian pianist living in Paris. We first glimpse him playing "a wild Hungarian rhapsody by an unknown composer with a crackjaw name" (even when Wilde wrote pornography, he never lost his sense of humor) and learn that "in no music is the sensuous element so powerful as in that of the Tsiganes."[3] Teleny's music evokes erotic longing as well as images of "vast plains, of bands of gypsies." But the novel's narrator, M. Des Grieux, finds Teleny problematic: "Was he my guardian angel or a tempting demon?" Of course an aura of sexual threat is a necessary part of the continental lover's appeal. "You cannot disconnect him from the music of his country," Des Grieux remarks while falling in love with Teleny, whose "features seemed to be overshadowed by a deep melancholy." (*See* Madness/Melancholy *below.*) The novel details various heterosexual couplings until Des Grieux and Teleny consummate their attraction. Teleny has all the qualities of the continental lover, from good looks to a beguiling accent—he tells Des Grieux, "in a low tone, in that musical tongue, 'My body hungereth for thee'"—as well as a sexual organ that inspires everyone who sees it (this is pornography, after all). After making love, the young men share "a partridge, with *paprika*, or Hungarian curry." (*See* Paprika.) Such as it is, the narrative cannot leave the lovers happily in each other's arms. Pursued by debtors, Teleny beds Des Grieux's mother, who offers to pay his debts, and he then commits suicide because he doubts that his lover will forgive him. Still, Wilde's homosexual fantasia did extend the activities of the Hungarian lover from women to men.[4]

While I doubt that Anaïs Nin read *Teleny*, she built on the stereotype. In the 1940s, Henry Miller, who was being paid $100 a month to write erotic stories, shared the work with her. When Nin's erotica was collected in *Delta of Venus* (1977), she opened the book with a story called "The Hungarian Adventurer." Her hero is known only as "the Baron" because "he had astonishing beauty, infallible charm, grace, the power of a trained actor, culture, knowledge of many tongues, aristocratic manners," plus a talent for "moving smoothly in and out of countries."[5] Needing money, he simply marries again, along the way seducing endless willing young women. The story has a dark side, though. It is, in fact, a story of incest—or as much of one as pornography allows. The Baron has an appetite for young girls, which he eventually satisfies with his own teenage daughters; when they aren't enough to solve the problem of a persistent morning erection, he even seduces his son. Nin has no moral concerns in this story, but she can't resist coming to the aid of her young victims with this unexpected final sentence: "Their rebellion against their father's folly mounted, and they abandoned the now frenzied, aging Baron."[6] Her Baron is the continental lover eventually gone to seed.

But Hungarian lovers aren't always as highly sexed as they appear in Wilde and Nin. Perhaps their intended audience makes all the difference. The other side of the coin—the Hungarian lover out of bed—is another matter. The world of romance, rather than sex, almost tames him. *Almost*. American writer Eleanor Perényi (née Stone), who tends to be associated with *Harper's* and *Vogue*, is also the author of a biography of Franz Liszt and the gardening classic *Green Thoughts*. Her Hungarian adventure began in May 1937, and she recounted it in a memoir, *More Was Lost* (1946), which has been out of print for decades. It begins with the details of romance fiction — sweet Hungarian champagne, blooming horse chestnut trees, Gypsies playing in the café below her hotel window. When her mother insists that Budapest "*is* a sinister city,"[7] Eleanor doesn't listen. At dinner that evening she meets a dashing young man, the Baron Zsigmond Perényi, who offers her a Czech cigarette from a silver case. It's love at first sight. Several months later they marry and move to his estate in Szöllös, Hungary. The memoir is actually a touching account of her life there. With the Second World War brewing, she learns Hungarian from the estate's servants and a Hungarian translation of Daphne Du Maurier's *Rebecca*. Eleanor turns out to be passionate *and* sensible. Her book recaptures a lost time and place as war closes in on the couple. After Zsiga is called to military service, they conceive a child as a gesture of hope for the future. But "nothing turned out as we planned,"[8] except for the child. Circumstances separate them in 1941, and Eleanor returns to America to wait in safety for Zsiga. Four years later he writes to her, explaining his absence. Repelled by the war's barbarism, and the persecution of the Jews, he had joined a Communist underground organization. They are not reunited.

For a Hungarian romance outside the vicissitudes of history and true feeling, one has to find a Harlequin Romance. And there is one. Jessica Steele's *Hungarian Rhapsody* tells the story of a young English woman, Arabella Thornlow, who visits Budapest to have her portrait painted by a prominent artist named Zoltán Fazekas. Expecting to meet a bent old man, she finds instead a fellow in his mid-thirties: "he was powerfully built but without spare flesh — and quite something!" For most of the book he treats her with impatience (a sign of interest), but eventually he confesses his love, along with his fear that her beauty might be only skin deep. Although he has only a slight accent, Zoltán does have great wealth and "cool grey eyes" that confuse the hapless Arabella. Finally she realizes that "Hungary must have woven some sort of spell over her while she wasn't looking." Published in 1992, the novel combines bad travel writing with its romance agenda. In a country that had just seen the end of forty years of Soviet rule, Arabella focuses on her clothes. It is the continental lover—not his country—who blinds her. She does blame Zoltán's one sexual advance, a chaste kiss, on music—"gypsy music, she decided, had a lot to answer for," and at that moment we aren't far from the world of *Teleny*, Harlequin Romances being a specialized breed of erotic writing. Unlike Wilde and Nin, or Perényi, Jessica Steele (if that is her name) promises her lovers marital bliss.[9]

CSÁRDÁS

From *csárda*, the Hungarian word for tavern, the *csárdás* (usually spelled czardas in English dictionaries) is a nineteenth-century courtship dance, in duple time, that alternates slow and fast sections. It has also become a popular name for Hungarian restaurants in North America, conveying as it does an image of passionate dancers swinging to the music of cimbaloms and tambourines. Perhaps the most famous *csárdás*, at least outside Hungary, "Die Klänge der Heimat," was written by Johann Strauss II for *Die Fledermaus* (1874). The most Hungarian of operetta composers was, in fact, Emmerich (Imre) Kálmán (1882–1953), whose 1915 masterwork *Die Csárdásfürstin* (The Csárdás Princess) blends the waltz tradition of the Viennese dance halls with, as one critic said, "the Hungarian soil."[10] Of Hungarian Jewish origins, Kálmán was such a popular figure that he was supposedly advised to leave Hungary during the Second World War by none less than the Admiral Miklós Horthy, after attempts to have him declared an honorary Aryan had failed. Diane Pearson took the dance as title of her popular historical novel about Hungary before the Second World War. Heavily researched (Pearson includes a bibliography), this *Csardas* (1975) is full of national clichés as well as one of the nastiest continental lovers, Hungarian style, I know of, whose pro-Nazi sympathies lead him into the Arrow Cross. At the novel's end, the charming aristocratic rotter is shot to death by his own mother. A perverse courtship dance, American-publishing style.

GOULASH (GULYÁS)

When the first Magyars arrived on the Hungarian plain in the ninth century, they brought along large, heavy cast-iron kettles (*bogrács*) for making soups and stews. Without refrigerators, they had to preserve their meat by drying it. Whenever they wanted a meal, some of the meat came out and was tossed into a pot, along with water, and reheated.

Goulash evolved over the years. While caraway seeds often appear in it, a proper goulash is never thickened with flour or sour cream, nor is wine added. A thicker stew is made by using less water; *gulyásleves*, or goulash soup, is simply a *gulyás* made with more water. Most families have their own versions, with small regional variations. For a true Hungarian taste, don't substitute low-cholesterol oil for the lard, and use only Hungarian paprika (*see* Paprika).

Goulash Recipe

2 tablespoons lard	1 tablespoon sweet paprika
2 onions, chopped	1 1/2 pounds stewing beef, cubed
1 tomato, chopped	1 teaspoon tomato puree
1 green pepper, seeded	2 teaspoons salt
and chopped	1 1/2 cups boiling water
1 clove garlic, minced	3 potatoes, cubed

1. In a heavy saucepan heat the lard, then brown onions until golden.
2. Add remaining ingredients *except* potatoes and water. Brown until meat no longer looks raw.
3. Reduce heat, add the water, cover, and braise for one and one-half hours.
4. Remove meat. Strain gravy, and return to pan along with meat. Add potatoes. Simmer for another hour.

GYPSY MUSIC

When Edmund Wilson became interested in studying Hungarian, he wrote this to a friend: "I think that Bartók's music really tells you a good deal about Hungary. I have always very much admired it, but it will interest me more now—the alternation between brooding depression and rousing peasant dances, with flashes of spirited self-assertion."[11] This sounds like a description of manic depression, a term that has been used to characterize the

Hungarian temperament (*see* Madness/Melancholy). Hungarian Gypsy music was an ersatz creation by Hungarian composers often performed by Gypsies in small string ensembles. Genuine Gypsy music does exist, as does old Hungarian peasant music, but they are far removed from each other and unknown to most people outside Hungary, except ethnomusicologists. The hybrid music had its origins in *verbunkos*, a style of Hungarian military dance music that developed in the 1700s and even influenced composers like Haydn and Beethoven. This music suited Hungary's growing national spirit and became associated with some legendary Gypsy performers. In the same way, the identification of "folk" music (or popular music, at that time) with national consciousness led to the development of the Hungarian song (*magyar nóta*). As László Dobszay noted, "The most effective medium for the spread of the *magyar nóta* was the gypsy band. Ever since their mass appearance in the eighteenth century, gypsy bands had no real repertoire of their own (least of all a gypsy repertoire). They played everything that pleased the merry-making public, in the twentieth century even fashionable dance music."[12] Although Franz Liszt (*see* Liszt, Franz) made a number of wild assertions about the importance of Gypsy music to the development of Hungarian music in *Des bohémiens et de leur musique en Hongrie* (1859), the facts of the matter eventually came to light when the composers Béla Bartók and Zoltán Kodály traveled throughout their country in the early years of this century and recorded old Hungarian music (folk music, here, in the modern sense). Both composers, and many after them, were influenced by their discoveries.

HOLLYWOOD'S HUNGARY
Hollywood's Hungary has ranged from Hungarians in disguise, like László Steiner (Leslie Howard), Arisztid Ort (Béla Lugosi), László Loewenstein (Peter Lorre), and Bernard Schwartz (Tony Curtis), to a few Hungarian performers who have learned to make a joke of their ethnicity—S. Z. Sakall (Szoeke Szakall) and Zsa Zsa Gabor (*see* Zsa Zsa) come to mind immediately. The moonfaced Sakall especially is a pleasure to see in forties films like *Christmas in Connecticut* (1945), where he mouths Hungarian complaints under his breath while Barbara Stanwyck sets out to get

her man. (Playing a New York restaurateur from Budapest, in one scene Sakall steps up to a pot of Irish stew, sniffs, looks into the pot and exclaims: "Goulash with turnips! *Catastroph!*" "I tell you, it isn't goulash," the cook, Norah, explains as he reaches toward her spice rack, grabs a can and says: "Paprika! That will fix it. Now it's goulash."[13]) (*See* Goulash; Paprika.)

Screwball comedies of the thirties and forties thrived on stereotypes of all sorts, and Hungarians were natural candidates during the years that might fairly be called the golden age of Hungarians in Hollywood. In *Midnight* (1939), with a screenplay by Billy Wilder and Charles Brackett, Claudette Colbert plays a charming American golddigger adrift in Paris. Soon she meets an impoverished Hungarian cab driver, Tibor Czerny (Don Ameche), and ends up posing as a Hungarian baroness to help a millionaire (John Barrymore) make his unfaithful wife jealous. Of course Colbert and Czerny-Ameche are destined for each other, but it takes the entire movie for them to admit it. Along the way, Hungarian jokes pile up. My favorite occurs during a breakfast party, after Colbert complains about her imaginary husband, the Baron (also played by Ameche): "When I married I didn't realize that in the Czerny family there was a streak of, shall we say, eccentricity." Sitting beside her, Barrymore nods in commiseration and adds, "The Czernys are all like that. I met an old aunt, the Countess Antonia. I thought she was an Indian. It turned out she used paprika instead of face powder."[14] Here we have the perfect blend of two Hungarian clichés — paprika and madness. (*See* Madness/Melancholy; Paprika.)

Deborah Kerr and Yul Brynner took on Hungary, and its 1956 uprising, in Anatole Litvak's *The Journey* (1959), a shameless ripoff of *Casablanca* (1942). Which reminds me that the greatest *invisible* Hungarian character in all Hollywood movies is the supposedly Czech resistance leader Victor Laszlo in *Casablanca:* never a Czech name, first or family, "László" is, of course, relentlessly Hungarian. Surely *Casablanca*'s Hungarian-born director, Michael Curtiz (né Mihaly Kertész) knew better.

Finally, no review of this kind would be complete without mention of Ernst Lubitsch's *The Shop Around the Corner* (1940) with that most American of actors, the lanky Jimmy Stewart, playing a young Budapest man about town who finds himself working in a leather-goods store which is "just around the corner from Andrassy Street—on Balta Street, in Budapest, Hungary,"[15] as the opening of the film announces. Stewart spars with his new coworker, Margaret Sullavan, in Beatrice-and-Benedick fashion, and soon loses his job. Unbeknownst to the antagonistic couple, they have been corresponding with each other as pen pals (he answered her newspaper ad) and even falling in love. Surrounded by genial eccentrics, they live in a sea of kitsch—musical cigarette boxes, indigestion from too much Hungarian goose liver, and various implausible accents. But Lubitsch is such a fine director that he can make anything work. All conflicts are resolved shortly after Sullavan, still in the dark, tells Stewart that her epistolary lover claims that "I remind him of gypsy music"—what else? Stewart is reemployed, the lovers are reconciled. Some years later the movie inspired a melodious Broadway musical, *She Loves Me* (1963), by Jerry Boch and Sheldon Harnick (of *Fiddler on the Roof* fame), which has had several revivals and recordings. But Broadway's Hungary has had less influence on North American stereotypes of Hungarians, although it does provide its own brand of kitsch.

JOKES, HUNGARIAN

Of course Archie Bunker told one in an episode of *All in the Family:* "A Hungarian is a guy who can follow you into a revolving door and come out ahead." But then Archie spared no one. My favorite comes from the Hungarian-born atomic scientist Leo Szilard. During a discussion of extraterrestrial life with Enrico Fermi, Szilard suggested that it was a genuine possibility. "And so," replied Fermi, "they should have arrived by now, so where are they?" "They are among us," Szilard declared, "but they call themselves Hungarians."[16]

LISZT, FRANZ, AND HIS HUNGARIAN RHAPSODIES

More people have probably heard one of Franz Liszt's nineteen Hungarian rhapsodies than any other piece of Hungarian music by a Hungarian composer. But what have they heard?

The world's first professional Hungarian (*see also* Zsa Zsa), Ferenc Liszt (1811–86) was born in Doborján, Hungary—now Raiding, Austria. His mother was the daughter of an Austrian draper; his father worked as a steward for the prominent Esterházy family, a clan that Eleanor Perényi, one of Liszt's biographers, compared to rich Texans.[17] The Esterházys became part of Liszt's legend, for he liked to claim that nobility had recognized his genius early on. At the age of ten he left Hungary with his father, who understood the significance of his son's talent. He didn't return for eighteen years. Liszt spoke no Hungarian, and near the end of his life, when he came back to Hungary to live, found that he couldn't learn the language. In the salons of Europe, however, he had made much of his background, even allowing audiences to think that he was part Gypsy and descended from a noble family.

When he returned to Hungary in 1839, a celebrity across the continent, Liszt was welcomed as a hero. Growing nationalist sentiment was ready for a spokesman, and prominent Hungarians looked to the pianist. They even offered him a saber on the stage of the National Theatre in Budapest, and Liszt accepted it as a souvenir. His contribution to the country would be music. He wrote to his mistress, Marie d'Agoult, "I have collected a number of fragments with the help of which one might well recompose the musical epic of this strange country, whose rhapsode I want to become."[18] In fact, Liszt's fragments came from the music of contemporary professional Gypsies who performed in a popular style they considered *tzigane*.

The rhapsodies themselves are ersatz Hungariana, but more than a hundred years of performances have made them part of the standard repertoire, at least for pops concerts. Although Liszt wrote a book about Gypsy music, he confused it with Hungarian folk music, as most of his biographers point out, including the sympathetic Alan Walker, author of a rich and probably definitive three-volume life.[19] (*See* Gypsy Music.) Liszt achieved a hybrid that suggests Magyar rhythms much in the way that Hollywood composers (who owe him a debt of gratitude) have learned to suggest a multitude of exotic locales in music that is stirring but empty. Despite their virtuosic requirements, the rhapsodies are a world apart from Liszt's profound piano Sonata in B minor.

A recent revisionist look at Liszt's rhapsodies includes no less a pianist than the meticulous Alfred Brendel, who suggests that the "urban" folk music of the nineteenth-century Gypsy style, seeking to be spontaneous and improvisatory, inspired Liszt in the way that jazz has inspired classical musicians a century later. He writes: "A multiplicity of pungent, darkly glowing and delicately languishing shades of tone coloration awaits rediscovery in the 'Hungarian Rhapsodies,' in addition to characteristics that the public at the turn of the century can hardly have appreciated and possibly did not even notice: the Mephistophelian humor, the inclination to grotesqueness, the readiness to indulge in irony mocking one's own intoxication."[20] For admirers of the rhapsodies, I leave the last word to Brendel.

MADNESS / MELANCHOLY

One scene in J. D. Salinger's *Franny and Zooey* (1961) typifies the North American image of Hungarians as unstable, even mad. Mrs. Bessie Glass, Zooey's mother, stands in the family's large bathroom (where much of the novella takes place) while her handsome actor son shaves. Ever ready with advice, she urges him to get a haircut: "You're getting to look like one of these crazy Hungarians."[21] Zooey smiles, ignoring her remark. He doesn't ask which Hungarians she has in mind.

Crazy Hungarians — the two words cling together, linking Hungarians with extreme behavior if not clinical madness. After all, everyone knows that decade after decade Hungary continues to have the highest annual suicide rate in the world, or at least in countries where such statistics are kept: 44 suicides per 100,000 people, or roughly 4,400 a year.[22] And Hungarians living outside of their birth country continue to have a high suicide rate. It seems no coincidence that in James Joyce's *Ulysses* (1922), Leopold Bloom's father, a Hungarian Jew from Szombathely who left his country and changed the family name from Virág (flower) to Bloom, later committed suicide.

I've spoken with Toronto-based psychologist and social worker Csilla Nagy (Hungarian, of course), who, consulting in clinical and community services, has specialized in multicultural issues. These "issues" amount to patterns of psychological behavior that occur in various ethnic communities. Hungarians, she assures me, are generally manic depressives. "The whole country," she adds, "is manic depressive. Look at its history." Known for rapid and unpredictable mood swings, Hungarians seem classic examples of the syndrome. Another specialist on national characteristics from the historical point of view, John Lukacs writes in *Budapest 1900: A Historical Portrait of a City and Its Culture* that the Hungarian temperament includes "a deep-rooted and (nonreligious) pessimism [that] is often broken by sudden bursts of appetite for life." [23] Certainly the melancholy that I associate with Hungarians is another word — albeit a more literary one, hence more attractive to me — for the way they often appear outside their borders, or families.

A song says it best. "Gloomy Sunday, with shadows I spend it all," sang Billie Holiday in her famous recording of 1941, "My heart and I have decided to end it all." This American classic is actually a translation of "Szomorú Vasárnap," written in Budapest in 1927 by László Jávor. Holiday, and many jazz singers after her, recorded the English translation with the original melody by Rezső Seress. But few of them may have known that the song had once inspired a style in student suicide, just as Goethe's novel *The Sorrows of Young Werther* did a century earlier. One account notes how several young Budapest students "each chose their own gloomy Sunday to climb the heights of the *Lánchid*, clad in black, where they left a flower and a copy of the song's text before leaping to their deaths." [24] The Lánchid, or Chain Bridge, is one of Budapest's oldest bridges over the Danube, linking Buda and Pest. Here the song "Gloomy Sunday" meets Strauss's "Blue Danube" waltz (*see* Blue Danube) to suggest the real Hungarian character. Strauss, after all, was an Austrian who wrote for the café society of Vienna. "Szomorú Vasárnap," written in the Kulacs restaurant at the corner of Dohány and Osvárt Streets, on the Pest side of the Danube, is the genuine home-grown product of Hungarian melancholia. It seems oddly just that it took Billie Holiday to make it an American song as well.

O'KEEFFE, GEORGIA, AND HER FLOWERS

When some viewers look at Georgia O'Keeffe's paintings of gigantic flowers, they also see slightly disguised female genitalia. Not me. From the start I thought of flower-trimmed Hungarian folk pottery and colorfully embroidered Hungarian blouses. This connection may not be entirely fanciful, or the odd confession of someone spotting a Hungarian behind every bush. Three of the grandparents of this most American of painters were immigrants from Europe, but her maternal grandfather, George Victor Totto, is of particular interest to me. Totto was a count from Budapest who fled to America after the failed uprising against Austrian rule in 1848, in which he had been an aide-de-camp to the revolutionary hero Lajos Kossuth. (Family legend claimed that Totto had been ransomed from jail with the family jewels.) Eventually he escaped to America and settled in Sauk City, Wisconsin, where he married Isabel Wyckoff (of Dutch descent) in 1855; they later settled in Sun Prairie. Unsuccessful at farming, in the 1870s George Totto left his wife and six children to return to Hungary, supposedly to claim his share of a family fortune. While he may have visited Wisconsin again, he died in Hungary. Georgia Totto O'Keeffe (her middle name after her grandfather, and her mother Ida's maiden name) was born in 1887, and probably never set eyes on George Totto, who was, as her biographer wrote, "worshipped, in absentia, by his daughters."[25] Surely Ida Totto told her children stories of their aristocratic grandfather, for in Sun Prairie it was thought that she had married beneath her station. Did George Totto ever send his daughters any Hungarian linens embroidered with folk flower motifs? Unlikely, yes, but there's no way of knowing for sure. In any case I think there's an element of high kitsch in O'Keeffe's overblown flowers, and even though I can't prove a connection with Hungarian folk flowers, I'll continue to associate the two. (This also leads me to the distinction between high and low kitsch, but that's a subject for another essay.)

PAPRIKA

"There is something about paprika itself that makes it synonymous with 'Hungarian,'" wrote George Lang, author of the definitive *The Cuisine of Hungary*, which is also a cultural history of the country. "'Fiery,' 'spicy,' 'temperamental'—all these adjectives suggest both paprika and the Hungarian national character."[26] (*See* Madness/Melancholy.) Aside from questions of national psychology, the history of the spice's introduction to Hungary is still a subject of debate. Is paprika the Spanish pimento pepper, brought back from the New World by Columbus? Or did it arrive from India, via Persia, with the Turks in the beginning of the sixteenth century? Or did the Turks discover it from the Italians, who in turn had borrowed it from Spain? Lang tries to sort out the complicated history from folklore, offering his own twist: In the sixteenth century the Turkish Empire included Bulgaria, where the Turks had taught locals how to cultivate the pepper plant from its seeds. When Bulgarians emigrated to Hungary, Lang contends, they brought the plant with them. However it got there, the result was culinary history.

Hungarians took to the fiery vegetable, especially when it was dried and ground into a spice. By the seventeenth century, it was used to season stews (*see* Goulash) and soups. Cheaper than imported black pepper, in time it appealed to all classes of society. As one might expect, however, the spice was first popular with peasants, taking at least a century to find acceptance with the country's gentry and nobility. (Hungarians adopted the ways of the French and Austrian courts, and the oldest Hungarian cookbooks include techniques and recipes associated with French cooking. Chicken paprikas did not appear on the menu of the National Casino, a club of the Hungarian House of Lords, until 1844.) The spice first appeared in a Hungarian cookbook in 1829, in the third edition of István Czifrai's popular *Magyar nemzeti szakácskönyv*, the Fannie Farmer of its day.

Made from the ripe dried pods of the red capsicum or bell pepper, paprika comes in varying degrees of pungency. There are, however, essentially two kinds of paprika—the hot spice and the milder, sweet rose paprika, which was the result of a refining process, developed in Szeged (now the paprika capital) in 1859, that removed the white membranes and seeds of the pepper, thus reducing the spice's fire. Because paprika is heated during the grinding process, each lot will vary somewhat in color, aroma, and taste. Rich in vitamins B_1, B_2, C, and P, Hungarian paprika is not to be confused with the commercial North American variants, which may include ground soybeans.

Chicken Paprikas Recipe

It is often said that the essence of Hungarian food comes from three ingredients—lard, paprika, and sour cream. Most families have their own version of chicken paprikas. Even my grandmother and her sister differed about adding green peppers: Grandma didn't, and they *don't* belong.

1 medium onion, finely chopped

3 tablespoons lard or bacon drippings

2 1/2 teaspoons sweet rose paprika

4-pound chicken, cut in pieces (you may add an extra breast)

1 1/2 teaspoons salt

several shakes of black pepper

1 1/2 cups hot water

1/3 cup water

2 tablespoons flour

sour cream, about 1 cup

1. Heat lard in a Dutch oven and sauté onions until golden.
2. Add paprika, stirring until blended. Do not simmer or it will be bitter.
3. Add chicken, simmering over medium heat until it takes on color. Stir to coat all pieces with paprika-onion mixture.
4. Add salt and black pepper. Let the chicken brown for five minutes.
5. Boil water, add 1 1/2 cups and stir. This is the base of the sauce. Cover and lower heat. Simmer for one hour.
6. In a one-cup shaker, place 1/3 cup water and the flour. Shake well, then fill to the top with sour cream and shake again.
7. Remove chicken from pan and add sour cream mixture slowly to the base. Stir—simmer—and when ready to serve, pour sauce over the chicken. Excellent with dumplings or rice.

SUICIDE: *See* Madness/Melancholy

VAMPIRES

Of course people immediately think of Count Dracula and his grim Transylvanian castle; then of Béla Lugosi, who played him in the 1931 movie (*see* Hollywood's Hungary). But there's another, far more interesting Hungarian vampire: Countess Erzsébet Báthory (1560–1614), who is claimed to have bathed in the blood of 610 young girls to preserve her youth. (It was Countess Báthory that Edmund Wilson had in mind when he teased a Hungarian friend that the two principal exports of Hungary were vampires and atomic scientists.[27]) Camille Paglia links Báthory to the Marquis de Sade, and suggests that she may have been sexually aroused while torturing and murdering her victims. For Paglia, Báthory is "the prototypical lesbian vampire of horror films."[28] Perhaps, but had Paglia dug a little deeper she could have found more than images from popular culture.

Erzsébet Báthory was the wife of Ferenc Nádasdy, one of the richest landowners in Hungary during the sixteenth century. According to contemporary rumors she was a vain woman obsessed with holding on to her youth with the aid of the blood of young serf girls. Stories spread from one village to another along the Vág (Váh) River in what was then northern Hungary, and by the spring of 1610 the palatine of Hungary ordered an investigation of the countess, who was charged with killing more than 300 serf girls, servants, and children of lesser nobles. Witnesses claimed that the countess used thorns to tear the flesh off the naked girls before throwing them into icy water or torturing them with hot irons. Too gruesome to be true? The countess, who spent the rest of her life in prison, may have been the victim of the Habsburgs, who eyed the landholdings of the wealthy Nádasdy family and produced a show trial to bring about their downfall. Land and money, rather than blood and sex, are probably at the core of this story. Báthory did, however, leave her name behind in the camp film classic *Daughters of Darkness* (1971), in which French actress Delphine Seyrig plays the vampire lesbian Countess Báthory in the setting of modern-day Belgium.

The source of Bram Stoker's Count Dracula is an infamous historical figure, Prince Vlad V of Walachia (1431–76), who was also known as Dracula ("son of the dragon") and Vlad Țepeș, or Vlad the Impaler. Honored today in Romania as a national hero, he fought the Ottoman Turks and on several occasions vanquished them, apparently with great cruelty. Stoker may have learned of the legend from a Hungarian acquaintance or any number of books in the British Museum; he was also indebted to Sheridan Le Fanu's novel *Carmilla* (1872). However, he updated his sinister source. The hero of his *Dracula* (1897) is the continental lover, Hungarian style—a suave and alluring aristocrat with a seedy castle back home in Transylvania (Dracula's particular area of that region now belongs to Romania). As A. N. Wilson observed in his introduction to the novel: "In its decadent forms, the cult of *Dracula* partakes, in a self-consciously comic way, of the taste for the kitsch."[29]

Blood isn't the only kind of nourishment in Stoker's *Dracula*. In the novel's opening pages, Stoker's young hero, Jonathan Harker, stops in Budapest, where "the impression I had was that we were leaving the West and entering the East." This is one of the recurring clichés in travel writing about Hungary. Later that night he is served "a chicken done up some way with red pepper, which was very good but thirsty. (*Mem.*, get recipe for Mina.) I asked the waiter, and he said it was called 'paprika hendl,' and that, as it was a national dish, I should be able to get it anywhere along the Carpathians."[30] (*See* Paprika.)

The association of vampires and Hungarians continues to this day. In an episode of *Murder, She Wrote* first broadcast in October 1993, mystery writer Jessica Fletcher has to solve a murder committed in her hometown, Cabot Cove, Maine. A mysterious dark stranger, Lawrence Baker, pays cash to buy an old boarding house called Borbey House. After his death, in order to expose Central European superstition in New England, Jessica becomes a expert on vampires. She asks the local sheriff, "Are you aware of what the name Borbey means in English?" Of course she answers herself: "I checked in the library and it's Hungarian for Baker." I don't know what dictionary Jessica Fletcher used, but the Hungarian word for baker is *pék*, while nothing quite like "borbey" exists in the language. (In the word *borbély*, which means barber in English, the "l" is silent.) Perhaps Angela Lansbury and her writers decided that there weren't enough Americans of Hungarian descent to bother with accuracy.

ZSA ZSA

Eva had her own line of wigs and appeared on *Green Acres*, Magda sold jewelry in Manhattan, but the most famous of the Gabor sisters is still Zsa Zsa. Whether she's costumed as Jane Avril and singing the theme song of *Moulin Rouge* (1953), John Huston's movie biography of Toulouse-Lautrec, chattering away to Merv Griffin on his talk show, or slapping a policeman across the face and then, briefly, doing time in a California jail, this most famous of Hungarians (at least in the United States) has entertained Americans for over four decades.

Born to a wealthy Budapest family in their fifth-floor apartment at 31 Múzeum Körút (Circle) just after her mother had helped herself to a dish of apricot *palacsinta* with cream, and christened Sári, after the great actress Sári Fedák, Zsa Zsa set her sights on the glamorous life early on. Her childhood, as she recalled it, is a study in upper-class Mitteleuropa kitsch: operettas with Richard Tauber and family jewelry shops, Madame Subilia's School for Young Ladies in Lausanne, Switzerland, Gypsy music in open-air cafés below the apartment. A rebellious teenager, Zsa Zsa decided to do something for her country, and lied about her age in order to enter the Miss Hungary beauty pageant. After winning, she was disqualified.

She may have left Hungary, but the country still means something to her. In her small prison cell in El Segundo City Jail (Los Angeles), in July 1990, after her diamond earrings had been taken from her, she thinks of "the legend of Zsa Zsa Gabor that my enemies have constructed—the legend of the glittering Hungarian heartbreaker (whom they accuse of being older than Methuselah yet still pretending to be seventeen)" and she begins to feel tears in her "badly made-up eyes." But help is in sight. She recalls her background, and the moment is saved by "my uniquely Hungarian talent for melodrama and self-dramatization." She even tells herself, "Remember that you are Hungarian, that the blood of Attila the Hun and Genghis Khan courses through your veins."[31] A historian she isn't, but that's hardly the point. Zsa Zsa is Zsa Zsa, sui generis.

The men in her life—Kemal Ataturk, Conrad Hilton, George Sanders, Porfirio Rubirosa, and, currently, Prince Frederick von Anhalt, duke of Saxony—have been as glamorous as the publicity about Zsa Zsa, who usually preferred marriage to less formal liaisons. If not exactly a great courtesan, she isn't a genuine actress either, but rather a personality whose specialty is her own brand of femininity, turn-of-the-century style, though in updated dress. With her accent, which she plays like a fine instrument, Zsa Zsa has offered up herself and her once-fragile beauty as a kind of kitsch icon, for like most women in Hollywood she has tried to age behind a mask of her former self. Most recently she was back in the news after Frederick's of Hollywood, the lingerie emporium, was looted during the Los Angeles riots of 1992. A twenty-four-year-old art student, Jim B., ran off with Ava Gardner's bloomers and Madonna's bustier, among other items, but eventually took them to a local priest, the Reverend Bob Fambrini, at the Church of the Blessed Sacrament in Hollywood. Once Father Fambrini returned the undergarments to Frederick's, Jim B. said that he had a clear conscience. But he went on to add, "I was really wanting Zsa Zsa's bra. That would have been hot."[32]

Visiting Pannonia

The ancient Roman province of Pannonia, lying to the west of the Danube, can be found on most maps of the Roman world and corresponds to the area sometimes referred to as Transdanubia, or western Hungary. After Roman occupation, a series of invaders—Celts, Huns, Franks, and Slavs—inhabited this land. When the Magyars arrived in the ninth century, they were simply the new gang on the block. Medieval chronicles often used Pannonia as a synonym for Hungary, but it meant more than that. A place where East met West, where Asia met Europe, Pannonia belongs to the geography of the imagination. As such it is a fitting name for a bookstore, which is how I first heard of it.

Over the years I've followed Pannonia Books in its various locations in Toronto, buying a calendar for my grandmother or looking out for Hungarian novels in translation. But only since I began studying Hungarian have I really come to appreciate it.[1]

I remember my first visit. Surrounded by books, I couldn't read a word of them. The authors' names on their spines and covers meant nothing. I was lost. Although the language of these books used the Roman alphabet, it might as well have been Cyrillic. At first. But as I made my way from one shelf to another, passing a wall of slim, oversized books apparently for children, I stopped: Mailer. Nearby were Malamud and Mann; on the shelf above, Louis Bromfield and Vicki Baum; on the shelf below, Lin Yutang. My sense of dislocation momentarily increased, for it's the rare bookstore that still has Louis Bromfield, Vicki Baum, and Lin Yutang on its shelves. This shop was in a time warp. But I had found an oasis of translations, although the titles gave little clue. What was *Az éjszaka hadai?* Until I leafed through its first pages for copyright information, I couldn't have guessed that I was holding *The Armies of the Night*.

Since I like to browse in bookstores of almost any kind, I'm even drawn to foreign-language shops. Like many large cities, Toronto has a good number of them. Yet for most people these stores are all but invisible. Toronto's Hungarian community grew after the revolution of 1956, along Bloor Street West. Pannonia stands roughly between Elizabeth's Meat Market and Tuske's Meats, two local landmarks where, on any Saturday morning, the language most likely to be heard is Hungarian. A handpainted sign at the doorway of number 472 designates Pannonia, above a camera shop.

You climb a steep staircase and on the landing, first door to the left, step into another world, although this may not yet be evident. Ahead stands a long, narrow table, shaped like the store itself, randomly piled with "special" items—books, records, and calendars. So far, nothing unusual, although the table is covered with a brightly embroidered cloth. At the front of the store, under its large, uncovered window, two old desks have been pushed together. Cluttered with papers, boxes of file cards, ledgers, and telephone books, they are working desks, not places to hold court. While the store doesn't seem to belong in North America, it's not of Europe either. It is a place in between, a fissure: neither/nor. This is part of what delights me. For a moment you might even think that you've walked into a used-books store; it has that kind of genial directness. In this, Pannonia is not unlike its owner.

Kate Karácsony has a heart-shaped face that reminds me of the young Vivien Leigh, short-cropped dark hair, and unusually small hands, which finger a pencil while we talk. I can almost see their fragile bones. This is the first time I've approached her with questions about the bookstore. Until now I've never wanted to cross the line from anonymous browser to a customer with a name, a job, a life outside Pannonia. The shop might not seem the same, and I didn't want to risk losing it: a browser's anonymity is part of the pleasure.

Kate seemed happy to tell me about Pannonia, after a fleeting expression of surprise passed over her face at my show of interest. She's obviously proud of the shop. Pannonia was founded in 1957 by George Elek, an engineer by training, shortly after he fled Hungary. It has moved several times since the original store was on College Street near Lippincott—from King/Dufferin, Spadina/Queen, and Bloor/Spadina, to the current one at Bloor/Bathurst. (I barely remember Elek, whose name I hadn't known at the time.) Ill with cancer, he sold the store to Kate and András Karácsony in September 1985. Kate had worked in an antique shop in Hungary, and her husband, a computer analyst, planned to write the program for their new business. They knew they were buying a bookstore with a significant inventory and the goodwill of a local community, and wanted to keep Elek's achievement alive. In April 1986, only a few months after they had begun to see the complexities of the business, Elek died. Kate remembers, "We had to discover everything by ourselves."

"Everything" included an elaborate system of file cards for university orders and invoices. Not only a retail bookstore but a large mail-order business, Pannonia sells anything of interest that Hungarians write and publish to libraries and universities around the world. With a stock of 16,000 titles, the range of books is great.

The Karácsonys publish their own catalogue twice a year in order to help them serve libraries at Yale University, UCLA, Indiana University, and the Library of Congress in the United States, the British Library in London, and the State Library of Queensland in Australia, to name only a few of their accounts. A substantial part of the business includes libraries across Canada, and Pannonia also supplies the Hungarian National Library with newsletters from Hungarian organizations around the world. Having spoken to Hungarian booksellers in other cities, I've been told repeatedly that any Hungarian bookstore has to develop a mailing list or it dies. But even by this rule, Pannonia has excelled. It is an important resource for anyone interested in Hungarian letters.

It's easy to overlook the importance that foreign-language stores have in their local communities. Bookshops like Pannonia provide a unique service, displaying posters for movies, concerts, and lecturers from the homeland — any event of interest. Apart from the cookbooks, travel books, art books, children's books, scholarly and reference volumes, popular novels, and collections of poetry, Pannonia sells records, tapes, CDs, Christmas cards, magazines, and a small selection of ceramic bowls and plates, and even rents videos of Hungarian movies through its video club. This inventory isn't unlike the range of items at some of the other foreign-language stores I know, yet the emphasis at Pannonia is on books.

After talking with Kate, I return to the shelves. Away from the window, the light turns blue, misty and still, like light at the bottom of a fish tank. The books here feel different from the lavish ones produced in North America. Their paper is thinner and less opaque, so that a heavy inking can make it difficult to read. (Yet I see no paper as ugly as the cheap pulp newsprint used here for mass-market paperbacks.) The boards used for covers are thinner too, and more flexible. The type is generally smaller — to conserve paper? — and few of the books have colored dust jackets or covers. I can't help but think that these are books produced by people for whom books still matter, still contain something they want to know. It's a relief to hold a book that hasn't been packaged to death, and to see that good design doesn't have to mean foil stamping or costly commercial art. Many of these books seem throwbacks to the better-designed books of the thirties and forties.

In a section of English translations of Hungarian books, I start to make my choices. Corvina, the distinguished Budapest publisher, has produced Gyula Illyés's study of Sándor Petőfi, the most celebrated Hungarian poet of the nineteenth century. Illyés is a sociologist cum man of letters, and his book is six hundred well-designed pages, showing care and taste, with only a white cloth cover, handsomely stamped PETŐFI in royal blue, and a simple dust jacket that repeats the cover's typographic design and adds a photograph of Petőfi. (A comparable North American book would never be so trusting of its audience.) Next I find a paperback collection of short stories by the twentieth-century novelist Zsigmond Móricz, also published by Corvina. It has a black-and-white photograph of a horseman riding on the Hungarian plain in a cloud of dust, with elegant, deep red typography for the title: *Seven Pennies and Other Short Stories.* It's a pleasure to pick up because it doesn't announce itself with a fanfare.

The most exciting thing about a bookstore where you don't know the writers is the sense of potential discovery. Even if you wander through the foreign-language sections of a good university bookstore, picking up titles by Goethe or Proust, you can't help having an illusion of familiarity. This is one of the drawbacks of a North American education — people can know something about books without ever reading them. And if you've read them, it's likely that it was in a university course, years ago. (I want to think that this at least inspires a respect for books, though it's a difficult notion to support.) But in a foreign-language bookstore you'll find so many unfamiliar titles that you can't guess the canon of classics, let alone their ranking: you're lost and have to decide for yourself what you like. Petőfi and Illyés are good examples. A Byronic poet, Petőfi fought in the revolution of 1848 to liberate Hungary from the Habsburgs and their allies, the army of the tsar. He lived the romantic life suitable for a revolutionary, died at twenty-six, all that. And I should like him — I know I should — but he tries my patience. Illyés, on the other hand, is the author of a study of poverty, *Puszták népe* (People of the Puszta), that reminds me of James Agee's *Let Us Now Praise Famous Men,* and I read it enthralled. I decide to buy *Petőfi* simply because Illyés wrote it.

But the books aren't all literary, for Kate's definition of "Hungarian interest" is a broad one. To my surprise I find *The Café des Artistes Cookbook* by George Lang. (On Central Park West in New York, this restaurant was recently the subject of a *New Yorker* cartoon where a young boy stood before his class for show and tell, holding a swizzle stick and describing the meal he'd eaten there with his parents.) I flip through the pages and then remember that Lang, its Hungarian owner, wrote *The Cuisine of Hungary*. The only things in this book that could even vaguely be called Hungarian are two torte recipes that Lang assures us have culinary roots in the nineteenth century. Okay. I'm still glad to find it.

Across the aisle I notice a stack of tapes, but there's little to claim my attention for long—just the Hungarian production of the musical *Les Misèrables, A Nyomorultak*. This isn't what I've come to find. Nearby, a rack holds Hungarian newspapers from around the world—sixty different ones, Kate says. That's more like it. I reach for a copy of *Szabadság*, the largest Hungarian American weekly, which my grandparents usually had around their house. I haven't seen an issue for twenty-five years and it looks just as I remember, only now the articles are about the Gulf War instead of Vietnam.

Before taking my purchases to Kate, I thumb through Pannonia's catalogue in case there's something I've missed. Fifty-six two-column pages, it opens with books in English, and then Hungarian titles, by subject: literature (including translations into Hungarian, from Ian Fleming to Leon Uris); biographies; poetry (a separate section); literary history; mysteries; children's books; philosophy; religion; history/politics (after literature, the longest section); dictionaries; language textbooks; reference books; art books; ethnography; travel books; atlases and maps; cookbooks; a few pages for hobbies, sports, and health; music; and even sheet music. But absent are sections on popular psychology and self-help books—those staples of any North American bookseller—and I'm inordinately pleased to discover the omission.

As twilight descends, the shop darkens. During my visit a man in his twenties called for an order, two women bought newspapers, and a frail, elderly man said a few words to Kate without buying anything. In between she sat at her computer, checking on orders to fill. What would it be like to own Pannonia, to come here every day?

While Kate totals my bill, I realize that Pannonia has gradually become familiar. The excitement I now feel comes mainly from the books themselves. After several years of learning Hungarian I no longer have the exhilaration of discovery based only on ignorance — my discoveries now depend on language, and are linked to it. Handing Kate my charge card, I feel reassured. Our talk is easy, cordial, yet with an edge of impersonality, as if we hadn't discussed Pannonia's history only half an hour before. Although I'd like to ask why she calls herself "Kate" instead of Kati, or Katya, the Hungarian diminutives for Katalin (Katharine), I don't. Perhaps as a girl she sat in a Budapest movie theater and fell in love with Katharine Hepburn, and North America. It's nice to think it happened that way. Instead I promise, when I come next, to bring the name and publisher of a book about Hungary recently reviewed in the *New York Times*. Kate would like to order a copy for the Hungarian National Library.

Time spent here always has a calming effect on me, and with my bag of new books I descend the stairs to the street. I know enough to head home directly. I won't even look into the window of the upscale pasta restaurant nearby, or the gourmet patisserie where for five dollars a slice the cakes never taste exactly fresh. Bloor Street's immigrant families and earnest grad students have moved farther west, replaced by two-income couples with amenities and the homeless who sleep in shop doorways. As this stretch of Bloor succumbs to gentrification, a few stores like Pannonia are congenial holdouts — at least until their rents skyrocket. When they do, I imagine that Pannonia will move on, as it has in the past, and I'll follow it to its new location. There's comfort in the thought.

Toward a Course on Central European Literature in Translation

During the fall of 1991, Árpád Göncz, the new president of Hungary, planned to visit Toronto for a festival devoted to Hungarian culture. A novelist and translator, Göncz was part of the movement toward democratization in Central Europe. Shortly before his visit I went to Toronto's Metropolitan Reference Library in search of background information about Göncz, whom I hoped to interview. The Robarts Library of the University of Toronto, the city's other important reference library, had none of Göncz's books in its collection, but I knew that the Metro library kept an extensive file of newspaper clippings on contemporary writers.

That afternoon the file drawers were locked, so I headed to the information desk in the literature section, where the librarian offered to open the file. She did not recognize Göncz's name, but I hadn't expected her to. At the filing cabinet she took out the folder for Hungarian writers. Given the size of Toronto's Hungarian population, I had expected a generous file, but this one was disappointingly thin. She looked inside to find only one article and handed it to me rather proudly. As soon as I saw its headline, I said, "But this is about Václav Havel." She didn't appear to recognize his name either, so I added, "He's a Czech writer. A playwright. And the president of Czechoslovakia." "You're sure?" she asked. I repeated that I was, to which she said, "Then what's he doing in here?" We looked at each other for a second and I suggested, "Well, I suppose H is for Havel and for Hungarian."

The librarian returned to her desk and I went home emptyhanded.

THE PLAN

Several months later, Stong College of York University—Canada's third largest university, located in a suburb north of Toronto—decided to offer the undergraduate course I had proposed on Central European literature in translation. Having looked through all of the catalogues of North American universities that I could find, I saw that my course would be the only one offered anywhere. Various departments of comparative literature listed courses, usually at the graduate level, in the different national literatures that make up Central European literature—Austrian, Hungarian, Czechoslovakian, perhaps Polish, perhaps Romanian. But these courses generally used books in the original language, not in translation. No department seemed to take the idea of Central Europe and a Central European sensibility seriously, although it has been an important subject, at least in Central Europe. What, then, would North American university students—notoriously uninformed even of their own history—make of it?

The course description I prepared had to suggest an academic rationale while also selling the course. I include it here:

The Quest for Central Europe: Literary Perspectives

The literature of Central Europe has been a powerful comment on events and trends in European history over the past century. In light of recent rapid changes, it is increasingly important to understand this unique cultural and geographic area. Some of the major historical events that have shaped it are the First World War, the rise of modernism, fascism and anti-Semitism, the Second World War and the Holocaust, and the impact of Soviet communism. This course studies Central Europe—past and present—by introducing students to a literature they would not ordinarily study, including novels, short stories, memoirs and letters in translation. (Some current newspaper and journal articles are also read.) Texts are explored in their historical and social context in order to develop an historical perspective as well as a sense of cultural evolution; they are also examined in terms associated with literary analysis. By studying various literary genres, students will also learn to identify some larger issues involved in reading, such as the validity of inquiry through cross-cultural comparisons, the relation of national boundaries to various genres, and questions about studying literature in translation.

Without saying it directly, I planned to explore the notion of a Central European sensibility, of a Mitteleuropa that was more complex than Viennese waltzes and *Kaffee mit Schlag*, and see how this sensibility was reflected in a culture's books. I also hoped that the exercise would make my students more aware of the arbitrariness of some of their own cultural assumptions.

THE BOOKS

Every university course is dependent on the books that publishers decide to make available and then to keep in print. Mainstream courses are naturally served with more competitively priced books as well as a greater variety of material. The marketplace is its own kind of censor (a thought worth remembering before any discussion of Central Europe). In addition, English-language translators and publishers have long favored the secondary languages of international commerce—French, German, etc.—and rarely bring out translations of books by writers from other languages. For example, Péter Esterházy, Hungary's most important contemporary novelist after György Konrád, has long been translated into German, French, Italian, Danish, and Swedish, but into English only in 1991. Translators have neglected most of the male writers and all of the significant women writers of Central Europe. This is particularly frustrating at a time when anyone teaching literary studies will want to include works by women in a new course. Margit Kaffka (1880–1918), one of Hungary's finest novelists, still awaits a sympathetic translator into any foreign language. Her novels, dealing with the plight of women in the patriarchal world of the declining gentry before the First World War, would be of special interest to English-speaking readers.[1]

In making up a reading list I had to accept the fact that I was planning a compromise rather than an ideal course. Fortunately, in the 1970s Philip Roth was general editor of an excellent paperback series focusing on writers from Eastern Europe, published by Penguin Books. (Although many of these titles are now out of print, some have been taken over by other publishers.) I also tried not to indulge my particular interest in Hungarian writers, even though four of the fourteen titles for the course are translations from the Hungarian. But Hungary was, after all, half of the Dual Monarchy. The reading list included:

Timothy Garton Ash, *The Uses of Adversity:*
   Essays on the Fate of Central Europe
Peter Handke, *Across*
Václav Havel, *Letters to Olga*
Gyula Illyés, *People of the Puszta*
Franz Kafka, *Collected Stories*
György Konrád, *The Case Worker*
Milan Kundera, *The Unbearable Lightness of Being*
Zsigmond Móricz, *Seven Pennies and Other Short Stories*
Robert Musil, *Young Törless*
Joseph Roth, *The Emperor's Tomb*
   The Radetzky March
Josef Skvorecky, *The Swell Season*
Andrzej Szczypiorski, *The Beautiful Mrs. Seidenman*

Stephen Vizinczey, *In Praise of Older Women*
Gregor von Rezzori, *Memoirs of an Anti-Semite*

Just as classes began in September, so did the problems. Although books had been ordered in June, it took the summer for publishers to admit that several of them were unavailable. Robert Musil's classic parable of the rise of fascism was out of print, with no new publisher in sight; Peter Handke's account of the rise of anti-Semitism in modern-day Austria was pending a reprint, as was György Konrád's *The Case Worker*, with no delivery dates in sight. Usually this means that a publisher is collecting back orders, and will later decide whether or not to put a title out of print.

When I heard that Joseph Roth's *The Radetzky March* and *The Emperor's Tomb* were out of print, I saw my course collapsing before me. One of the vagaries of Canadian publishing is that while a small number of houses distribute books for U.S. presses, they often have little interest in selling them. In light of Nadine Gordimer's recent article praising Roth in the *New York Review of Books*, it seemed strange that any publisher would put his most famous novels out of print, so I decided to ignore the Canadian distributor and telephone the editorial offices of Overlook Press in New York City. There was plenty of stock in their warehouse, and books were shipped immediately. Since translations of books by Central European writers are seldom considered a priority by the North American publishers who include them on their lists, it is wise to keep a simple moral in mind: Question anything a publisher tells you. Your course depends on your skepticism.

THE STUDENTS: 1

While teaching at Princeton University in 1959, Hannah Arendt wrote to Karl Jaspers that her students "didn't even know that there had ever been such a thing as Austria-Hungary."[2] I had no reason to believe that my students would have discovered it in the intervening years.

Twelve first- and second-year students enrolled in the course. To my surprise, only three had backgrounds associated with Central Europe—Austrian, Polish, and Croatian. And only one, a young woman of Polish extraction, knew her family's native tongue. It is worth noting that North American students of Central European descent often find that their ethnicity is overlooked by their society and even their universities. Two recent studies of the ethnic origins of Canadian students illustrate this point. A University of Toronto survey on race and ethnicity, conducted in the summer and fall of 1991, included in its 35 categories 11 related to European background: British Isles, Dutch, French, German, Greek, Italian, Polish, Portuguese, Spanish, Ukrainian, and "Other European," which made up 8.2 percent of the total student population. Students from Austrian, Czech, Hungarian, Romanian, and Slovak backgrounds had to select "Other European."[3] At York University a similar survey, done in the winter of 1991, listed 22 categories, with 14 related to Europe: English, Scottish, Irish, Italian, French, German, Greek, Ukrainian, Polish, Scandinavian, Dutch, Portuguese, "Other East European," and "Other West European."[4] At least York's students had a somewhat wider choice, and this posed an interesting political question: does one regard Hungary, for example, as part of Eastern or Western Europe? And what about Czechoslovakia? At any rate, "Other East Europeans" made up 4 percent of York's student population, and "Other West Europeans" 2 percent. Both universities listed "Jewish" as a separate category, although most of the students who claimed "Jewish background" (3.5 percent at University of Toronto, 6 percent at York) probably had ancestors from Russia or Central Europe. These surveys suggest that university administrators are blind to Central European identity—a lack of interest that mirrors the attitudes of North American society.[5]

During the first class, I asked my students to write a paragraph about why they had chosen this course, and their answers covered a wide spectrum. There were, naturally, some personal reasons ("As I child I lived in Poland. There is a culture, an atmosphere, a 'pull' which Europe has for me." Or, "I find myself bombarded with required courses. I needed a course that was different enough to expand my horizons and which was completely my choice"). Other reasons included the political ("I hope to understand the feelings and emotions of an opressed [*sic*] people" and "I am interested in history and politics and this course, although it is essentially an English course, has overtones of each of these interests"), intellec-

tual curiosity ("[I want] to stimulate and strengthen my appreciation for literature from all sectors of the world" and "I am familiar with some American writers, but not as many from Europe"),
the pragmatic ("I was very limited in my choice of courses that fit
into my schedule"), and the bizarre ("I looked at the fact that this
course was offered by Stong College. I was told that Stong has a
strong athletic presence in the university and because I intend to
play rugby for York this seemed a sensible choice").

When my students wrote another paragraph defining Central
Europe, their ideas were more startling. Several offered vague
and all-encompassing descriptions ("Central Europe would begin
around Greece and spread out from there to neighboring countries." Or, "All the countries that are located on the main part of
Europe, including Germany, Austria, Italy and the former republic of Yugoslavia, yet not including England and other countries
detached from the main land"). A few, however, had almost no
idea, and included Britain (2), France (1), Germany (4), Greece (3),
Ireland (1), Italy (3), Poland (3), Rome (1), the Slovick [*sic*] states
(1), Turkey (1), and Yugoslavia (2). "Rome and all the exotic and
fascinating places that I've never been," one student wrote, while
another confessed, "I think Central Europe includes those countries formerly under the control of the USSR, such as Germany. I
had never heard of the term 'Central Europe' before, just 'Western'
Europe. Whatever countries it may involve, I have never been ex-
posed to any European literature besides English literature so all
of it is new to me." Only two students specified Austria, Hungary,
and Czechoslovakia, although several thought that Central Europe
included countries previously controlled by the Soviet Union. My
favorite definition came from the student who wrote, "Such countries as Poland, Czechoslovakia, Hungary and Germany are considered centrally located within Europe and have very unique qualities." *Centrally located*, the jargon of a real-estate agent, may not
be inappropriate for a region that has seen its borders change so
frequently.

At first I was surprised by these answers, but I soon realized
that I should have predicted them. When I asked about the history
courses my students had taken in high school, the following list
emerged: European history from 1200 to 1940 (1); European his-

tory from the French Revolution to the Korean War (1); world history since the Second World War (1); ancient history (3); Chinese
and Japanese history (1); American history (1); Canadian history
(1); American/Canadian relations (1); Russian and German history
(1). In other words, my class of twelve had taken only eleven history courses over a common four-year period—less than one per
student. If this sample is typical (and I have no reason to doubt
it), these students provide a grim example of what is not being required in North American high schools.

SOMETIMES THE PLAN WORKS

In October 1992, as reports of "ethnic cleansing" increased from
the former Yugoslavia, and Western governments seemed para-
lyzed in their attempts to deal with the worsening situation, the
Canadian government held a national referendum about its new
constitution. The event was largely reported in the United States
as a vote for or against Quebec's potential separation from Canada.
While Quebec sovereignty was an essential element in the referendum, so were the rights of individual provinces, of Canada's
native peoples, and other minority issues. As Canada becomes an
increasingly multicultural country, the old tensions between its
English and French communities often seem irrelevant. At the
same time, conflicts between the Quebecois and non-English immigrants have grown in recent years, and they usually center on
Quebec's language laws, which prohibit even immigrant children
from speaking their native languages in local schoolyards.[6] Along
with the referendum, my course's contemporary background included the promises of change that dominated the American presi-
dential campaign, the growing neo-Nazi movement in Germany,
and the breakup of Czechoslovakia. As the academic year pro-
gressed, parallels between the decaying Dual Monarchy at the turn
of the century—and its struggles with increasingly vocal ethnic
groups—and current events were not lost on my students. History
was more interesting than they had expected.

After realizing that the class had a weak background in history,
I juggled the reading list to begin with selections from Timothy
Garton Ash's *The Uses of Adversity*, and gave an informal two-hour
lecture that surveyed a thousand years of Habsburg rule, from the

Holy Roman Empire to the final years of the Dual Monarchy. The books became pieces in a puzzle that would be completed only at the end of the course. The class enjoyed Roth's novels and Móricz's short stories, mainly because both writers used a realistic style. By the time we finished discussing Roth, students were pointing out similarities between the ethnic conflicts that fueled the decline of the Dual Monarchy, and the growth of nationalism that accompanied it, with current events in Europe. However, they were more interested in parallels with North America, where racial and ethnic conflict is not yet associated with widespread bloodshed. "The future's pretty clear," one student pointed out. "We're facing a race war." I did not interrupt. "Can't it be avoided?" another asked.

"I didn't think we'd talk so much about war," a student remarked several weeks later. Before I could reply, another student said: "But it's in all the books." He was right, of course. "It's like when we were talking about the referendum," he continued, "and no one thought we'd go to war if Quebec separated." I remembered that brief but troubling discussion. Two students had argued that Canada would never send soldiers into Quebec because Canadians were a peace-loving people, until another student, a political science major, mentioned a recent conference where several historians had suggested that the idea of war with Quebec was not farfetched. These students were the young men who would fight that war, and the prospect appalled them. "What about military intervention in Serbia?" I asked. "It's the rich old guys who like war," our rugby player offered. "It makes them richer." Before I could ask him to elaborate, he added, "Look at what Roth says." We returned to *The Radetzky March* without any prompting.

Kafka was another matter, and they shook their heads in exasperation at "The Metamorphosis" and "The Hunger Artist." Particularly vocal, the rugby player called these stories "dumb and sick." I picked up on his point, and spoke of the spiritual condition Kafka wrote about as a malaise that might indeed be characterized as "sick." Then, when I suggested that we consider Kafka in his historical context, as a Jew resisting assimilation in turn-of-the-century Prague, they began to see his plight. It was a small step from Kafka's sense of alienation to their own, and discussion soon turned to the grim economic opportunities facing them after university, along with their own sense of betrayal. Modernism now seemed familiar. Although few had read Douglas Coupland's novel, they knew what Generation X was all about.

THE STUDENTS: 2

Gradually the students brought their own interests to the course, even looking for reflections of themselves in the books. Before the Christmas break, Iza, the young woman of Polish background, said that she wanted to try to read some women writers in Polish, so I recommended several novelists. As I mentioned before, the women writers of Central Europe have not yet been translated, although there is a large body of translated autobiographical writing about the Holocaust by Central European women. While these memoirs have little literary merit in the traditional sense of belletristic literature, they are examples of witnessing, with a unique kind of power. I gave a list of them to Iza, who decided to present a ten-minute seminar report about women and the Holocaust. To my surprise, the other women students (half the class, in fact) were not as bothered as I was by the course's lack of women writers. Whenever possible we looked at women's lives, and as we developed a picture of this subject during the Dual Monarchy, its relentlessly patriarchal nature became clear, even oppressive.

Since there were no Jewish students in the class, it was necessary to present the Holocaust to people who had few associations with it. Of greater concern was the fact that several students revealed a barely hidden anti-Semitism, while one was quite casual about it, without even recognizing his prejudice. "Jews," he once remarked, "aren't doing badly in the current recession." Without asking him to elaborate, I gave an impromptu talk on scapegoating and the changing legal status of European Jews in the last two centuries. Then, during our next class, I showed Alain Resnais's short film documentary *Night and Fog*, hoping that its vivid pictures of Holocaust victims — of people as commodities — would make a strong impression. I rarely use films as teaching aids, preferring to think that books explain themselves if you ask good questions. Since these students came from high schools that no longer emphasize even the most basic historical knowledge, it seemed necessary to show them what horrors people have inflicted on each other in the service of nationalism. And they did find Resnais's images extremely disturbing. Our discussions of Andrzej Szczypiorski's novel about life in the Warsaw ghetto, *The Beautiful Mrs. Seidenman*, took on a new edge, as if the class suddenly felt a stake in the suffering it recounts, and a genuine sympathy for the characters trying to escape it.

AS THE COURSE CONTINUES

By the end of the first term we had developed a vocabulary for studying Central European literature, a set of concerns that kept arising from one book to another: the idea of empire, the emperor, and honor; order, tradition, authority, and convention; patriarchy; the church; the outsider; the Jew; the duel; woman as mother, wife, and mistress; ethnic oppression; language rights; social decay; social change. Rather than exploring the sensibility of Central Europe, we were studying its literature as a commentary on society and politics, as well as the social agendas of various writers. But sensibility and politics began to merge. Aesthetic concerns, such as the way various writers handled the same genre, seemed less compelling than the social dimensions of these books. I saw this as a reflection of the power of books in Central Europe, a power that is difficult for North Americans to appreciate. In a culture of visual images — of movies, television, and music videos — we can hardly recall a time when novels really counted. And it is inconceivable for us to imagine Gore Vidal, say, or Toni Morrison, elected to political office. We think politics is too important to entrust to anyone but politicians — a frightening notion if you spend any time with it.

When planning the course, I had intended to hand out newspaper clippings and magazine articles, mostly as background information. These ranged from essays by Václav Havel and Milan Kundera, reprinted in the *New York Review of Books*, to straightforward reports of neo-Nazi activities in Central Europe, to Janet Malcolm's *New Yorker* account of a visit to Prague, where she retraced childhood haunts and discovered a common dislike of Kundera's fiction, which many Czechs consider a distortion of their lives that panders to Western intellectuals. As the academic year went on I added to my pile of clippings, for the steady flow of grim news from Europe almost seemed tailored to the concerns of my course.[7] Since universities are now more scrupulous about photocopying articles without copyright clearance, I passed out original copies, so that only a few students read the same articles. This actually became an advantage in class discussions, and suited a small seminar course. Yet the first articles were greeted with a blunt question: "Will we be tested on these?" No, I assured everyone, but you still need to read them. Soon the articles elicited curiosity, then enthusiasm. They proved that literature was not simply the study of books written by dead people. And after Christmas break, two students remarked that over the holidays they had explained the history of several current European conflicts to relatives who were impressed by their newly acquired knowledge. In spite of a heavy reading load, four essays, and a final exam, the course was paying off. No one had expected it to be relevant.

At times the students joked that I must have foreseen the dramatic changes happening in Central Europe: there were just too many coincidences between the subject matter of the course and the headlines in the daily news. Watching out for the potential dangers of reducing literature to sociology, or to a grand lesson in reading the newspaper, I spoke of metafiction as a genre, and of the blending of historical fact and fiction. Looked at in this context, novels by Roth, Skvorecky, Vizinczey, and Szczypiorski took on a new dimension. (Roth's *Radetzky March*, in which Emperor Franz Josef appears on several occasions, falls properly into the genre, but the other novels share some of its characteristics too.) Most of the writers that we dealt with had set their novels back in time by at least fifty years, and we tried to understand why. I wanted the students to see for themselves that it is possible to use the past to comment on the present, and that in authoritarian regimes the device was often a subversive one. We talked about allegory, which the students found relentlessly uncontemporary, until one of them, who had been able to find a copy of Robert Musil's *Young Törless*, called it "a Habsburg *Lord of the Flies*." Everyone knew that book, and allegory began to make sense. The class concluded that Central Europeans needed allegory more than North Americans. This seemed a wise observation. Allegory, they saw, particularly suited writers in countries where more direct forms of political dissent were heavily censored.

One afternoon, near the end of the second semester, a woman student remarked that the young heroes of the last few novels we had read were obsessed with sex ("they're all horny over there," she said). This led to a discussion of the pursuit of sexual identity as a mask for the inability to claim public or political identity. At first the class ignored my notion that an emphasis on sexual life can be a kind of failure. I decided to let the idea pass. The following week, while discussing Kundera's novel, it came up again. Several students had rented videos of the films based on Vizinczey's and Kundera's novels, and the visual images of lovemaking brought the point home. I then turned to Janet Malcolm's *New Yorker* article, in which her cousin, a Czech window-washer, attacks the image Kundera has given the West of all Czech intellectuals as sex-obsessed window-washers. "If Vizinczey says they're horny, and Skvorecky says they're horny," one woman student offered, "then maybe Malcolm's got it wrong. Maybe Kundera got it right. Men are just like that." Of course everyone laughed. It was the voice of Generation X—skeptical and world weary. "You sound like one of the characters in *The Emperor's Tomb*," I suggested, thinking of Roth's apathetic young Viennese before the First World War. "But we're not nostalgic about anything," one student insisted, almost proudly. Perhaps she was right. At least she had read Roth carefully.

At our final class I asked the students to discuss a short passage from Timothy Garton Ash: "Central Europe is not a region whose boundaries you can trace on the map—like, say, Central America. It is a kingdom of the spirit."[8] They looked at this passage from several angles, and decided that history is sensibility. If there is such a thing as a Central European spirit, today it may have to be kept alive by writers living outside the region—Kundera in Paris, Vizinczey in London, von Rezzori in Tuscany. And what, we thought, was the connection between nostalgia and sensibility? Plagued by an almost deadly nostalgia, and old fears of multiculturalism, Central Europe has been struggling with an identity crisis for most of this century. The region never had time to resolve the psychic wound left by the treaties after the First World War, which redefined its borders, before it faced German occupation, and then Russian occupation. "But all that suffering made people think," one student argued. Generalizing with abandon, we even wondered if it helped to account for the richness of the region's literature. This notion seemed a hopeful way to end the course.

THE FUTURE

The course is scheduled again for the upcoming academic year, but it will not be a straightforward re-run. No one can predict the future in Bosnia, or anywhere else in Central Europe, for that matter, although the recent proliferation of nationalisms does not bode well. I cannot even guess the surprises that various publishers hold in store. Recently the distinguished Czech translator Paul Wilson mentioned that one of the best contemporary German translators was learning Hungarian with an eye to translating some of that largely untapped literature. I found the news encouraging. If my course is to have a lasting life, its reading list will need to metamorphose, like the shifting realities of Central Europe itself.

The Poet
as Translator
Margaret Avison's
"Hungarian Snap"

Several years before the publication of her first volume of poetry, *Winter Sun* (1960), Margaret Avison was walking through the then-outdoor courtyard of Toronto's Royal Ontario Museum, admiring its Chinese tomb lions. Nearby, Marshall McLuhan sat entertaining two Hungarian émigrés, Ilona Duczyńska and her husband Karl Polanyi. Spotting Avison, he motioned her to join them, saying, "Here's a poet you should use in your project."[1]

Thus, as with many collaborative efforts, a fortunate accident was at the start of this one. The Polanyis wanted to publish a collection of translations of some of Hungary's greatest twentieth-century writers, including Attila József, Gyula Illyés, and Ferenc Juhász, and as an outcome of the impromptu meeting with Avison, her translations were destined to be part of that volume. Entitled *The Plough and the Pen: Writings from Hungary, 1930–1956*, it was published in 1963, with an introduction by W. H. Auden.[2] In her collection *No Time* (1989), Avison included one of these translations, revised, and she offered several of them in her *Selected Poems* (1991). Her translations are exemplary, deserving study for themselves and for the issues they raise.[3]

The poet as translator has a long, impressive history, especially when poets work with languages they know well. But it makes for a fascinating sideline to this tradition when poets take the risk of dealing with languages they don't understand. William Butler Yeats's lack of Greek never stopped him from translating Sophocles. Auden and Pound worked with poems in languages they couldn't read, and more recently Robert Lowell, W. S. Merwin, and Elaine Feinstein (to list only a few) have enriched our sense of the possibilities of English while introducing unfamiliar writers.

Although the reasons for undertaking such translations differ from poet to poet, certain technical concerns remain constant. Lowell raised many of these in the preface to *Imitations*, his collection of translations of Western poetry from Homer to Pasternak. "I have been restless with literal meaning," he confessed, "and labored hard to get the tone. Most often *a* tone, for *the* tone is something that will always more or less escape transference to another language and cultural moment."[4] Like many poets faced with writing in an unknown language, he had to rely on intermediaries. Of Pasternak he wrote: "I have rashly tried to improve on other translations, and have been helped by exact prose versions given me by Russian readers." This is "an old practice," as he recognized — an old practice that yields new poems twice removed from the originals.

Inevitably a poet brings to the act of translating personal associations with a language, culture, or writer. Avison recalls that the Polanyis were her first experience with European intellectuals: "something I'd known from novels, and here it was in the flesh." Both had been active in leftist politics in Hungary before becoming exiles. After meeting in Austria, they settled in England during the 1930s. Duczyńska taught science, and became an Associate Fellow of the Royal Aeronautical Society; Polanyi taught in Vienna and London, and eventually became a professor of economics at Columbia University. Fortunately the Polanyis were able to overcome Avison's fear, stemming from their country's policies during the Second World War, that all Hungarians were anti-Semites. Duczyńska was Jewish, Polanyi a Christian, and they represented a side of the Hungarian character new to Avison. She had admired the revolution of 1956, and had been appalled when the West encouraged the freedom fighters and then "dumped" them. The Polanyis intrigued her because of their commitment to both politics and literature.

And Avison—who knew some German and high school French—came to be fascinated by the Hungarian language itself. The effect of spoken Hungarian reminded her of Finnish, which she happily associated with girlhood school friends. (Hungarian and Finnish are both part of the Finno-Ugrian language group, and distantly related.) While the pronunciation of Hungarian words tends to evenness, there is often a slight stress on the first syllable, giving the hint of an accent. Musicians have called this stress the "Hungarian snap," thinking of such composers as Bartók and Kodály. Avison immediately liked the sound of spoken Hungarian.

Duczyńska made the initial selection of poets. Her reasons for choosing them, Avison recalls, were partly political—a way of introducing her view of non-Stalinist Hungary to the West. Since the revolution of 1848, Hungarian writers have been a major political force in national life, preserving Hungarian identity and speaking out against oppression. The Populists, who emerged in the early 1930s, were a loosely formed radical movement of peasant intelligentsia. Attempting to do for letters what Bartók had done for Hungarian music, they studied the sociology of rural life and advocated partition of the great landed estates. Some followed Marxism, holding to its early humanist vision; others converted to communism; and still others wanted to reform the Communist Party. Many of Hungary's leading writers between the two world wars were part of the group, or touched by it in a significant way. They were, in effect, the progenitors of the revolution of 1956.[5]

Avison was particularly drawn to the work of Illyés and Juhász,

writers associated with the Hungarian landscape. Initially Duczyńska offered her translators little choice when she assigned poems,
and Avison had to compete with Kenneth McRobbie for Juhász,
eventually sharing the poet. Illyés's descriptions of the Hungarian
plain—a region much like the prairies of Manitoba familiar to Avison from her youth—especially appealed to her, and she also felt
sympathy for his despair at the onset of the Second World War, a
despair she found particularly bleak considering her own "pacifist
growing-up period, which made the Illyés intensity natural to me
too. It said something."

Hungarian poetry can of course be read apart from the country's historical and cultural situation. But a quest to preserve
national identity is central to all of the poets Duczyńska asked Avison to translate. While Communist poets such as László Benjámin,
Zoltán Zelk, and Lajos Tamási were important in the national context, their poems—expressing first idealism, then disillusionment
with party corruption—were not especially well suited to translation. They were effective in the Polanyis's anthology mainly as
examples of Hungarian writing of the period, but Avison was wise
not to include her translations of Zelk and Benjámin in her own
collections. On the other hand, Attila József (1905–37), Gyula Illyés (1902–83), and Ferenc Juhász (b. 1928) wrote poems that invite
a wider audience, and translation.

Hungarian is a notoriously difficult language, with a unique system of grammar and few crossover words. It has little in common
with the more familiar Indo-European languages. Based, in part,
on an elaborate system of suffixes, it is an agglutinative language
that offers particular problems for translators of poetry: Hungarian syntax and word order differ greatly from English. Simply
by the nature of the language, poetry in Hungarian is bound to
be more compact than most poetry in English. At the same time,
the Hungarian language may seem more formal because it has not
undergone as rapid a shift to colloquial usage as North American
English.

Initially Avison was given the Hungarian texts, marked with the
accents of the language and the metrical stresses of the verse, as
well as notations of "rhyme and assonance patterns, number of syl-
lables and rhythmic pictures."[6] Literal translations accompanied

each poem, with the corresponding English word under the Hungarian original, so that she could recognize each word and gauge its weight in the original poem. There were also free-flowing prose translations, although Duczyńska urged Avison not to work from them. Instead, they went over each poem together, word by word. Finally, tapes were made of the poems so that Avison could hear the sounds: "And I played the tapes and played the tapes and played the tapes, and once I got to know what the words literally meant, I tried to see if I could get an English one that was at all able to echo it." Avison also listened to recordings of Hungarian music. She especially loved the Bartók string quartets, and recalled them as "the thing that keyed me most of all in that period."

Each translation went through more than twenty drafts. Avison spent long hours with the Polanyis, even staying overnight at their home and working on into the next day, "battling over four or five lines, sometimes." When asked if the process had been frustrating—especially for a writer accustomed to working by herself—she laughed, saying, "If it hadn't been for the enormous appeal of these two people, I couldn't have stayed the course." This process ran over a period of four years, and was often spotty, since Duczyńska was involved with other translators as well.[7]

Translation is not simply a linguistic act. It is also an interpretative one, where affinity matters. The "optic heart" in Avison's poems, the heart that *sees*, is not far removed from the concern with consciousness and perception in Juhász's "Farm, at Dark, on the Great Plain" ("Tanya az Alföldön"), which opens with a rhapsodic evocation of the natural world of a farm at night, emphasizing the universal molecular life where "breathless, matter lives."[8] Not until the beginning of stanza 13 does a speaker say, directly, "I lie in drenched grass," establishing the struggle for individual consciousness on that

> strange, blissful night, primal, voluptuous—
> random—with nothing of passion's single-mindedness.
> Plant cannot guess—nor planet—the knowledge a
> human bears.

The speaker turns his attention to the farm below with a simple, intimate "I love you"—an almost shocking shift in tone. The subsequent portrait of an aging farm couple (perhaps Juhász's parents, who are mentioned frequently in his work) facing the hardships of their rural existence momentarily distracts the speaker, who then returns to the issue of consciousness, confessing his love for the earth, and for an absent partner:

> Only with you I believe, I feel at one,
> nor need my heart at last go so mercilessly alone
> to its corruption.

The moment of consciousness carries within it the desire to escape and merge, to return to the anonymous "glimmer" of the natural world that closes the poem. These few passages alone should suggest the richness of Avison's translation, and the affinity she felt for Juhász.

Technical or linguistic matters, however, shape the affinity. Avison generally followed the stanzaic order of the original poems, although she did not maintain exact meters or line breaks. In stanza five of Juhász's poem, for example, she made two sentences out of three, included a parenthetical clause, and expanded the diction:

> The moonlight's liquid glass
> wells over the earth
> and quells the very silence in its clasp
> to crystal blocks,
> glass turrets,
> tinkling vine-stems.
> Still—how this silence (silvery bushes,
> half-guessed-at-stalks, dim files of foliate)
> entangles and engulfs the din of empty space
> and murmurous flower-scent from the garden-beds.

> *A holdfény folyékony üveg*
> *amely vastagon a világra csurog,*
> *anyagát e csönd dermeszti meg.*
> *Üveg-tömbök,*
> *üveg-tornyok,*
> *üveg-liánok csengenek.*
> *Ez mégis a csönd. Áttetsző bozótok,*

sejtelem-szárú növényzetek
fonják, növik be az űr zaját,
*s a szagos virágos-kerteket.*⁹

Juhász repeats the word "glass" (*üveg*) four times, including it
in a descriptive series, while Avison uses it only twice, substitut-
ing "crystal" once, and deleting it the final time. The incantatory
quality of the original has been changed to something more ornate,
yet this ornateness is not false to the original. (As Lowell said, a
translation catches *a* tone, not *the* tone.) In the second stanza of
the same poem, Avison's translation reads:

> Glass-petalled flowers, leaves of thin glass
> are incandescent, as
> our anguish.

> *Üveg-virágok, üveg-lombok*
> *izzanak,*
> *mint a gondok.*

More literally translated, the stanza would read:

> Glass-flowers, glass leaves
> are incandescent,
> as our troubles.

While "anguish" is too strong a translation of the Hungarian word
gond (care, worry, anxiety, trouble), which Juhász uses in the plural form, the lushness of Avison's version suggests the tradition of
English Romantic poetry, and this is not entirely inappropriate to
Juhász. His diction and imagery, his concern with human isolation and use of the Hungarian landscape as an emblem of states
of mind, resonate with familiar echoes that Avison powerfully con-
veys.¹⁰

When asked if she felt any kinship with Attila József's "Ars
Poetica," Avison admitted that she had to overcome her lack of
sympathy with the poet's self-assertive stance: "One of the things
I don't like about it is its superiority towards other people who
are caught." Unlike Juhász's poem, which can be enjoyed inde-
pendently of his other work and apart from its Hungarian context,
"Ars Poetica" requires some background. József, who committed

suicide in 1937 at the age of thirty-two, is considered by many Hungarian critics to rank with the nation's greatest poets, Sándor Petőfi (1823–49) and Endre Ady (1877–1919). Consumed by self-analysis, he watched with increasing horror as the forces of fascism swept across his country. Yet for all his championing of the people — József is a true socialist poet — the source of his writing often seems to be a more private suffering, and Avison was not incorrect in sensing this. It is part of the tension that makes his poetry worth careful reading.

"Ars Poetica" opens with a bold assertion: "I *am* a poet. What do I care / about Poesy?"[11] although the character of the original is missing (*Költő vagyok — mit érdekelne / engem a költészet maga?*).[12] By breaking the Hungarian sentence into two statements — a separate declaration followed by a question — a quality of arrogance, of swagger, enters the speaker's voice, and this is not present in the original. The necessary shift in word order — *költő* (poet) opens the original, while "I *am*," with an italicized verb for emphasis, opens the translation — solidifies this impression. The use of "Poesy" bothers Avison today: "I remember hating the second line and [also] putting the word 'Poesy' in, but Ilona insisted." Translated literally, the poet's question is "Why should I be interested in poetry itself?" "Poesy" is not the best solution for *költészet maga* ("poetry itself") because it has archaic and arch connotations for a modern English-speaking audience that the word *költészet* lacks for Hungarian readers. Since Duczyńska not only provided the literal translations but also edited the anthology, Avison's translations were subject to the potential pitfalls of any collaborative work. Though admirably translated, "Ars Poetica" is not likely to win readers to József's work.

No such problems occurred with her translations of Gyula Illyés's "Ode to Bartók" ("Bartók"), "The Plough Moves" ("Megy az eke"), and "Of Tyranny, in One Breath" ("Egy mondat a zsarnokságrol"). And her inclusion of the ode in several collections attests to her estimation of its power. Speaking of Illyés, she said: "There is nothing that gets in the way, there's no ego that gets in the poems, there's just utterance." This "utterance," as she called it, "was always a combination of reasonable statement and enormous power of feeling." Avison, who is not thought of as a political poet, was in fact drawn to Illyés's politics. In a note added to the ode for her own collections, she explained the unusual circumstances of its publication, which are worth relating here not only for what they suggest about the poem, but also because they may have contributed to Avison's sympathetic reading of it. Written in the autumn of 1955, when the Rákosi regime was urging Hungarian writers to follow the dictates of socialist realism, the ode paid tribute to Bartók on the tenth anniversary of his death. The composer's music, then banned in Hungary, was a rallying point for anyone unsympathetic to Rákosi. Published in a popular weekly Budapest entertainment magazine, *Szinház és Mozi* (Stage and Cinema), with a print run of over 60,000, the poem had a powerful effect, and several days after its appearance the police removed all remaining copies from the newsstands.

The ode is a stirring call to freedom, first linking it with artistic creation, principally Bartók's use of folk material in his music ("O speak for us, / stern artist, true musician").[13] Only from the discord of his creations can true harmony emerge. Illyés contends that Bartók's music has the power to solace a suffering people because it embodies their song, their dream; it is crucial to the survival of the nation. This was a dangerous poem to have written at that time, and Avison admired Illyés for taking the risk.

Again she followed the poet's stanzaic pattern, although the shorter concluding stanzas of the original have been linked together, for a soaring effect. Regarding her version, Avison wrote that "an attempt has been made to echo the sound and syllabics of Illyés's poem in the English translating."[14] This was no easy task, as the opening stanza indicates:

> "Jangling discords?" Yes! If you call it this, that has
> such potency for us.
> Yes, the splintering and smashing
> glass strewn upon earth—the lash's
> crack, the curses, the saw-teeth's screeching
> scrape and shriek—let the violins learn this dementia,
> and the singers' voices, let them learn from these;
> let there be no peace,
> no stained glass, perfumed ease

under the gilt and the velvet and the gargoyles
of the concert hall, no sanctuary from turmoil
while our hearts are gutted with grief and know no peace.

"Hangzavart"? — Azt! Ha nekik az,
ami nekünk vigasz!
Azt! Földre hullt
pohár fölcsattanó
szitok-szavát, fűresz foga közé szorult
reszelő sikongató
jaját tanulja hegedű
s éneklő gége — ne legyen béke, ne legyen derű
a bearanyozott, a fennen
finom, elzárt zeneteremben,
míg nincs a jaj-sotét szivekben![15]

Clearly the original is a much more compact poem. Avison's pyro-
technic sounds, however, have caught the Hungarian, even suggesting its brilliance. Phrases like "the saw-teeth's screeching /
scrape and shriek" and "gutted with grief" recall Gerard Manley
Hopkins, and remind us that a good English translation will contain echoes of the tradition of English poetry as it introduces
another tradition. Yet Avison's use of alliteration and assonance
(especially on the letters s, c, and g), like Illyés's, evokes Bartók's
musical line, and is true to the tone of the original.

Regarding her revisions to the ode, made before including it in
No Time (1989), Avison said: "Some of them were for ear. If you
remember the 'glass flashing' — my ear was offended and I was sure
in the original it couldn't have been quite so blatant. And sometimes because I thought the logic was easier to follow with a little
more care, just so that it would be a little more syntactically correct. The Hungarian seemed to be constructed in logical as well
as musical terms, and I thought we sacrificed something there as
I went over it. I think Ilona would not have minded." This is not
the place to enumerate all of her revisions, but several examples
are worth noting. In line four, for example, "glass flashing from
earth" was aptly changed to "glass strewn upon earth." In stanza
four, line six, the "T" in "That," which begins the line, has been
capitalized to establish the following ten lines as part of a continu-

ous—though twisting—phrase, also giving it prominence over the use of the lowered-case "that" in the opening of the next several lines. More important than these small changes is the fact that Avison chose to make them in work published years before. Such revisions suggest the care that she has taken with her writing.

The poet-speaker of Illyés's "The Plough Moves" equates a plough slowly digging a furrow with a hand writing a book. As the details of this metaphor are developed and sustained over five stanzas, farmer and poet merge into the same "immutable creative force"[16]: "Your story, Hungary, is being written / here in these furrows." With the "vast plain his book," farmer and poet share a similar fate—they make gestures to the future, to "all that still lies ahead." This is Populist poetry with a vengeance, and yet its simplicity is moving. (Duczyńska and Polanyi clearly took the title of their anthology from Illyés's poem.) Written in the rhythm of popular folk songs—a rhythm also associated with the poet Petőfi— "The Plough Moves" must have been difficult to translate:

> The plough moves and the moving furrow slowly
> builds up the row
> like a hand writing in an open book
> for all to know;
> its paper the vast plain, a feathery ocean
> the heavens span
> from brim to brim; the writing hand one aging
> hired man.

> *Megy az eke, szaporodik*
> *a barázda*
> *mintha egy nagy könyv íródnék*
> *olvasásra.*
> *Papirosa a határ, a*
> *tengerszéles,*
> *a tolla meg az a szegény*
> *öregbéres.*[17]

Whereas her translation of the ode is suitably cacophonous, Avison here used a less ornate language, as the poem demands. She maintained its rhyme scheme: row/know (*barázda/olvasásra*), span/man (*tengerszéles/öregbéres*), and came close to some exact correspondences (*barázda* = furrow; *olvasásra* = to be read; *tengerszéles* = sea wide; *öregbéres* = aged farmhand). In Hungarian poetry, assonance is a common form of rhyme, and such partial rhymes are valued for their originality. Avison's pure rhymes (row/know), here based on one-syllable words, do not suggest the original's more complex pattern. She was, however, writing an English poem, not a Hungarian one, and her poem needed to work in the conventions of its own language.

For Illyés's "Of Tyranny, in One Breath," which did not appear in *The Plough and the Pen* but instead in *The Dumbfounding*, Avison used a similarly direct poetic line and diction. An indictment of political oppression (specifically the Rákosi dictatorship), the poem is made up of one sentence that runs for forty-six short stanzas, varying from two to four lines in length—an almost breathless technical feat. Beginning with Bren guns and questioning police, it becomes an exhaustive catalogue of all forms of tyranny, from the overt actions of a totalitarian state to the ways in which tyranny can overwhelm a society, informing daily life until "*you* / are the prison bars you're staring through."[18] An example of what Avison regarded as Illyés's "combination of reasonable statement and enormous power of feeling," the poem is held together by repetitions—"where tyranny settles in . . . ," "for tyranny is . . . ," "it is . . ."—until "tyranny" becomes a looming, inescapable "it." As in the Bartók ode, the tone of urgency here has a hallucinatory quality; it comes from the tension between Illyés's statements and the depth of his attachment to freedom—a tension that Avison found sympathetic, and successfully conveyed.

While some poets decide to translate poetry during difficult creative periods (as Lowell admitted in *Imitations*), others find that translating can accompany a rich time of personal work. Avison made her translations during the heady years of her debut as a poet. The acclaim for *Winter Sun* gave her both an audience and a social role that was a creative stimulus—"recognition, like it or lump it, helps." This new status, together with the collaborative nature of the translation project, and the friendships it brought, may have affected the preparation of her next collection, *The*

Dumbfounding (1966). As Avison recalled, "It was just a nice synchronizing of things."

The shift in tone between her first and second collections, which many critics have discussed (in some cases linking it to her religious conversion), may have also been related to her translations; as Ernest Redekop wrote: "Sometimes, indeed, it is tempting to think that she may have been influenced by some of the images and concepts that she had translated."[19] Yet such speculations are difficult to prove, and to look for comparable "images and concepts" is to ignore the collaborative process that shaped Avison's translations. Equally conjectural, my own suspicion is that Avison's meetings with Ducszyńska may have had a subtle effect on the questions she asked herself in revising her own poems—in fact, on the entire process of revision. The intensity that characterized their sessions together, and the emphasis on clarity, precision, accuracy, and feeling, could not have been lost on someone as thoughtful as Avison. When asked if, after her experience with Hungarian poetry, she ever wanted to translate other poems, she replied, with a wry smile: "I don't like writing. I never tackle a piece of writing if I'm not asked to, persuasively enough—that's the trouble." That no one asked her is our loss, for her Hungarian translations—and especially of Juhász's "The Farm, at Dark, on the Great Plain" and Illyés's "Ode to Bartók"—belong with the finest translations made by contemporary poets.

Introducing Péter Esterházy

Not since György Konrád's novel *A látogató* was translated into English as *The Case Worker* (1974) has a Hungarian writer caught the attention of North America. With luck this may soon change, because Péter Esterházy deserves a wide readership here. His books have already been translated into French, German, Danish, Italian, Polish, and Swedish. The recent publication of the English translations of his novels *Helping Verbs of the Heart* (1991), *The Book of Hrabal* (1993), and *The Glance of Countess Hahn-Hahn* (1994) finally gives Western readers the chance to discover one of the most original writers in Europe today.[1]

Think of the Medicis and you begin to sense the power and glamour of the name "Esterházy" in Hungary. An aristocratic family that can trace its ancestors to the twelfth century, they have influenced affairs of state, built famous palaces, been patrons of musicians like Joseph Haydn, and even founded one of the first Hungarian communities in Canada in 1886 — Esterhazy, Saskatchewan, named after Count Pál Esterházy. The latest to add his own stamp to this name, Péter Esterházy was born a count in Budapest in 1950. Yet there is nothing about him that suggests the dashing mustachioed stereotype the title brings to mind; in fact, he bears an uncanny resemblance to John Lennon.

After studying mathematics at the University of Budapest, Esterházy published his first book, *Fancsikó és Punta* (Fancsikó and Punta) in 1976. A collection of linked stories in which the child hero invents two trickster-like friends to help him deal with the adult world, it immediately drew attention to an idiosyncratic young writer. Unwilling to tell a story straight, Esterházy refused to be confined to the limits of the page or the dictates of realism. His work uses satire, parody and pastiche, jokes and wordplay, archaisms and slang, references to European art, literature, and philosophy, autobiographical details, political observations, comic asides, and direct addresses to the reader — any number of elements that are sometimes associated with metafiction and also postmodernism — to create a universe in which readers can't predict where they're heading. Esterházy solidified his reputation as Hungary's most exciting young, experimental novelist with *Termelési-regény* (Production Novel, 1979), a satire about industrial production and the institutes devoted to it that includes a set of notes longer than the novel itself. Yet the book is much more than a send-up of the socialist-realist fiction that the Communist Party encouraged, for it contains autobiographical episodes and some deadly serious tongue-in-cheek meditations on the act of writing, as well as characters like Goethe's Johann Peter Eckermann, Comrade Gregory Peck, and Marilyn Monroe. Although he writes in a language unrelated to any of the major European languages, Esterházy shows a rich awareness of contemporary European and American fiction.

It would be too simple to call Esterházy a postmodernist and be done with it, despite his obvious connections with the term. After all, postmodernism is not a monolithic movement but more of a set of assumptions, perhaps even an umbrella term. In a series of lectures about Hungarian fiction at the University of Amsterdam, Richard Aczel, one of Esterházy's translators, noted that Esterházy has claimed that in Hungary "there is postmodernism, even though modernism is yet to have its day, never having been allowed to run its course."[2] It is an appealing—though contentious—idea. Aczel, however, builds on it:

> What has become clear over the last few years is that rather than experiencing the death throes of "late" capitalism, we are seeing capitalism—together with its attendant liberal democratic ideology—enter a new, vigorous and revolutionary phase. Far from being on its last legs, it has finally smashed totalitarian regimes of Eastern Europe. Postmodernism may not prove to be a "post" aesthetic ideology at all, but, on the contrary, a prelude to a new chapter in the grand historical narrative. One day, cultural historians may look back and see that what was once called postmodernism was in fact the moment that prefigured a new experience of modernity in both East and West.[3]

In this speculative context, Aczel even goes on to suggest a radical way of seeing postmodernism: "Could postmodernism itself finally turn out to be a kind of premodernism, a secession, a *fin-de-siècle* decadence before the discovery of a new modernity in the 21st century?"[4] The question perfectly suits Esterházy's work, and one might begin to address it with a sideways glance at the past that connects Esterházy with one of his great literary forebears.

Recently Esterházy wrote an introduction to the English translation of Dezső Kosztolányi's 1924 novel, *Skylark*. One of Hungary's finest writers, Kosztolányi (1885–1936) drew praise from Esterházy for both his vision of the world and the reforms he brought to the Hungarian language itself. An original contributor to *Nyugat* (West), the important literary magazine that almost single-handedly created modern Hungarian literature, Kosztolányi was both a poet and a prose writer. His circle of friends included Sándor Ferenczi, one of the founders of psychoanalysis, and many writers outside Hungary, such as Thomas Mann, who wrote an epistolary preface to his novel *Darker Muses: The Poet Nero.* In 1936 he became the first chairman of Hungarian PEN. I include these details not only because they give a sense of Kosztolányi's personality, but also because they suggest that he may have been a kind of role model for Esterházy. In a country where writers can feel isolated by the very nature of the language they use, Kosztolányi's internationalism made it possible for the next generation of writers to see themselves as part of a larger community. On the surface, Kosztolányi is a realist, but his realism, by turns, can be ironic, satiric, dispassionate, and visionary.[5]

When Esterházy praises Kosztolányi as "a representative of *l'art pour l'art,* a writerly writer," he reveals his own literary values; and he further develops the idea when remarking of Kosztolányi: "Courageously and coquettishly he chooses the 'babbling surface' as opposed to the 'silent depths.'"[6] This passage, I think, says more about Esterházy's aesthetics than Kosztolányi's novels, and I suspect that anyone who has read Kosztolányi's *Skylark* or *Anna Édes* will agree. Esterházy's obsessive use of literary quotations gives his own work a "babbling surface," as writers from one generation and another echo and collide with each other. There are moments when Esterházy's use of quotation and disjointed fragments seems too clever by half — a weakness his work sometimes shares with other postmodern fiction — but even at such moments of literary display, Esterházy writes with a kind of aristocratic *sprezzatura* that makes the reader want to continue. "Kosztolányi does not seek his own authentic face," Esterházy suggested, "but the authentic mask."[7] In the sense that Kosztolányi is closer to Chekhov than Tolstoy, this is true, but again, it says as much about Esterházy — if not more — than it does about Kosztolányi.

Like Kosztolányi, Esterházy is not interested in writing a grand historical-national narrative, or in solving his country's many problems. In fact Esterházy's distrust of language builds into a distrust of narrative itself to the point where, in good postmodern fashion, nothing exists outside the text itself. Breaking from Soviet realism (which had plagued Hungarian writers of the fifties and sixties) and even from realism itself, Esterházy refuses the didactic as well as the confessional mode. This becomes a more serious break with the Hungarian tradition than Western readers might guess. In Hungary, where the political and the polemical have been a crucial part of literary life, Esterházy's commitment to an individual text rather than to any external claims on it is a radical departure. In this sense the Hungarian context of postmodernism is quite different from the American or the French. His debt to modernists inside and outside Hungary is acknowledged in his foreword to *Helping Verbs of the Heart*, and I will cite only nine of the forty-three names he lists—Donald Barthelme, Jorge Luis Borges, Peter Handke, Gyula Illyés, Lautréamont, Robert Musil, Jean-Paul Sartre, and Ludwig Wittgenstein, along with Saint Paul.

Esterházy's vision needs scope, and he found a way to shape it in a loosely structured cycle of novels called *Bevezetés a szépirodalomba* (Introduction to Literature), which were collected in 1986. Here he ranges over a large cast of varied characters. "Daisy," for example, the first story in *Ki szavatol a lady biztonságáért?* (Who Takes Responsibility for the Lady?, 1982), is set in a transvestite nightclub where the moody night world serves as backdrop for a black comedy about love and, by implication, the futility of all human relations. It is paired with "Ágnes," in which a French publisher's reader reveals his growing love for the wife of his best friend in a report he's writing about a text that unfolds before the narrator (and reader) at the same time. The story's epigraph — "The situation is hopeless, but not serious" — serves as a good introduction to all of Esterházy's books. Tossing out references to Paul Klee, Rilke's Berlin, and Konrad Adenauer, as he does in "Ágnes," Esterházy is a tremendous juggler, and this makes him a natural essayist.

Whether writing a novella in verse like *Fuvarosok* (The Transporters, 1983), or a novel using dictionary-like entries reminiscent of Ambrose Bierce (*Kis Magyar Pornográfia*, Small Hungarian Pornography, 1984, a collection of anecdotes about Hungary's national obsessions), Esterházy continued to upend realism's favored conventions. *The Transporters*, the English translation of *Fuvarosok*, turns the 52-page verse "novel" (as Esterházy called it) into a prose story, in keeping with Esterházy's version of that text as a prose work when he included it in his *Introduction to Literature*. The story takes place in a country house in late summer, where family talk runs to making plans for mushroom picking or visiting the neighboring countess, who "has seen life and a few places, like Pozsony, Szabadka, even Pest."[8] Chekovian at its start, the narrative soon breaks into a dark world of erotic longing and sexual violence. Zsófi, the young narrator, recounts the daily life of her mother and older sisters while she watches some lorry drivers camped near their property. For a moment the story becomes a celebration of primal maleness, as Zsófi observes the men — "their thighs are of heroic proportion, their trousers cannot help being tight"[9] — with fascination. But this is a novel by Péter Esterházy, after all, and the irony here is dramatic.

The text of this lyrical prose poem is woven through with quotations from a wide range of religious writers — Pascal, Kierkegaard, Teilhard de Chardin — blending the metaphysical with the personal until they seem one. The quotations are buried in the text itself, and appear without the drumroll that sometimes accompanies such references in Esterházy's work. As a result, "The Transporters" has the luminous quality of visionary realism. Zsófi, who believes that "things can be beautiful only if things can be ugly as well,"[10] refuses to acknowledge the brutish, degrading events that transpire before her. The story thus develops a double vision of its events, beautiful and ugly, held together by Zsófi's manner of telling. Esterházy's apparent distrust of language also becomes a distrust of seeing and knowing; his heroine shares his obsession with epistemology. The simpleton who accompanies the transporters at first troubles her with questions of belief — "He says the stars are so many barren rocks, the lamp is not a lamp, table is no table, children are no children,"[11] until Zsófi's mother nicknames him "Dummy." But the girl comes to know better, and she calls him "Knight," with an echo of Don Quixote. Dummy even fights to save Zsófi when one of the transporters attacks her, before retreating to chew on an old rind of bacon while running in a circle he can't break out of.

By the end of the story Zsófi and her sisters come to call stars "barren rocks," but she still maintains her double vision. The story concludes with rapturous prose, and I want to quote a longish passage to suggest Esterházy's achievement. At the start of it, Zsófi refuses to disown her attachment to Dummy:

I loved him, I say. So you loved him, the tall girls cry, you loved him, you say, she loves him, they exchange incredulous glances, she loves the fool and mascot of a transporter . . . You idiot! Couldn't you see what these people were?! Couldn't you see what they were up to?! Would you mess around with people like that?! You good-for-nothing treacherous slut, they are coming at me threateningly, they draw sharp bodkins, die, Szófia, die you must, so die all traitors. I am about to commence my last prayer, my sisters are reeling with laughter, reel back to their beds, they are sprawled out on the stained yellow butterfly-patterned blanket, they are rolling about wrestling, panting, their teeth flashing. Oh you! Mummy brought in warm water and a mug of milk. Lay the table. Make the bed. Stoke up the fire. Set the dogs loose for the night.

There is no dog. I am sitting in the washbasin. Scraping off, like the enamel earlier, dried flakes of blood. This is my blood. Douching does not hurt me. We have come through again, my sisters say panting in ecstacy. Yes, yes, we have come through, my darlings, mummy says, she is stroking my hair with her heavy old hand, we have come through, and we have salt, potatoes and parsley.

We all break into the laughter of heartfelt relief.[12]

For someone who loves irony as Esterházy does, this is indeed passionate writing. Yet he has not fallen to the temptation of "fine" writing. This prose is heightened to mirror a heightened consciousness that has been growing before the reader.

Esterházy's collection of essays entitled *A kitömött hattyú* (The Stuffed Swan, 1988) is filled with the reversals common to his fiction. In "On Laziness" (which appeared in translation in *Partisan Review*) he begins with the axiom "Whereon one cannot act, thereon must loaf" and proceeds to reject it, explaining that the lazy are nibblers, content with little, and a bit old-fashioned, though in fact not passive, but "prepared for everything."[13] It is the hardworking who are "machines, cold, stiff, plaster-like, predictable," while the lazy remain "organic, warm, soft. They are soil, independence, landscape, faith." And then, just as you're ready to throw over your life and hit the road, Esterházy can't resist a final turn, proclaiming: "I will chase away this dreadful dawn with work. This is still my best solution."[14] Though the ground may seem to be shifting, the values of humanism remain a constant, even when hidden behind bitter humor.

Unfortunately the North American publication of *Helping Verbs of the Heart* was largely ignored, except for a few paragraphs in John Banville's roundup review of new Central European fiction in the *New York Review of Books*, which included novels by Tadeusz Konwicki and Bohumil Hrabal, along with Esterházy's. Yet Banville admired his novel, saying: "It is a puzzling, and at times an infuriating work which, despite its determinedly playful, nonchalant air, stays in the mind long after one has finished reading it. I know of few novels (one thinks of Peter Handke's trilogy *A Sorrow Beyond Dreams*) which communicate so poignantly the grief and confusion, as well as that strange, febrile euphoria, which attend the loss of a parent."[15] Banville only hints at the richness of Esterházy's novel.

Any reader who opens a copy of *Helping Verbs of the Heart* will immediately notice its unusual design. The type area of every page is bordered with a thick black line reminiscent of mourning bands or the edging on death announcements. Even before the act of reading begins, Esterházy challenges his reader's conventional associations with death and grief as they appear in modern fiction. Within these frames, the top portion of each page contains the book's central story while a parallel text, in capital letters, runs along the bottom of the page. This design would be a futile exercise in didacticism if Esterházy's novel didn't equal it in stark emotion. Fortunately it does.

The novel is a double dream of mourning, with its own dream logic. In the first half, the narrator—a grown man—visits his family at the time of his mother's death; in the second half, the mother mourns her own life, and the family she has left behind, from the vantage point of death, whose mystery she never reveals. With language that is concise, hallucinatory, deadpan, and comic, Esterházy explores family conflict in its many combinations. The largely unnamed main characters are primal figures from a fairy-tale world—"Mother," "Father," "my sister," "my brother." We come to know them through their attributes and preferences—

his sister's "careless makeup," his brother's "usual breezy flair."[16] None of these characters really knows anyone else, but they all sense how to inflict the deepest pain or provide the gentlest consolation.

As they meet and argue during one of the most private moments of a family's life, Esterházy's portrait of their situation pulls the reader in several directions at once. At a small family breakfast before the funeral, for example, "the table was laden with a wicker basket of soft-boiled eggs and plates of salmon, cold roast beef, clams, Transylvanian and boiled bacon, tomatoes, peppers, various kinds of bread and toast," creating a ridiculous sense of abundance that almost turns the intimate meal into a state occasion.[17] What happens, however, has little to do with the grandeur suggested by the table. As the characters remember breakfast traditions of the past, the narrator calmly suggests that everyone refrain from crying at the funeral—"I've got some tranquilizers here," he even offers. For a moment the scene threatens to explode, but everyone decides to go on eating. As the family continues its funeral preparations, the lower, second text of capital letters comments on the process: " 'WE THOUGHT LIFE WAS A FEAST AND SOMETHING WAS AWAITING US.' "[18]

After the mother's burial, the second text remarks, " 'CORPSES DECOMPOSE NOISELESSLY.' "[19] But Esterházy goes on to prove otherwise. Halfway through the novel, at the end of the first part, the narrator is lost in mourning and sees something like the ghost of his mother. Hamlet-like, he cries out to her, "Can't you hear me, Mother, Beatriz, Beatriz Elena, Beatriz Elena Viterbo,"[20] adding each unit of her name until he names her fully. He is, here, evoking not only Dante's lost Beatrice but also a character from Borges. Suddenly the novel's narrative focus shifts, and the mother takes over the narration.

Her first address to her son takes us into a world of acceptance and forgiveness, but we glimpse it for only a moment: "My son. My little son. My darling little son. So that's how it is, you there, me here, me here, you there, I don't think at all. I've accepted your death mindless and wordless. You have died, and I am no more. And so on. You no longer exist, yet you are. You are: the one who died. You and only you are the one who died. My tears have dried now, but whenever I think about being your mother, whenever I think, *I* am your mother, I am moved by my own self. The thought of you numbs me so I'm sometimes startled I don't drop the things I've been holding."[21] At first she stutters his name, just as her son had to slowly build hers. But the mother's monologue eventually turns into a litany of resentments, longings, and bittersweet recollections of her youth. It is a monologue of a spirit looking back, at once personal and impersonal. *"There is no place I should wish to be,"* the mother finally admits (in italics) as if to comfort her son. Mostly, she remembers details of her life, from a caterpillar with a light green head, "the same color as the faded cover of Győző Határ's Sterne translation in the 1955 edition" to passages of almost surreal absurdity: "I should also note that I was present at Pope Paul VI's funeral. I wore a black mantle and a white porcelain chamber pot."[22]

After the mother describes eleven versions of her son's funeral, the narrative shifts one last time, into an extended recollection, by the son, of a time before his mother's death, when he helped her from her hospital bed to the toilet. A poignant evocation of the fragility of the sick and the old, this scene concludes the novel with a moment of quiet recognition. The scene is told matter-of-factly, as if the two characters were, say, washing dishes together, only here they discuss rumpled bedsheets and toilet paper. Suddenly the mother looks at her son and admits, "I'm going to die." "Ah . . . ," he replies, and she says, "I'm afraid, my son." Abruptly the novel ends. Esterházy has taken language and memory to its very limits—there is no more he can tell. The second text, however, has the last word: "SOME DAY I'LL WRITE ABOUT ALL THIS IN MORE DETAIL."[23]

I have quoted several passages at some length to give the flavor of Esterházy's prose, or at least its flavor in translation. Esterházy refuses to let a linear narrative dominate his novel, as if it would simplify and distort the requiem. A kind of stream-of-consciousness eulogy, *Helping Verbs of the Heart* refuses to accept ordinary distinctions between the living and the dead. Helping verbs—auxiliary verbs—have a unique role in most languages. The novel's second text even reminds us that "HELPING VERBS MAY EXPRESS NEGATION."[24] They are necessary to complex language, and in fact make complex statements possible, allowing for distinctions and even marking the passage of time. Like the novel's motto from Wittgenstein — "He who can hope can speak, and vice versa" — the image of helping verbs of the heart suggests the powerful connection between language and feeling, or language and living. In this sense, an act of mourning becomes an affirmation of life in spite of the pain it inevitably carries.

Esterházy has always enjoyed writing in various historical styles. He followed the collected *Introduction to Literature* with a novel called *Tizenhét hattyúk* (Seventeen Swans), under the pseudonym Lili Csokonai. The controversial book purported to be the autobiography of a young cleaning woman in contemporary Budapest, although it was written in the prose style of sixteenth- and seventeenth-century Hungarian. Shortly after its publication, Esterházy admitted authorship. His recent novel, *The Book of Hrabal* (*Hrabal Könyve*, 1990), pays homage to the great Czech writer Bohumil Hrabal. It tells the story of a Hungarian writer and his wife, Anna, who are visited by two angels, Gabriel and Blaise, intent on stopping the abortion of the couple's fourth child. This is not, however, an antiabortion tract, but rather a book about giving birth: the writer struggles with his new novel; Anna falls in love with its hero, sharing her deepest thoughts with him; God, directing the action through a walkie-talkie, battles his own problems, including an aging mother; and two angels, in human form, frighten everyone as they drive around in a Lada with the license plate A1, associated with the Hungarian secret police. The narrator is not the writer, as might be expected, but various characters including God, the angels, Anna, Hrabal, the writer's mother, and an omniscient author, using letters, dialogues, interior monologues, and religious meditations. But it is Esterházy's frenetic energy that dominates the book, making it a tour de force.

Esterházy's usual interests appear, including quotations (from the likes of Swedenborg, Wittgenstein, and Tsvetayeva) and interruptions to the narrative about a wide range of subjects (the Gulag, the nature of angels, the Central European temperament, and American jazz musician Charlie Parker, to mention only a few). The novel, however, seems to have grown out of the emotional territory of *Helping Verbs of the Heart*. It is filled with the autobiographical elements that increasingly characterize Esterházy's fiction. While Esterházy has always shown a special empathy for his female characters, Anna stands out among them. She exposes the most intimate domestic details of a woman's life—from a growing bond with her mother-in-law to her tender, weary love for a self-absorbed husband who gives her "the simple life of a literary widow." [25] Left to find her own consolations, Anna examines fragments of memory that reveal Hungary's history of Stalinist oppression. She becomes the book's heart and conscience as it turns into a meditation on the passage of time.

Esterházy's portrait of a marriage, however, exists within a larger narrative frame about the dilemmas God faces, which remain unresolved at the novel's end. In a dark comic vision, he closes the book with "the Lord" picking up Charlie Parker's old saxophone and blowing an off-key sound that "crashed mightily through the universe" as its maker awaits his own apotheosis—a curious inversion of Baroque Catholicism. But Esterházy doesn't stop here. He goes on to call the perverse note an "admission of its own failure, a choking sob, a supplication" much like "the last, resounding word of the novel." [26] Artistic creation—difficult but essential—is shown to be a kind of religious act, or statement, but even the Lord has trouble with it. Esterházy's unnamed writer, who "would have much preferred to be a good writer than a good Catholic," still considers himself Catholic, like "people who are neither true believers nor true nonbelievers" because they see "some *trick* in faith." Naturally "he believed that he'd end up serving the Lord *anyway* with his work." [27]

Anna, at least, knows that her interests—and God's—aren't the same. The story of the garden of Eden stands behind Esterházy's celebration of literary domesticity: mankind falls, only to fall again and again. *The Book of Hrabal* should make anyone familiar with Esterházy's work recognize that he is a religious writer, first and foremost, and that he has always been one.

In *The Glance of Countess Hahn-Hahn: Down the Danube* (1994), Esterházy has gone about as far as possible to erase the line between fiction and nonfiction. Not exactly a novel or a travelogue, or a commentary on writing about the Danube River— and Central Europe—his elliptical book is partly in homage to a wide range of writers who have shared Esterházy's concerns, including Joseph Roth, Elias Canetti, Italo Calvino, Peter Handke, and Bruce Chatwin. In the novel's present, a writer (Esterházy himself) known as the Traveller is hired by the Contractor to voyage along the Danube and describe his experiences "in his own very individual style, spiced with ironical reflections."[28] Along the way, he recalls traveling as a teenager with a charismatic family friend, Uncle Roberto. But there is no hint of a plot like that of Graham Greene's novel about travels with an unpredictable aunt. And at first there are few observations about the natural world, for the Traveller has a relentlessly urban perspective: "I have always found Nature rather boring, ever since my childhood, as they say. I never understood, and thus never accepted, its privileged status."[29] Instead, he offers a jumble of historical anecdotes, family gossip, and critical remarks about Central European pieties.

For a reader who always skipped the descriptions of nature in novels, Esterházy turns out to have an exacting eye, seeing the Danube not only as a river but as "the totality: the Danube is the form."[30] Danubes, Esterházy might have written, in the plural. The river becomes a "self-creating work of art,"[31] similar to the novel itself as well as its narrator. Esterházy shifts back and forth between first- and third-person narrators while maintaining for both a Woody Allen kind of mask of beleaguered innocence. Regarding first-person narration, he writes that he could say, "I am Madame Bovary. Or I could say, pleading for attention: P.E. — *c'est moi*. And then again, I could simply say: I, but this 'I' is not some fabricated figure, but the novelist, who knows his business, a bitter, disappointed man."[32] The last two adjectives seem a harsh self-assessment. Yet they may be as true as all the other partial truths that make up this curious spiritual memoir. As Esterházy writes: "To sum up: a West European speaks about an object, there *is* an object, and he examines it, sometimes, albeit, in a very subjective manner; an *East* or *Central* or kind of *in-between* European, on the other hand, speaks about himself, there *is* this thing himself, and he speaks about it, albeit through an object."[33] In this sense, the Danube and Esterházy become one.

A kind of extended pirouette, *The Glance of Countess Hahn-Hahn* has the quality of a bravura performance. An unsympathetic reader — especially one with little interest in Central European culture, history, and politics—might become impatient with its flashiness. Esterházy is aware of this risk, but he takes it anyway. Early in his novel, the Contractor chastizes the Traveller, asking, "How are you going to demystify the self-admiration of postmodernism?"[34] The narrator denies that he is a postmodernist, but the term fits and he knows it. As mentioned earlier, Richard Aczel has spoken of postmodernism as "a secession, a *fin-de-siècle* decadence."[35] Certainly Esterházy shares the fin-de-siècle tendency toward summary, even though he distrusts official history and grand gestures.

Philip Marsden, in one of the first reviews of the novel, in the *Times Literary Supplement*, objected to its lack of "story": "An almost palpable horror of realism pervades Esterházy's writing. It is a horror that gets him darting off down dark allusive alleys, into semi-real childhood scenes, into comic sexual fantasy, into pastiche, into endless skits and jokes. These passages work well, sometimes dazzlingly well. But you long in the end for something fluent, something as dark and inevitable as the Danube itself."[36] Marsden gets carried away with his own prose, but Esterházy's distrust of story, and emphasis on discourse, have resulted in a novel that is easier to admire than to care about. Such a distinction may sound old-fashioned, but I think it suggests one reason why people read fiction. Impulses like Esterházy's to survey, document, and dispute ultimately create—alongside various official histories—another kind of history. It too has limitations. Still, anyone remotely concerned with the future of Central Europe will want to find a copy of *The Glance of Countess Hahn-Hahn* at once.

Perhaps in response to the rapid changes Hungary has undergone in recent years, Esterházy currently writes a regular column for a weekly alternative newspaper in Budapest. While Western observers persist in seeing Hungary as part of the Eastern bloc, Hungarians know better. Their identity is first national, then Central European. Esterházy has kept apart from the more nationalistic strain of Hungarian writing, emphasizing instead this European side of his heritage. And like his fellow Central European writers, who are among the world's most political, he is concerned with living in a country that often seems on the margin of history. Hungary's recent dismantling of Soviet-brand socialism has changed that, at least for the moment.

In another *Partisan Review* essay, Esterházy observed: "Time was when a native like me interested in knowing what was going on here and how it tallied with the latest in world trends had only to open a decent Western newspaper to feel like Snow White: Hungary was invariably the fairest of them all. Yet as much as he read, he knew he was one of the dwarfs—ugly, puny, poor, and trudging through the mines knee-deep in lies."[37] Hungary (and Central Europe) now pose a different set of problems for themselves and for the West: "On the one hand, we Central Europeans have maintained quite superciliously that Central Europe can be truly understood only from within; on the other, that to be Central Europeans means not to know ourselves."

After casually claiming that nothing can be understood anyway, Esterházy reminds us that the language Hungarians use is "alien and strange even after translation. Out of joint. Its reference system is different; it doesn't use words in a 'leftist' or 'liberal' or 'sixties' kind of way; it's more lyrical, I'd say, masterly or masterless, but in any case highly personal—verbal bouquets for facts, metaphors for theories. And to make matters worse, we speak a language so personal that for the last forty years we haven't known who the person is."[38] But Hungary is a country where writers have long been at the forefront of any debate about national independence and social reform, and Esterházy's remarks have a historical ring to them—possibly to remind himself of that tradition.

"What Comes After" Hungarian Voices, Summer 1993

For the past five years I have been working on this book, yet until recently I had never visited Hungary. Last year the time finally seemed right. In particular, I anticipated seeing the village my grandmother left in 1909 — a village no one from my family had visited. While my mind was filled with pictures of the "old country," courtesy of Grandma's memories and André Kertész's photographs, another world would confront me at every turn. Baroque stucco churches and fin-de-siècle architecture seemed only a backdrop, and I grew more curious each day about the way people faced the change from communism to a "market economy" — the currently favored euphemism for "capitalism," a word that seems to embarrass both the media and politicians, as if it evokes limitless greed. That spring, the most popular joke in Budapest went like this: "You know what's the worst thing about communism?" "No," I would say politely. "What comes after it." Of course I laughed— it was expected. I was about to hear "what comes after."

One evening, several days after arriving in Budapest, I'm sitting in an outdoor cafe with friends from Toronto who had just come from Prague. We are, naturally, speaking English. One of them is annoyed that all over Prague people kept playing the Beatles, especially "Let It Be." "What can that mean today?" she asks. "It doesn't mean anything."

Suddenly a handsome young man at a nearby table leans over and asks if we're British. We shake our heads, laughing, and tell him that we're from Toronto. His face breaks into a wide smile.

At twenty-three, Gábor spent two years living in Hamilton, Ontario, with his Hungarian girlfriend. He regrets returning to Budapest last year, where he now lives with his parents. He hadn't planned to return, but when he saw a Canadian immigration officer about becoming a landed immigrant, Gábor admitted that he wanted to be a writer, and a poet at that. "We don't need those," she told him, "we have enough writers"—or so he remembers. With hindsight, he says, he was too honest. So he is back in Budapest, attending its best university, where he studies English and Hungarian literature.

I tell Gábor that he was fortunate to return. He distrusts my remark, but admits that he had missed his native language. "It's difficult to write in the shadow of great writers," he adds, "and Hungary has great writers."

I suggest that writers need their own languages and cultures, and explain that I'm also a writer and a teacher of creative writing. Gábor asks where, and when I tell him his eyes cloud over. He would like to have attended university in Canada, he says. I explain that some of my best students, who have just graduated, are unemployed and without prospects.

"So it's no better there," he says.

"It's different there," I reply.

Gábor finally admits that life in Canada wasn't ideal. He speaks of the frustration he felt with the English language: "For three months I wouldn't speak a word of it. After a year I was okay, but I missed Hungarian. I can only say my deepest feelings in Hungarian."

Conscious of being older than the eighteen-year-old girls at university, who prefer the boys with money (or so he believes), he works with disabled Gypsy children to help pay for tuition.

"Doing what?" I ask.

"Teaching them not to spit on each other, not to use bad words —to be human."

I'm surprised by the last phrase.

"They have terrible lives," he adds.

We plan to meet several days later, when he will show me the best bookstores in Budapest. He is eager to practice his English.

Gábor reminds me of Krisztina, a young woman I met several years ago when she worked as a nanny for friends of mine. She was particularly pleased that they played in the Toronto Symphony, for she came from a musical family in Budapest. Welcoming the chance to learn English, she planned to return home after a year, to her job in a flower shop, whose aging owner had promised her coownership. A slight woman of twenty-one with a mane of dark, Pre-Raphaelite hair, Krisztina seemed sure of her future.

Now, at twenty-four, she is less certain. When we meet in Budapest I remark that she looks well, and that Hungary must agree with her. She laughs bitterly and cuts me off: "You are wrong." I hadn't meant the compliment as an empty one, but I'm taken off guard. Hungarians are like this—forthright, and unafraid of speaking their minds. Despite years of foreign occupation, they haven't acquired the North American habit of concealment behind politeness.

Krisztina currently lives with Paul (not his real name), who waits outside the lobby of my hotel in his new sports car. Paul is a private currency trader. A slender, fortyish man wearing a white T-shirt, brown leather vest, faded jeans, and scruffy white tennis shoes, without socks, he talks easily, and is genuinely curious about people. Everyone in Budapest seems to know him. Over dinner, on the terrace of a new restaurant near the Canadian embassy, I hear about their lives.

Krisztina's arrangement with her previous employer fell through, and she has spent the last year waiting to open her own shop. She has picked the location and believes it is only a matter of time before the right space becomes available. Bristling with unfocused energy, she wishes that she could return to Toronto — she knows she would make her way there more quickly. Also, she regrets that she is forgetting her English. I suggest that opening a business in recession-worn Toronto would be difficult too, but she is impatient to have her own shop: not having one seems like a tragedy. In the context of life in Budapest I can understand why. During the past few years scores of new businesses have been opened, and often by people between twenty-five and thirty-five. The older generation, I'm told, lacks the taste for risk that goes with opening a business, and of course they have little business experience.

Hungary, Paul claims, is like North America around 1985, before things began to sour. It is an ideal place to make money if one has a taste for speculation. As a currency trader, he naturally follows all the stock market and banking news, from 6 A.M. to midnight. "The point," he explains, "is not how much money you have, but which currency you're holding. At the end of the day you need to be holding the right currency." In order to speculate, he adds, you need nerves of steel, "a nose," as he calls it, and half a million dollars at least. Anything less and you can't cover ordinary losses. The "nose" isn't really a talent for making money but for watching it — an instinct for shifts in the money market. Paul manages only his own money now, but Budapest is a good base to work from. Any number of wealthy retirees of Hungarian origin are returning to Budapest with half a million dollars at their disposal. I'm reminded of the CNN news announcer who cheerily commented, while I was preparing to meet Krisztina and Paul: "The world is a 24-hour marketplace. It's a 24-hour economy."

Hungary draws black-market money, a condition Paul assumes will change in the next few years. "Where will the currency traders go next?" I ask. "Everything's moving east," he says. "Maybe China.

Mongolia. Who knows?" There is a touch of Gatsby in Paul, and I'm charmed by it. Like many self-educated men, he is extremely clear about what he knows. "Being an entrepreneur isn't always rewarded," he cautions Krisztina. "Not even a good one." I mention Gábor, and his difficulties in adjusting to Hungary, but she shows little interest. All her friends are worried about the future, she says. Many are unemployed, but this doesn't stop them from getting married and having children. "Everyone wants to buy things. After years of not buying, not having—of little variety—they want things."

I offer a feeble bromide: all the television commercials, magazine advertisements, newspapers ads, shop windows, reinforce this desire.

No one responds, so I tell them about Klára, a researcher in family studies at the Institute of Sociology in Budapest. She is around forty, and a single mother. I repeat her remark that Hungarians tend to marry young but have one of the highest divorce rates in Europe.

Krisztina nods, then shrugs, and I decide not to quote a comparison Klára made: "The young," she said, "are very disturbed about the future of Hungary. Those who are older are simply exhausted from years of change, especially all of the ideological shifts."

"It isn't a tragedy not to own your own flower shop when you're twenty-four," Paul adds. "Krisztina's still young."

I agree, but we sound like middle-aged men closing ranks, and I'm embarrassed. We turn to politics, but when I ask their opinion of FIDESZ, both shrug.

Once made up mainly of students, the untarnished League of Young Democrats (FIDESZ) has recently allowed people over thirty-five to join. It has also been involved in a scandal, along with the center-right ruling party, the Hungarian Democratic Forum (MDF). Both parties, possibly by secret agreement, flipped a valuable piece of property in downtown Budapest that had been given to them during the recent distribution of state's assets to political parties. With a general election expected in 1994, the campaign coffers of FIDESZ are full. As if this scandal weren't enough, journalists have just discovered that FIDESZ owns a luxury car-rental dealership, with Porsches and Ferraris available for $200 to $400 a day.

Paul thinks that the Socialists will be important in the next coalition—a view I hear from others, too. And if they are, this means that some Communists, who became Socialists, may be back in power. "But politicians aren't important, they don't run anything. Only money does," Paul adds. I begin to object. "Well," he allows, "you do have to worry how a politician will be affected by money." Since recent polls have shown increased support for the Socialists, people are naturally talking about them. Hungary, like its Western counterparts, will soon have to face the way polling affects election campaigns, perhaps even election results.

Inevitably we talk of Serbia, Bosnia, the possible spread of the war. They are both convinced that Greece and Turkey will become involved, and maybe Hungary. The Serbian war-machine poses a special threat to Hungarians, who fear the spread of ethnic cleansing to the large Hungarian community in Serbia's Vojvodina region, a former Hungarian territory ceded to Yugoslavia in the Treaty of Trianon. Twenty percent of its population is ethnic Hungarian, mostly concentrated in Subotica, less than an hour's drive from Szeged in southern Hungary.

"Remember, this is Eastern Europe," Paul cautions. "It may look Western, feel Western, but it's not. Ten years ago Yugoslavia was like Hungary, with charming cities—a civilized place—then, overnight, this war. Something like that could happen here too. You never know for sure."

Local rumor has it that 60 percent of Hungary's national debt is owed to private Japanese banks, which will not, of course, write off any part of the debt. Though there are no facts to back this up, that is irrelevant—people live by beliefs, not facts. And until several years ago most Hungarians believed the Soviet system to be strong and if not eternal, close to it. Then one winter the system began to unravel and collapse. Everyone I talk with is still puzzled that this could have happened.

Meanwhile, the international financial community is monitoring Hungary's worsening economy. The International Monetary Fund has demanded deficit reductions in relation to increased loans; the European Economic Community hasn't yet welcomed Hungary as a member; and the United States has threatened to remove Hungary's most favored nation status unless it recognizes international patent rights, especially for pharmaceuticals. During my visit, President Bill Clinton acknowledged Prime Minister József Antall's invitation to be part of the 1996 World Expo in Budapest without committing the United States to a pavilion there. The message is clear: Hungary—the former-Soviet satellite most likely to succeed—had better behave if it wants to be part of the West.

With my Toronto friends, whose visit to Budapest overlapped the first days of mine, I explore the old Jewish section of the city. There we meet Zoli, and they rent a flat from him for several nights.

Zoli is a fixer. In his early fifties, he wears a frayed white shirt that is immaculately clean. A collection of nervous tics, he offers the flat, a taxi to the airport, and excellent *chollent* ("I can get"), but never his full name or address. He says he can be reached every day at Hanna's Restaurant, between noon and 1:30, since he always eats there. Hanna's is a kosher place behind the old Orthodox synagogue; at best it can be called utilitarian. We remind him that it's now 3 o'clock in the afternoon. He says we should just leave a message for him. His eyes are haunted.

In the apartment, on Síp utca, toilet paper has already been torn and set in small piles for Orthodox tourists rigorously observing the Sabbath.

While visiting the synagogue on Dohány Street, reputedly the largest in Europe, we fall into conversation with a bearded man in his fifties who sells postcards and other souvenirs at the entrance. Seeing me look at a tape of Hungarian cantors, he invites us to hear him at the Friday evening service that night. He is the cantor, he tells us, at the Rabbinical Seminary, and of course he knows Zoli.

When I learn the man's name—Emil Tóth—I'm puzzled, for Tóth is not a Jewish name. It is several days before I learn his story, and then only from someone else.

Though the service begins promptly at 6:00 P.M. the congregation continues to talk during it, greeting each other, exchanging news. It is as varied a group of people as one might imagine: young people dressed in jeans and brightly colored shirts, frail, elderly single women, a few clearly prosperous families, many shabbily dressed aging men. More striking is the fact that it is such an accepting group, full of welcome. The cantor has a rich, melancholy tenor voice, and as I listen, without understanding the Hebrew words, I wonder how it was possible for decent Budapesters to have looked away as the Arrow Cross, Hungary's Nazis, marched the city's Jews to the bank of the Danube and shot them in the back.

The service over, Emil invites us upstairs to Kiddush. A prominent guest, a rabbi from Belgium who studied at the seminary, will speak briefly. It is still early, so I join my friends, who are eager to go. Neither speaks Hungarian, but that seems a small matter.

After wine and challah, a young man reads a short exegesis on the next morning's text. (He is a double for Barbra Streisand in *Yentl* and I try not to smile.) Then the Belgian guest begins to speak, admonishing the young man for reading his words instead of memorizing them. Silence fills the room as people look at each other, or at their glasses. The visitor goes on to say that he regrets to see that the seminary isn't holding to the high standards it had once set for Jewish intellectual life. Shaking his finger, he turns into the cartoon of a hectoring old man unknowingly lamenting lost youth.

Several days later I go to the Jewish Museum, beside the Dohány Street synagogue, where I meet a woman who offers to trace my family tree. She needs only a few dates, or documents, to do a complete job. And three hundred dollars, American. Of course we talk, and she speaks of the nuns who educated her and other Jewish children, of the last days in Auschwitz, "before the Americans defeated the Nazis," and of her son, who is studying medicine in the United States after a career as a computer programmer. Naturally she shows me his picture, and points out that his wife, who didn't like America, has returned to Hungary. But I am most interested to hear about her friend Emil. Born and raised a Roman Catholic, he converted to Judaism after the war. I don't need to ask why.

At the museum I copy a map of the streets that defined the

Budapest ghetto during the years of the Second World War: Szabó utca, Dohány utca, Király utca. Later, after my friends leave the city, I walk the edge of the ghetto. I am not a Jew but I want to remember.

Seventy-two-year-old Judit, wearing a navy blue dress with small white polka dots, resembles an aging school teacher. Over coffee at the Gellért Hotel we speak of a mutual friend in Toronto. Then she advises me about the train to Győr, a city halfway between Budapest and Vienna. She says, rather gaily, that she can ride all trains, subways, and buses for free now that she is over seventy. "But only inside of Hungary," she adds. "It's from the old system." *The old system*—I hear that phrase often.

The current government hasn't met the people's expectations. For the first time Hungarians face high unemployment and inflation. "I read that unemployment is 13 percent," I say.

"Oh, no," Judit says. "Not that much. The government made a big mistake in giving people shares to compensate for old property. How can you give someone 20 percent of a house, or of a farm? You can't. But they gave shares, which were useless. It would have been better to give nothing. People would have said, 'What's lost is lost.' Instead they had expectations."

"What happened?" I ask.

"It was worst for people with land." Judit continues to work, part-time, as a researcher and translator at the Museum of Agriculture, and she knows what she's talking about. "Before, the land belonged to cooperatives. Now it's been returned to individuals. But who owns the tractors? The tools of agriculture? You can't farm without them, and no one has the money to buy them. The reparations have destroyed agriculture here.

"And industry, too. Hungary never had a lot of industry, but we sold to Russia, to other eastern countries. We had markets. Now we don't have markets and we produce very little."

Hungary used to produce the goods it needed—even simple items like bottled fruit juice and laundry detergent. Today these are imported, mainly from Austria and Germany. They may be of slightly higher quality, but they are much more expensive, and entire industries (and jobs) have been lost. The worst unemployment is in eastern Hungary, where there are more untrained workers and Gypsies. Yet the low unemployment rate under the Communists was not only a matter of industrial production. The Communists held to a policy of enforced retirement—age sixty for men, fifty-five for women. The system is now changing, and both men and women will be allowed to work until they are sixty.

"Everything we need has to be imported from expensive companies in the West," Judit continues. "And at a time of high inflation." Shaking her head, as if to change the subject, she says, "I hope there won't be a war."

War—the subject on everyone's lips. "Do you think there will be?" I ask, aware that I'm feeding her questions. Yet she doesn't appear to mind. It amazes me that she can say, so casually, "a war" and not "another war," for she has lived in Budapest all her life and knows war firsthand.

"I hope not. But who can say?"

Her stories of living in Budapest cellars during the final months of Hitler's war help me understand how some Hungarians could have ignored the Holocaust going on nearby—they simply didn't know what was happening.

Unlike the worn people Klára described, Judit doesn't seem the least bit exhausted. But she comes from an upper-class family and has probably learned to conceal her truest feelings from strangers —perhaps even from those close to her. But I prefer to think that she is forthright.

It is difficult not to be impatient with Hungarian inefficiency. It takes nearly an hour at Cooperative Travel to book a hotel room in Győr for two nights. By the time I finish, four young women have become involved with the process: making the call, losing the paper with my name on it, reserving the wrong number of nights, talking with each other or on the phone, or simply staring blankly at a calendar that features a photograph of Venice. Perhaps the Communists allowed a system where several people did the job of one, but I can't see Western businesses, or a market economy, allowing this system for long. And the result will be additional unemployment.

A five-minute walk from my hotel, the Lukács Institute is at 2

Belgrád Rakpart, overlooking the Danube from the Pest foot of the Liberty Bridge, in the fifth-floor apartment where Georg Lukács was raised. His books were an important influence on my generation, the New Left of the 1960s. Today, on the first floor of the building, is Nero Bar, a small bar/casino where young people sit at video machines playing a game called "American Poker." I walk past it, toward a bookstore that sells *Budapest Week*.

Amazingly, Budapest has four English-language weeklies: *Budapest Week, Budapest Sun, Daily News,* and *Hungarian Times.* The *Sun*, obviously aimed at the invasion of Western businesses, is sympathetic to this trend and related concerns. *Budapest Week* would be a good alternate newspaper in any city. The dour, bi-weekly *Daily News* was founded in 1967 and is Hungary's oldest English-language newspaper, with numerous ads for "privatization advisers." Finally, the recently founded *Hungarian Times* advertises itself as a newspaper for "decision makers," which means it knows what the business community cares about. On the help-wanted page, one ad stipulates: "Only dynamic, results-oriented team players need apply." Each week, as these newspapers pile higher on my desk, I feel increasingly bleak about the prospects of Hungary's future. The country has so far survived four major occupations: by Turks, which lasted roughly 150 years (1526–1683); by Austrian Habsburgs, lasting almost a century longer (1683–1918); by Germans for only a few years during the Second World War; and by Russians, about four grim decades after it. Hungary now faces a new occupation, that of international investment. While it may seem premature to comment, signs already portend bad times ahead.

Sooner or later, well-heeled visitors to Budapest end up at Gundel's, one of the legendary restaurants of Europe, so I decide to try it, too. Its reopening, with the help of twelve million American dollars, is considered a local triumph. Somehow Hungarian American restaurateur George Lang convinced the Communist government to sell him Gundel's. An entrepreneur as well as a cook and writer, Lang is author of the comprehensive *The Cuisine of Hungary.* He is, as well, owner of the popular Café des Artistes in Manhattan. With the help of the American Lauder family (of Hungarian origins), he oversaw the renovations. And he even persuaded the distinguished Hungarian American historian John Lukacs to write about the significance of the opening of the "new" Gundel's in a lavish brochure given out by the restaurant, which also includes testimonials from *The Times* of London, the *New York Times*, the *Washington Post*, the *San Francisco Chronicle*, and *Newsweek*. It assures you that previous guests (with regular tables) included the King of Siam, Thomas Mann, Charlie Chaplin, Richard Strauss, and, more recently, Elizabeth II for a state dinner. As if this weren't enough, the brochure promises: "If you visit often enough you'll eventually meet everybody worth knowing."

The restaurant, certainly, is beautiful—restrained and sophisticated, especially because it eschews Habsburg kitsch and recreates the world of international café society in the 1920s. Yet the food is another matter. In fact it is some of the worst I find in Budapest. A cold wild-rice salad has absorbed its sour vinaigrette so that each bite releases a sharp, acrid taste; the strangely bitter chicken paprikas without sour cream (cited on the menu as a "Lauder family recipe") can only be considered an aberration; the tortes are leaden—and all this can be had for fifty dollars a person. After an equally unsuccessful second visit, I conclude that the best way to enjoy Gundel's is to buy some cherries (or whatever's in season) in the fruit market at the foot of the Liberty Bridge and take these along for a snack after walking through the restaurant's lobby, which affords an excellent view of the dining room. This way you can see what twelve million dollars can accomplish without getting indigestion.

Round-faced, with a small mustache, Attila drives a white Mercedes instead of one of the ubiquitous Lada taxis of Budapest. I hire him several times for day trips. His car is mercifully air conditioned, since Budapest is having its third year of record-breaking heat in early summer: stifling, mid-August temperatures in May and June. "The ozone layer," everyone concludes.

In his mid-fifties, Attila recalls leaving for school one October morning in 1956 and finding that the trams weren't moving. He fell in with school friends and, as word passed, they went to an unguarded depot where Russian arms and ammunition were stored, and took as much as they could carry. That night, when he went home and told his parents, they were so frightened they refused to let him leave the apartment for the rest of the brief revolution. Attila speaks without bitterness about the way Hungarians felt betrayed by supposed allies in the West. They had believed the radio broadcasts that encouraged them to resist the Russians and promised troops on the way. "UN troops," he specifies, "which we knew meant American." Of course they never arrived.

I am more struck, however, by an earlier memory of his. During the winter of 1945, while Germans and Russians fought for control of Budapest, he recalls going outside one snowy morning—he must have been four years old—to see dead horses in the street. Like any child, he identified with the horses, and wept for them. Then he noticed that people were coming out of their buildings, going up to the animals, and cutting chunks of meat from their bodies. Starving for months, Budapesters had seen little fresh meat that winter.

With Attila I discuss István Csurka, the renegade MP who has just been expelled from the ruling MDF party for his right-wing anti-Semitic views. Yet Attila says Csurka is not a rabid nationalist, like Serbia's Slobodan Milošević, but a notable playwright who simply argued that Hungary has long been controlled by foreign or nonnative groups: Germans and Jews. "Both of Hungary's times of Communism are associated with Jews," Attila explains, and I let him reveal his views (held by many): "First Béla Kun, in 1919, and then the secret police after World War II. These are facts. Csurka is right in pointing this out—he's simply wrong in the conclusions, which went too far. Jews who settled in Hungary in the nineteenth century worked hard, like your Vietnamese and Koreans. They made Hungary a modern country. They became influential in its social, intellectual, and political circles. These are facts," he repeats. "The second generation of children of the wealthy, like Georg Lukács, became Communists and sat around in cafés dreaming Utopian dreams—they didn't have to work, not like their fathers or grandfathers. Lukács had a monthly stipend from a Swiss bank. Unfortunately, Csurka used the term 'Judeo-Bolshevik,' the same term Hitler used in *Mein Kampf*. Csurka wouldn't kill a Jew, but some of his followers might. They wouldn't kill a banker, who advances the interests of international money, but they might kill a decent shopkeeper."

I finally object. "But he did propose an ethnic cleansing of Hungary."

"He didn't see how his conclusion might appeal to 'real' anti-Semites." Attila reminds me that Csurka wants the current regime purged of former Communists. "This has been distorted by the international press—especially the American press—as anti-Semitism rather than anti-Communism."

"They mean different things to him?" I ask. Perhaps sensing my dismay, Attila tells me that he knows the historian John Lukacs. "Last year, when he was in Budapest, we talked for two days about his books. He said he should get me a job lecturing in an American university."

Attila also thinks that North Americans misunderstand what is happening in Serbia. Like many Hungarians, he assumes that Russia will back Serbia. "Russia will never turn away from Serbia. And Milošević is like Hitler, he understands power. The real threat of war is that it will spread." Attila concludes, frowning, "People don't learn."

Attila, who voted for the Free Democrats in the last election, is not alone in his frustration with current Hungarian politics. Everyone assumes the next government will be another coalition. As Attila says, "No party can win in Hungary." Of course the coalition shifts, depending on the person I'm speaking with. Attila thinks the next government will involve FIDESZ, and others agree. "They are career politicians, modern technocrats, perhaps opportunists. They're young and smart and they want a share of the power. But they have no real platform or ideology," he warns, fearing that the future of Hungary will be in the hands of such technocrats.

More reflective, Judit says that until several months ago she—and many others—wouldn't have agreed with this assessment, but that it now seems reasonable. FIDESZ is likely to be part of the next coalition: "They have not only youth in their favor, but the fact that they can't claim—truly or not—that they fought in World War II, or in '56, or whenever. Also, since they were too young to be part of the past regime, they can't be accused of being Communists." She goes on to say that not all those who previously worked in the government, or found a place for themselves in it, were Communists. "Some were intelligent people, people with talent. No one likes to admit he isn't intelligent. Some of the people who claim they could have succeeded during the previous regime simply lacked talent—and they want to blame others for their own deficiency."

Like most people I speak with, Judit thinks the next government will be a shift—if only a slight one—to the left. Everyone knows there will be another coalition government. The only question is how the coalition will be made up—which reminds me of the old joke: "If you have three Hungarians locked in the same room, you end up with four political parties."

Privatization of agriculture came at a time when the Soviet bloc—two-thirds of Hungary's market for agricultural goods—collapsed. The remaining third of Hungarian production is consumed at home. A rich and fertile land, Hungary is developing new markets in Germany, Finland, and Sweden. Practicing traditional, generally chemical-free farming rather than using industrial methods, the country produces high quality corn, wheat, sunflowers (for oil), and other agricultural products. Although Attila believes that small groups of farmers will form genuine cooperatives—renting machinery they can't afford alone—his view is decidedly more optimistic than Judit's, or Jenő's.

Jenő is my grandmother's nephew. At sixty-five, he looks much older. He often repeats, "I'm not old, just tired," and "I could tell you so many things." An emotional man, he likes to talk—a trait I find in most of the Hungarians I meet.

In 1909 my grandmother, Mari, and her young sister left their village to visit their older sister, Rózsa, who had immigrated to America—this is the start of any immigrant saga. Mari intended to visit for several months and then return home, but neither she nor her sisters ever went back, even to visit, nor did any of their children. I'm the first in the family to come, and as I look at Jenő, who meets me in Győr, I regret that Mari never returned. Yet she didn't put Hungary behind her. She read Hungarian newspapers, wrote letters home, sent packages of clothing, large bundles I remember helping her take to the post office. As Jenő reaches to embrace me I think of all my grandmother's unresolved emotions because she never saw her home or parents again. And I hate myself for falling into the trap of the language of my time—*unresolved*—as if one could ever accept the loss of a country. It has to be a permanent wound, the immigrant wound. Throughout my childhood I sensed her loss without knowing what it was.

Before my visit, Jenő wrote that he would introduce me to my relatives. I replied that I wanted to see the graves of my grandmother's parents. When Jenő and I meet, it takes no time to see that he has an agenda for the day. The visit is not mine alone. Jenő confesses that his family had been hurt that no one from America had visited them. Other villagers had happily received American relatives. I try to explain why my grandmother never returned: she had no money for traveling, then the Depression came along, and she had children to raise. He nods with understanding—he knows how life can change our plans. But he insists: "She should have come." I say: "She often talked of Páli, of her family. Dying, at ninety, she said, 'I wish my father would come for me.'" Jenő likes this, and I decide to tell the unvarnished truth. "Grandma always said that she was afraid to see her father again because if he asked whether she was happy, she would have to say no—she couldn't lie—and anyway he would see the truth in her face." *This* Jenő understands. "Yes, yes," he says, shaking his head.

A trained auto mechanic, Jenő also worked for several years in Budapest as an electrician at the Ministry of the Interior. He is quick to add that he has never been a member of any political party, including the Communists'. He says that he was lucky to have had "three professions," for he counts being "a peasant by blood" as a profession. During the 1956 revolution, he was working as an electrician in the countryside and collecting money from the peasants for their electricity. Almost inevitably, villagers who believed he was a Communist, because he worked for the government, made threats on his life. He wanted to flee to America that winter, but he had two small sons—Laci, a year old, and little Jenő, two months old. (My grandmother, he recalls, wrote letters saying that she expected him to come to America.) Jenő saw no way that he could walk to the Austrian border with two babies. Also, he was his parents' only child, although, he adds, they encouraged him to emigrate.

"First they took away the land from the aristocracy," Jenő says. "Then from the rich peasants, then from the poor ones. Always they said 'Now take care of yourselves.' Today there's no one left to take things from." In the early years of the Communist regime, when cooperative farms were formed, Jenő's father was told to sign a paper saying that he voluntarily gave up his land. He refused, and in the middle of the night he hid in a neighboring village. In the next weeks he moved his hiding place two more times. Finally the police caught up with him and punched him in the face, knocking out two teeth. He signed the paper, saying that he would rather give up the land than his life. Some years later, shortly before 1956, the Communists were going to confiscate a pig from Jenő. Hoping to prevent this, he spoke with a friend who was in the party, asking for his help. Instead, Jenő was called to party headquarters and punched in the face. "But they didn't take the pig," he now says proudly.

Jenő wonders if the next government will take back the things people have gained from the present one — not because he objects to a new coalition, but because that seems to be the way governments work. He explains that the offer to return land to the peasants is pointless. They lack the means of farming it: they don't have money for farm machinery or for the petrol to operate it; they are often too old to do the work alone; and their children have left the villages to work in nearby towns. Only six hundred elderly people now live in his village, Pápoc, a ten-minute car ride from Páli.

These villages are made up of single-story stucco houses along both sides of the two-lane asphalt road that cuts through them. The houses are well kept, with rose gardens in front. Usually there is an old church — in Jenő's village, one from the twelfth century; in my grandmother's, a pinkish Baroque building on the site of the original sixteenth-century church. The old houses are long and narrow, like the property behind them. Many once had outside corridors with Roman archways, most of which have been incorporated into the houses as small extra rooms. This, however, is not the case at the house where my grandmother was born. About 130 years old, it is lovely in its simplicity. I wonder what will happen to it, and to these villages. When I later ask Judit, she suggests that younger people will start to live in them again and commute to their jobs in nearby towns, since the roads are good. And artists and writers are buying old village houses rather than building new cottages, especially in the resort region of Lake Balaton.

Grandmother's house is now owned by Mariska, the wife of my grandmother's youngest brother, Antal, who died thirty-four years ago. Mariska is seventy-two, and the planes of her face reveal that she was once a great beauty. We are drawn to each other immediately. She has torn down the stables behind the house, but she still works a large stretch of land in back of it. Like her neighbors, she raises oak and fir trees that she sells to a Hungarian firm that sells them in the Netherlands and France. She shows me her tract of trees, which are barely knee-high, and then confides, "I hope you didn't think we would be primitive."

Occasionally she can find a local boy to help with the trees, but the job of tending them is largely hers. After admiring them we go inside and she offers wine and salami, which I'm offered again and again that day, sometimes along with Pepsi and Sprite. And she shows me, with great pleasure, a Christmas card sent last year by the company that buys her trees. It is printed in three languages — Hungarian, French, German; the most fulsome message is in Hungarian.

Next week Páli will have a religious procession, and Mariska regrets that I'm going to miss it. Every June, for the past forty-five years, she has decorated the front of her house with wreathes made of twigs, leaves, flowers, and ribbons. She recalls: "When I first came here, I wanted to put up flowers for the festival, but I hoped no one would mind. Antal assured me it wouldn't matter." I want to ask why she never married again, but the question would be rude.

"What can I send to your family in America?" Mariska asks as I prepare to leave. They would be happiest with her greetings, I say, and we embrace.

As yet few of these villages have telephones. In Pápoc, Jenő's village, the telephone in the post office can be used from 8 A.M. to 3 P.M. But most of the villages have cable for television. Jenő and his friends complained to their mayor that they needed telephone lines before they needed television cables: "Our children don't live near us any more, and we want to talk with them." Television cables are what they got.

Jenő's house is larger than Mariska's, and surrounded with old nut trees. In the stable behind he keeps pigs, chickens, ducks, geese. One pig, to be butchered and cured later in the fall, is for his sons. "Young people no longer keep animals," he says. "Just dogs and cats."

I could listen to his stories for days. My favorite took place in 1945, during the last months of the war. Jenő was sixteen and hadn't yet been drafted, although his father had been conscripted into the army. He remained with his mother, Lujza, in the house he lives in today. That spring seven young Russian women soldiers were billeted with them, from April until October. They had day jobs nearby in a makeshift Russian airfield, and Jenő's mother had to cook for them. One night, early in their stay, Lujza made an elaborate cake. Suspicious, the soldiers insisted that she taste a piece first, in case she meant to poison them. The thought had probably never crossed her mind, and in no time they fell in love with her cooking. Often several of the soldiers stayed with her during the day to learn to cook her recipes, which she wrote out for them. By October, they said they didn't want to return to Russia, though they had little choice. One of the women even wrote to Luzja after returning to her village near Kiev.

Jenő remembers working in a field that summer, when an American plane flew low to the ground, shooting at the villagers. As everyone hid, he wondered if any of his American relatives were in that plane. Apparently my grandmother's oldest sister had written that one of her sons-in-law was a pilot and had flown over Lake Balaton, and the image stayed in Jenő's mind. (After the war, she sent a parcel of clothing to Lujza that included an American soldier's coat, which had belonged to this son-in-law; Jenő has it still.) By then, the Russians had occupied the right bank of the Rába River, while the Germans held the left. Three times the Russians nearly took the village, and Jenő could hear soldiers cry out as they were shot. Their blood reddened the river, and twenty-five civilians were also killed in the battle. (Jenő likes vivid details.) As the Russians moved closer to Pápoc, Jenő recalls someone telling the boys that in order to save Hungary they had to save their own land. An old man, who had fought in the First World War, over-heard this advice and remarked, "If you want to save your country, what are you doing sitting around? The Russians are almost here." The boys, who were frightened, knew where several casks of local wine had been hidden, and got very drunk from them: "Sick drunk," Jenő says with an embarrassed smile. The Russians, who arrived the next morning and found the boys hung over, of course wanted to know where all the liquor was.

Our visit passes with such stories, and I never get to the graves of my great-grandparents. But Jenő insists that I come back next summer and stay for at least a week, saying, "There is so much I could tell you."

After leaving Páli in a summer thunderstorm, I return to my hotel in Győr. I flick stations randomly on the television, looking for CNN, which my hotel doesn't carry. Instead there is a Hungarian version of *Wheel of Fortune*, and a situation comedy, dubbed into Hungarian. I watch it for several minutes: wealthy Grandpa can't figure out how to change his grandchild's disposable diaper, so he uses his own handkerchief instead. Is the program from American television? Or German? It won't be long before all of Hungary is linked to such television. I switch it off, change my shirt, and go for a walk through the quiet streets of Győr, a beautifully preserved Habsburg town of cobblestone lanes and two-story stucco buildings painted white, beige, lemon yellow, Habsburg gold, and dusky rose. The lovely courtyards are filled with blooming flowers, giving off their night scent. I turn a corner and the painted white sign on a clothing shop proclaims: "Nothing is more American than Levi's."

Back in Budapest, I attend a rally at Heroes' Square to mark the anniversary of the Treaty of Trianon, where Hungary lost two-thirds of its land and sixty percent of its people. It is a gray drizzly evening that turns into rain, and only a thousand people show up, including several groups of flashy skinheads who stand apart, some with motorcycles. People in the crowd wonder if Csurka will appear—this is his constituency—but it seems unlikely. Instead, the crowd hears from Izabella B. Király, another MDF MP who was expelled, along with Csurka, for right-wing views. With a grim expression, but long earrings tossing about, Király laments the losses of Trianon. She has been much in the news as a critic of her party, which recently ratified a treaty with Ukraine that renounced all territorial claims to its land. There are Hungarians who still dream of an international review of Trianon, and the issue is not merely an academic one, nor a right-wing cause. Many Hungarians want associate membership in NATO, whose officials have been reluctant to include the country. Among reasons commonly cited is that if Hungary belonged, NATO would be faced with the problem of the status of ethnic Hungarians in neighboring countries.

Beside me, a blond boy in white T-shirt and shorts sips a magenta-colored drink that has turned his lips bright red. He is six or seven, and I wonder what wars he will have to fight in. As far back as I count, no generation of Hungarians has escaped a war or revolution.

The next day, organizers of the demonstration blame poor attendance on bad weather. But it would be fairer to suggest, as recent polls do, that most Hungarians have lost interest in Trianon. The promise of freedom of the last few years has congealed into high inflation and unemployment — both of which have more immediate claims on their attention.

Before I leave Budapest, I make one last sentimental stop, at the home of Hungary's greatest modern poet, Endre Ady (1877–1919). The Yeats or Rilke or Lorca of Hungarian writing, he created Hungarian modernism, and embodied the spirit of the country in his work, which, sadly, has no first-rate translation.

I climb the stairs to his fifth-floor apartment at 4–6 Veres Pálné utca, which has been made into a museum, and enter the foyer. No one replies to my greeting, so I walk in. Turning to my left, into a room that was clearly Ady's study and bedroom, I see a woman with white hair curled up asleep on the poet's bed. The museums of Budapest are filled with elderly women guards, usually talking to each other or surreptitiously chewing on a small piece of cheese or salami. This is my first sleeping guard. I call out to her. No reply. I can't resist the temptation to take out my camera and shoot several pictures. Even the flash doesn't wake her. "Jó napot!" I call out again. Good day! Is she dead?

I approach the bed and lean over the red-velvet rope hung around it. "Jó napot!" I hate waking anyone, and regret the look of confusion on her face. Then she smiles, bemused, and I explain that I want to see the rooms.

Of course she is embarrassed and quickly climbs off the bed. But she has survived such matters as war, inflation, and where the next conqueror will come from, and begins to show me Ady's collection of Hungarian paintings (anyone could have walked off with the wonderful landscape by Lajos Tihanyi while she slept) and lets me hold the pen Ady wrote with. For a moment she seems the emblem of old Hungary, weary and asleep in the bed of past triumphs.

I buy a handful of postcards and, since I'm leaving the next day, give her a handsome tip. She grins, and wishes me a good journey home.

A year has passed. In May 1994 Hungary held its election. The new ruling coalition did move to the left, but without FIDESZ. It is made up of the Socialist Party—which includes former Communist bureaucrats—and the liberal Free Democrats. Most Western newspapers ignored the election even though Hungary is an American ally with a strategic border on Serbia. In fact the Western media too often ignore Hungary. But my visit had made that impossible for me. Hungary's present and future, as well as its past, now claim my imagination. My associations with the country are no longer from other people's lives—my family's, or favorite writers'. I have people to correspond with and to see again.

The
Third Generation
and the "Problem"
of Ethnicity

During a recent conversation about this book, an old friend asked what my ethnicity meant to me. The question surprised me, since we've known each other for almost twenty years. I began by saying that ethnicity could be many things—mask, weapon, consolation, sentimentality, gesture, even a kind of inner voyage. On a roll, I gave examples of these, some historical, others anecdotal. But I didn't speak of myself.

My friend listened patiently and then persisted: "What do you feel about being Hungarian?"

Finally it occurred to me that I should tell a story. When I decided to visit my maternal grandmother's village in Hungary—the village she had left in 1909—no one in my family had written to any of our relatives there since her death over a decade ago. I found the address of her sister's only son, Jenő, and sent a letter to him in case his mother had died in the intervening years. A month later he responded with enthusiasm to my suggestion that we spend a day together in Páli, a two-hour drive west of Budapest. He added that as soon as my letter arrived he went to a box of "American letters," leafed through them and found a picture of me—at eighteen months. And immediately I remembered the boxes of Hungarian letters my grandmother had saved on the top shelf of her bedroom closet, along with the small black-and-white photographs stuffed into some of their envelopes.

During previous trips to Europe, I always found a reason to ignore Hungary. It was too far from Paris, from London, from Athens. It was out of my way. I never asked myself why I didn't make time for a side trip, or make a special trip in itself. Nor did my family ask. Everyone seemed to assume that there were other places to see first. It wasn't until Magda, my Hungarian teacher, said, "You have to go and get over your first trip," with an expression that allowed for disappointment, that I began to understand why I hadn't visited there before.

Sociologists might call me a textbook case. They repeatedly advise that ethnic identity has a short life in North America. Inevitably, the first generation learns how to accommodate a new country, making adjustments that lead to upward mobility, if not exactly assimilation. Their ethnic identity helps and hinders the process in various ways. The second generation may still speak their parents' mother tongue (with varying degrees of expertise and some unlikely accents) but they often reject, or put aside, an ethnicity that belongs to their parents. The third generation has usually lost the language skills that shape ethnic identity, while ties to religion and the "old country" seldom claim their imagination. Ethnicity has now degenerated into traditional holiday foods, sentimental gestures toward belonging, and memory.

Caught in my desire to recreate a past known only secondhand while even acknowledging the futility of that desire, of course

I dreaded what I would find in Hungary. Everywhere I read of changes in Budapest—franchises of Pizza Hut, Burger King, and Dunkin' Donuts; the popularity of Woody Allen movies—as if Hungary had come to the end of its own unique history, and all that loomed ahead was shopping at the mall. Even though I knew that "Hungary" existed mainly in my mind—and that my real relation was with these images, and not a place—I wanted to hold on to the images. Could I find what I wanted? Surely the personal meaning of a place is always subjective. The only way to lose a sense of place is to lock into the sadness or desperation of not finding it in the externals; a place rarely corresponds to externals anyway.

Nostalgia and the search for roots belong to our fin-de-siècle mood; they can be a simplification of other historical moments, times we would probably never want to belong to. Often, too, our nostalgia is coupled with irony—an irony that critiques what we feel. This irony is a central feature of the postmodern narrator, someone usually left alone with self-awareness, fragmented and supposedly beyond illusions. It's a stance I find suspect and want to resist. Yet several days before leaving for Hungary I gave in to it. I had an onset of spring allergies—the worst in years—and hoped they wouldn't run their usual four-week course. Perhaps, I thought, the notorious pollution of Eastern Europe would have killed all the pollen in Budapest, and I'd be able to breathe again, even if it was only industrial waste.

All of my associations with Hungary came from other people's lives, and I have to admit the prejudice I had about Hungarians from childhood.

My parents lived in the lower flat of a duplex and my maternal grandparents lived in the flat above, so I knew them well until I left home at twenty. They rarely spoke Hungarian, except when they had something to say they didn't want the grandchildren to understand, or late at night, when they sat on the porch, talking— I guessed—of the old country. Sometimes they sang Hungarian songs to themselves as they worked. But Hungary meant little to me. My grandfather once said, "Hungarians are always fighting with each other." I'm *sure* he said something like that. I recall one

Saturday night, when he was babysitting (I must have been eight or nine). It was late, I couldn't sleep, and we had already watched *Gunsmoke*. So he taught me how to count to ten in Hungarian: *egy, kettő, három, négy, öt, hat, hét, nyolc, kilenc, tíz*. By morning I had forgotten the words. What good were they to me? Just Hungarian numbers. And Hungary was the bad place my grandparents had left in order to make a better life.

Later, when I began to study history, I wondered why Hungary was always on the wrong side of the worst wars of the twentieth century. I made a list of reasons, but they never quite convinced me. Of course I wanted to hold up the freedom fighters of '56 as heroic, noble, but I never quite believed myself. Even now, as I write this and recall Attila, my driver in Budapest, mentioning the frustration that young Hungarians felt while waiting for UN troops, I keep thinking, "Yes, it was a betrayal, it was wrong, but look what you did to your Jews. . . ." I hate admitting this because I know, rationally, that there is plenty of guilt and blame to go around. After Hitler's war, nearly a million Hungarians were imprisoned by the Soviets or sent to work in the labor camps in Siberia. They were beaten, brutalized, raped. Most died after a few years — "the Gulag ate them," Attila had remarked. "Yet during those years, foreign intellectuals — especially the French, and the Americans — were so impressed by the accomplishments of the Soviet Union that they looked away from the sufferings of the Hungarians, and everyone else in the labor camps." Attila's words remain in my ears, as if he were challenging me not to look away.

Some years ago, I wrote a short story called "Hide and Seek," about a boy who is fascinated by two young Hungarian cousins who come to live in his family's house after the 1956 revolution. Part of his interest stems from his own growing sense that life is not as simple as the optimistic American system of education tended to envision. The boy is particularly intrigued by the younger and more handsome cousin, who always wears a black leather glove over an artificial hand. Only recently, after reading the story in my collection, did my mother confide that the young cousin I modeled the story on had once calmly observed: "Hitler had a few good ideas. He was right about getting rid of the Jews." Perhaps that was why my grandfather seemed so unhappy with his nephews — I'll never be sure. I don't like telling this story, but it is also part of what I know. Unfortunately I can never think of "Hide and Seek" in the same way again.

Writers and academics are often sentimentalists, although most would deny it. Given the opportunity to see Hardy's house, or the pen Keats wrote with, they're off and running — sometimes even convincing themselves that this is part of scholarship. Years ago I wrote a doctoral dissertation on James Frazer's *The Golden Bough*, and several days before leaving for Budapest I looked up Hungary in the index to the twelve-volume edition. There are eight references, most related to fertility rites and customs:

> Hungarian story of the external soul, xi, 140
> Hungary, continence at sowing in, ii, 105;
> > "Sawing the Old Woman" among the gypsies of, iv, 243;
> > the harvest cock in, vii, 277;
> > custom at threshing in, vii, 291;
> > woman fertilized by being struck with certain sticks
> > > in, ix, 264;
> > Midsummer fires in, x, 178 *sq.*
> Hungary, German, Whitsuntide Queen in, ii, 87[1]

I read each one, and found myself amused that for the first time in years I had a reason to consult this elephantine compendium of superstition. But my sentimentality also included André Kertész's Hungarian photographs, which preserved a dying way of village life. This is the world I wanted to see, the world of Grandma's memories — almost a pastoral, fertility rites and all. I wondered how much her native village had changed in the years since she left it. And I knew I'd want to write about it. For a thousand years, even longer, people have been writing about traveling. They always assume it's a good thing, but what are they actually doing? Perhaps they have understood that a trip doesn't take shape, doesn't have meaning, until you're done with it. And sometimes it takes years to understand what a trip meant. This weighs in against the modern obsession with travel — always on to the next place. I don't mean this objection to be simple, or puritanical, either. Perhaps we are what we visit.

But I didn't want the countryside alone. I've written elsewhere about the way Edmund Wilson learned Hungarian at the age of sixty-five. During a month-long visit to Budapest in April 1964, he lived in the Gellért Hotel, a Budapest institution rather like New York's Algonquin Hotel. I had anticipated staying there too. On arriving, I was disappointed to learn that it had been built in 1918, at the end of the Habsburg reign, after my grandmother had left Budapest. It is a prominent local monument, at the foot of Gellért Hill, but she wouldn't have seen it. Grandma worked as a nanny for half a year in Budapest, though I don't know on which side of the Danube—Buda or Pest. I have only the vaguest memories of our talks about those years, and find no clues in them. Perhaps she never told me.

The Budapest telephone directory included four Telekys spelt with a *y*, an uncommon ending: Gyula, Jánosné, László, Pál. The last, Paul—a doctor—had the same Christian name as father. There were more than forty Telekis with the *i* ending.

My name has always been a problem in North America. As a child I often felt it a badge of foreignness; now it makes me impatient with the carelessness of North Americans. It is regularly misspelled as Telekey, or Teleki, or Telki, but far more fanciful versions are also common: Teleski, Tellery, Telsky, Tekely, and even the bizarre, like Peleski. In mail from a university where I taught for nearly fifteen years it is misspelled in one of three ways, but their preferred version is Teleski. It seems that people refuse to believe the letters they see on the page, as if they've spotted an error and want to correct it.

Yet my name is one of Hungary's oldest, and most aristocratic, and this poses another problem for me: how did my family end up with it? Tracing my father's family to Tarcal, in northeastern Hungary, in the heart of Tokaj grape-growing land, I come on nothing like aristocracy. My great-grandfather had many stories told about him—he lived to 105 years of age, and buried six wives. Perhaps he was the youngest son of another youngest son, cut off from landed roots by the laws of primogeniture. This seems plausible, since I do know that he was a Calvinist minister, teacher, and choirmaster.

I'm of two minds about what I don't know. The curious and stubborn parts of my personality want to persist in finding an answer even though I know that, eventually, my father's family history will be lost to time. So the version I've constructed of a displaced son satisfies me for the moment. In fact I rather like not knowing. Sooner or later I would hit the wall of uncertainty.

I've always been drawn to people with a strong ethnic identity. I want to hear their stories, taste their food, read the books they knew that I've never heard of. Yet I drew a line at church pageants where people wore idealized peasant costumes, like the dolls my sister collected—a kimonoed geisha, a Greek evzone in his pleated skirt. Adults dressing up like that were enacting a ritual of the imagination that reminded me of children, of little girls playing at being bride. I was impatient with such nostalgia, which seemed perversely literal and empty. I was dismissive because I didn't understand it. And I was wrong. Nothing is as simple as I once thought those old-country costumes to be. They told of longings, memories, and accommodations with a new life that had its own rewards but endless disappointments. How could I not have seen? Yet my family had nothing to do with such doll-like displays of colorful ethnicity, the kind that gets paraded on religious or national feast days. Not my family. They took their ethnicity straight up—no rocks, no water. This may be one reason why I had to go in search of roots, and why I postponed the search for so many years. I never needed to react against the kitsch of ethnicity.

The question "What does your ethnicity mean to you?" troubles me less than the word "ethnicity" itself. I've never liked the way a life can be summed up so easily by a word. To put it another way, American foods like baked beans, maple syrup, or hush puppies are all "ethnic" food to someone living in Hunan or Szeged. "Ethnic" too often means foreign, although it lacks some of the harsh connotations of that word. Derived from the Greek *ethnos*, for a nation or people, the word suggests a people who were not Christian or Jewish—hence, heathen. It is, of course, not far removed from the Greek *ethos*, which suggests the distinguishing characteristics of various groups.

Yet my friend's question stayed with me in spite of my objections. Wasn't my answer contained in my Hungarian language studies, and in my reading and writing? They satisfied me. But perhaps I needed to satisfy others. In the last few years I've often found myself in a similar position with people—usually strangers, but sometimes colleagues—who ask what I'm writing. When it comes to fiction, it's easy to say that I don't talk about a work in progress. People may be curious, but this reply seems to satisfy them—it makes a kind of sense. When I mention my Hungarian studies, however, I notice quite a different reaction. Sometimes puzzled, as if they hadn't heard correctly, or sometimes interested, people rarely know anything about Hungary. A few mention the Hungarian restaurants along Toronto's Bloor Street, but that's about it. Or they ask, "Are you Hungarian?" as if no one else could possibly devote himself to the subject (as if there were, even, one subject). I used to be annoyed by that question, but now I act like the Ancient Mariner about to snag another unsuspecting wedding guest. I spout statistics, tell stories, recommend books. Learn something new, I want to say.

My "ethnicity" isn't simply an additional way of seeing myself or my world, which would make it external to me, a kind of psychological decoration, a tattoo. It is more intrinsic than that. I can't imagine myself without it. As far back as I can remember, the stories I heard included Hungary, just as fairy tales have forests and castles. Hungary is part of my imagination. Which may explain why it took so long for me to find it—I took it for granted, as if I knew it better than I did, the way one takes a hand, a foot, for granted. I can't name all the bones in my right hand, but I rely on that hand.

Now I have names for many of the bones of my ethnicity. They include the St. Roch chapel in Budapest, the novels of Dezső Kosztolányi, the corner of a small cafe in Győr, an anonymous painting, in Esztergom, of Christ disguised as a gardener appearing to Mary Magdalene, the man who sold me sour cherries at the Pest foot of the Liberty Bridge, my grandmother's golden eyes, the taste of her *almás rétes* (apple strudel), my favorite poem of Endre Ady, "Szeretném, ha szeretnének," which loses too much in translation. My "ethnicity" is made up of details, endless details, which make me think of the old adage, often attributed to Flaubert, that "God is in the details." So is ethnicity.

Inevitably I return to language, since it is through studying Hungarian that I've clarified some of my thoughts about ethnicity. And I'm not alone in linking the two. Richard Rodriguez, in *Days of Obligation: An Argument with My Mexican Father,* speaks of the power of the Spanish language in America as a private code rarely known outside the walls of home; Alice Kaplan, in *French Lessons: A Memoir,* explores the attraction of an American child to another language that, for her, embodied an alternate world; and Eva Hoffman, in *Lost in Translation: A Life in a New Language,* laments the loss of a world, self, and culture that she had to leave behind when her family emigrated to North America. All of these responses to language relate, in some way, to the connection between language and ethnicity, and they mirror some aspects of my own response to the subject. Rodriguez sees power in the secrecy of a familiar language just as Kaplan sensed another way of life hidden in the French language. But none of them exactly repeats my situation.

Recently I read that Mordecai Strigler, editor of the *Forward,* the Yiddish labor newspaper founded in New York in 1897, has had difficulty locating contemporary journalists who can write in Yiddish. The paper "is written in a dying language for a geriatric population."[2] In my local deli, signs are often taped to the wall offering Yiddish lessons for a generation whose experience of the language is confined to a few colorful words that their parents may use, but that have also become commonplace in American culture. The problem faced by the editors of the *Forward* confronts everyone interested in "ethnic" publishing. For several years I've taught a course in immigrant literature, and one afternoon I asked the students to bring their community newspapers to the next class. Chinese, Portuguese, Italian, Caribbean, Greek, and East Indian papers piled my desk the following week, along with the Hungarian ones I'd brought. Many of these newspapers serve newly arrived communities and I wonder how long they will exist. I can't help recalling that the Hungarian American *Szabadság* (Freedom), once a daily, now appears weekly, just as the *Forward* has been a weekly for the last decade.

Too often the study of ethnicity undervalues the importance of language to ethnic identity, perhaps because few scholars are genuinely bilingual. However, the sociologist John de Vries has argued that " 'language maintenance' is a *necessary* condition for the maintenance of ethnicity—though not a *sufficient* condition."[3] Examining, as well, the changes that signal the weakening of ethnic identity, especially in the third generation (declining residential segregation or marriage outside the ethnic group), de Vries emphasizes the significance of language as an ethnic "marker." Ethnicity needs language, and associations with it—cultural, religious, political, familial. Yet if I were to study Italian, say, I would never feel connected to that ethnicity, even though I would inevitably have a rich set of associations. I would be more like Kaplan with her French than Rodriguez and his Spanish, or Hoffman and her Polish. There would always be something impersonal, even willful, or arbitrary, in my connection with Italian; I would have chosen it, and not the other way around. Yet on a deeper level, ethnicity, like human life, seems an accident of fate. The fact that I was conceived at all, and then by Hungarian American parents, is contingent on a set of events that make me think of the pure chance that goes into making any human life—that two people for even a moment were drawn together in an act that created another human being. In this sense, ethnicity is always arbitrary. One might, after all, not have been born.

Is it arbitrary, then, that I decide to explore that ethnicity? I do have other interests. Perhaps there will always be some element of arbitrariness in the world of any third-generation immigrant. Certainly I have missed most of the more painful implications of ethnicity that first-generation immigrants seldom escape. Ethnicity can, for us, rarely be a matter connected to nationalism or nationalistic pride. Our political lives have been so shaped by the schools of North America that we can know our ethnicity mainly through familial, cultural, and linguistic ties. We can read about national ties, or listen to stories that deal with them, but they will never have the same resonance for us that they do for someone born in the old country.

Several years ago the novelist Mary Gordon (of Irish Catholic and Lithuanian Jewish ancestry) wrote a splendid essay about Ellis Island in which she admitted that the Americana of Plymouth Rock, Gettysburg, and Mount Vernon "inhabits for me a zone of blurred abstraction with far less hold on my imagination than the Bastille or Hampton Court."[4] These places, which purport to be her history, "are not mine," she writes. "Ellis Island is, though; it's the one place I can be sure my people are connected to." This made perfect sense to me. Despite recent debunking of the melting-pot theory of American history, there is still a kind of American distance from ethnicity, as if we should all be American in the same way. The same distance occurs in Canada, which officially advances an idea of multiculturalism, but always in relation to a dominant culture that knows its identity as truly Canadian. In both countries ethnicity is still a weapon that can be used against immigrants, or their children.

Oddly, exploring my ethnicity became a way of exploring the arbitrary nature of my own life. It was not so much a search for roots as for a way of understanding rootlessness—how I stacked up against another way of being. It involved my dissatisfaction with much of North American culture, its assumptions and its materialism, which may in fact have produced the desire to know more about another way of life. Soon after I began making the effort of learning another (albeit familiar) language, I saw that I had fallen into a kind of intellectual black hole into which I could pour endless effort and time and money. I persisted in my decision, which became a kind of commitment, because I wanted to know where it would take me. In this sense, exploring my ethnicity led to a greater appreciation of the arbitrariness of my life and the particular set of conditions that made it up. Yet this sense of arbitrariness tied me to others, living and dead, and to the fragility of all human life. It made me appreciate the way people have struggled to find a good life for themselves while also giving me a new vocabulary— a new language, and new points of reference—for their struggle. What is arbitrary suddenly became the core of the human experience, more essential than roots and more enduring than the particularities of any one people and their history.

Last year, in a fiction-writing workshop I taught, I had an unusually talented young writer with a classic Hungarian surname. None of Andrea's stories touched on ethnicity, which made me curious. During an interview in my office she told me about her parents, who had come to Canada after the 1956 uprising. Andrea knew a smattering of Hungarian and had wonderful stories to tell, but hadn't yet found a way into them. This isn't unusual, but her next confession was. She had been adopted by the Hungarian Canadian couple and had no idea of the ethnic background of her biological parents. Of course I was fascinated. Her ethnicity—and her feelings about it—were a social construct. Think, for a moment, of orphans who can never know their ethnic background. Are they less fortunate than others? As I said before, I'm of two minds about ethnicity, so I'm tempted to answer both yes and no. Someone else's ethnicity (or nationalism) can always seem like sentimentality, or chauvinism, after all. Yet I'm glad to say that Andrea is now writing stories that include her Hungarian background as well as issues about adoption. She has found a subject uniquely her own. (Through a recent, unexpected chain of events, Andrea has since found her birth mother. And it turns out that her maternal great-great-grandfather was Hungarian. Of course the coincidence seemed too good to be true.)

In "Playtime," I mentioned the son of friends who refused to speak as early as his parents wished. Several years have passed since then, and Marc speaks—and reads—with enthusiasm. In fact, he now attends a parochial school where he is learning Hebrew and Yiddish as well. And I can't help thinking that his ethnicity is just as arbitrary as Andrea's, or my own. Without the infusion of language, religion, and culture that occupies him, what—and who—would Marc be? English, after all, is the mother tongue of his parents, whose interest in Judaism has grown since they had children. Raised by other parents, he might remain unilingual. Or he might inherit another ethnic tradition, as Andrea did, and eventually claim it for his own. His language skills will matter if he has the chance to use them outside his school. Language, after all, belongs to community.

During the past summer, Krisztina, the would-be florist from Budapest, returned to Toronto for six weeks to attend an English-language refresher course at the university. I'm glad to say that, against the odds, she has managed to open her own shop in a busy section of Budapest. Krisztina worried that she was losing her English, and we commiserated about the problems of maintaining a new language. To speak fluent Hungarian I would need to live for a time in Hungary, something I don't foresee in the immediate future. And, since I have few opportunities to speak the language, to practice and develop it, my Hungarian remains a language of the written word. Of course this situation faces everyone who learns a language in isolation from a community.

Perhaps I've been drawn to people with a strong ethnic identification because they had, at least, a dual perspective on the world. Or perhaps I assumed that they understood the artificialness, and arbitrariness, of the world in which they lived their daily lives. Yet I am not one of those writers who is finding himself in his roots, reclaiming the sufferings done to immigrant forebears. As an American who has lived in Toronto for twenty-five years, I still feel like an American in Canada; but, in the United States, I feel like a Canadian in America. Educated with a sympathy for European art and music—for all of European civilization, in fact—that many Americans might not share, I'm convinced that ethnicity is always remaking itself in relation to circumstances, forces, and institutions beyond our control. For the second- and third-generation children of immigrants, ethnic identity often depends upon what they can get from their ethnicity—they can pick up their ethnicity when it's needed and drop it when they like. In this sense ethnicity is not simply a matter of having a strong ethnic identity and, perhaps, losing it. Ethnicity is a constructed thing even for first-generation immigrants who, more than many people, have to pick and choose who they are. Yet I do not feel entirely comfortable with the anti-essentialist position. Valuing ethnicity, even as a means to understanding how a culture makes arbitrary choices for us, doesn't automatically lead to a sense that ethnic identity (or cultural behavior) is relative.

I wish I could say that my Hungarian studies have made me feel less dissatisfied with my own culture, able to forgive it for some of the details of its own particular and insistent way of being arbitrary. But I can't. Instead, I wish that North America would immerse itself in the study of otherness—which *other* doesn't especially matter. It might even learn that the truths and traditions it regards as eternal are merely arbitrary conventions. And if it learned that, it might also understand that some of its conventions are better than others. Being human involves making judgments and having preferences. Understanding the complexity of this simple fact — which a study of one's own ethnicity can illuminate — makes it possible to be more fully human. Grandma kept her "Hungarian letters," and Jenő his "American letters," because they knew this instinctively.

Notes

Playtime: Adult Language Learning,
Edmund Wilson, and Me

1. Edmund Wilson, *Upstate: Records and Recollections of Northern New York* (New York, 1971), 214.
2. Ibid., 249.
3. Ibid., 215.
4. Éva Janikovszky, *Ha én felnőtt volnék* (Budapest, 1965), 1.
5. Edward Pcolar, conversation with author, January 1991.
6. Carol Gelderman, ed., *Conversations with Mary McCarthy* (Jackson, Miss., 1991), 39.
7. Wilson, *Upstate*, 225.

"What the Moment Told Me":
The Photographs of André Kertész

1. The context I have in mind is examined in such books as John Lukacs's *Budapest 1900: A Historical Portrait of a City and Its Culture* (New York, 1988) and Mary Gluck's *Georg Lukács and His Generation, 1900–1918* (Cambridge, Mass., 1985), as well as by two recent traveling exhibitions of Hungarian art with book-length catalogues: *A Golden Age: Art and Society in Hungary, 1896–1914* and *Standing in the Tempest: Painters of the Hungarian Avant-Garde, 1908–1930*.
2. André Kertész, *Kertész on Kertész: A Self-Portrait* (London, 1985), 15.
3. Ibid., 23.
4. Colin Ford, *André Kertész: An Exhibition of Photographs from the Centre Georges Pompidou, Paris* (London, 1979), 9.
5. Ibid., 24.
6. Ibid., 36.
7. Ibid., 30.
8. André Kertész, *Hungarian Memories* (Boston, 1982), 30.
9. Kertész, *Kertész on Kertész*, 37.
10. Sandra S. Phillips et al., *André Kertész of Paris and New York* (New York, 1985), 19.
11. Kertész, *Kertész on Kertész*, 29.
12. Ibid., 15, 105, 76.
13. Ibid., 38.
14. Ibid., 80.
15. Ibid., 33.
16. Ibid., 32.

17. Oliver A. I. Botar, *Tibor Polya and the Group of Seven: Hungarian Art in Toronto Collections, 1900–1949* (Toronto, 1989), 2.
18. Keith F. Davis, *André Kertész: Vintage Photographs* (New York, 1985), 6.
19. Many artists who settled in Paris at this time made a similar move to abstraction.
20. Kertész, *Kertész on Kertész*, 53.
21. Ford, *André Kertész*, 22.
22. Kertész, *Kertész on Kertész*, 90.
23. Phillips et al., *André Kertész*, 109. Weston J. Naef curiously misses the point with his phrase the "Americanization of Kertész." In fact, the photographer never developed an American fondness for scenic subjects, while it was his Europeanness that caused his work to be undervalued, as Kertész admitted.
24. Kertész, *Hungarian Memories*, 194.
25. Ibid., 96.
26. Ibid., 99.

The Archives of St. Elizabeth of Hungary

1. St. Elizabeth of Hungary Church is located at 9016 Buckeye Road, Cleveland, Ohio 44120-0175. Before moving to the present location in September 1893, the parish met for one year at St. Joseph's Orphanage on Woodland Avenue.
2. In addition to my discussions with Endre Ritly, information about the history of St. Elizabeth's Church comes from two pamphlets prepared by it for various anniversaries: first, the Golden Jubilee Pamphlet of 1942, which includes essays in English and Hungarian; second, the pamphlet prepared for the 95th anniversary, in 1987, which also includes essays in English and Hungarian. The earlier pamphlet is the superior of the two.
3. There are two excellent studies of Hungarian immigrants: Julianna Puskás's *From Hungary to the United States (1880–1914)* (Budapest, 1982) and Steven Bela Vardy's *The Hungarian Americans* (Boston, 1985). A good survey devoted to the important Cleveland community is Susan Papp's *Hungarian Americans and Their Communities of Cleveland* (Cleveland, 1981). Various short articles about St. Elizabeth's Church and Father Charles Boehm have been consulted in *The Encyclopedia of Cleveland History*, edited by David D. Van Tassel and John H. Grabowski (Bloomington, 1987). As well, William Ganson Rose's monumental study *Cleveland: The Making of a City* (Cleveland, 1950) contains information about the city's Hungarian community and its association with St. Elizabeth's.
4. "The 1920 census listed over a million Americans as born in Poland, 900 thousand from Austria and Hungary, and 1.6 million as natives of

Italy. By 1920, there were around 17 million American Catholics, out of a total population of around 105 million." F. Michael Perko, S.J., *Catholic and American* (Huntington, Ind., 1989), 223.

5. An example of the "enlightened" stereotype of the Hungarian immigrant circa 1920 appeared in a volume of the Yale University's Chronicles of America series, Samuel P. Orth's *Our Foreigners* (New Haven, 1920): "Over 338,000 Magyars immigrated to the United States during the decade ending 1910. These brilliant and masterful folk are a Mongoloid blend that swept from the steppes of Asia across eastern Europe a thousand years ago. As the wave receded, the Magyars remained dominant in beautiful and fertile Hungary, where their aggressive nationalism still brings them into constant rivalry on the one hand with the Germans of Austria and on the other with the Slavs of Hungary. The immigrants to America are largely recruited from the peasantry. They almost invariably seek the cities, where the Magyar neighborhoods can be easily distinguished by their scrupulously neat housekeeping, the flower beds, the little patches of well-swept grass, the clean children, and the robust and tidy women. Among them is less illiteracy that in any other group from eastern and southern Europe, excepting the Finns, who are their ethnic brothers. As a rule they own their own homes. They learn the English language quickly but unfortunately acquire with it many American vices. Drinking and carousing are responsible for their many crimes of personal violence. They are otherwise a sociable, happy people, and the cafés kept by Hungarians are islands of social jollity in the desert of urban strife" (175–76).

6. The impact of World War I on immigrant Catholic groups is an important subject rarely examined. A brief discussion of the response of German Catholics in the United States appears in a volume edited by Jay P. Dolan, *The American Catholic Parish: A History from 1850 to the Present*, vol. 3 (Mahwah, N.J., 1987), 327–29.

7. This subject merits further study. Hungarians were not assimilationists, as Dolores Liptak writes in *Immigrants and Their Church* (New York, 1989): "Unlike the middle-class Irish-Americans who wanted to blend into American society, however, most of Slavic, Hungarian, and Lithuanian immigrant groups preferred to develop parishes that maintained their separateness from other American institutions" (137).

8. Anti-immigrant and anti-Catholic prejudice often combined in the early years of the twentieth century. See chapter 7 ("The Anglo-Saxon and the New Immigrant") by Lewis H. Carlson and George A. Colburne in *In Their Place: White America Defines Her Minorities, 1850–1950* (New York, 1972) and also John Higham's *Strangers in the Land: Patterns of American Nativism, 1860–1925* (New Brunswick, 1955).

9. One of the finest examples of the social history of immigrant culture, with an emphasis on religion and community affiliations, is

Josef J. Barton's study of Cleveland ethnic communities, *Peasants and Strangers: Italians, Rumanians, and Slovaks in an American City, 1890–1950* (Cambridge, Mass., 1975). The numerous community activities sponsored by St. Elizabeth of Hungary Church are part of the pattern Barton describes: "Growing numbers of cultural groups appeared in the 1890s to celebrate Irish, German, Czech, and Hungarian culture; these societies came to dominate much of the cultural life of the city in the early 1900s" (22).

10. Michael J. Hynes mentions Charles Boehm and his pioneering work with Hungarian Catholics in the United States several times in *History of the Diocese of Cleveland: Origin and Growth, 1847–1952* (Cleveland, 1953). Unfortunately Boehm is not even noted in Albert Hamilton's *The Catholic Journey through Ohio*, published by the 1976 Catholic Conference of Ohio. Hamilton concentrates on Irish, German, and Polish Catholics.

11. Charles Boehm, *Magyarországi Szent Erzsébet Amerikai Hirnöke* (Cleveland, 1893), 1.

Without Words: Hungarians in North American Fiction

1. Mary Gordon, *Good Boys and Dead Girls and Other Essays* (New York, 1991), 172.

2. Gay Talese, "Where Are the Italian-American Novelists?" *New York Times Book Review*, March 14, 1993, 23.

3. In March 1906, for a Budapest newspaper, Ady wrote: "The Magyars of America make speeches and send their blessing. They are orphans and strangers there in a world whose life is complicated. America, which is only a few hundred years old, has galloped thousands of years ahead of Europe. And even more ahead of Hungary. And the Hungarians of America emigrated from here with an out-of-date ideology— an ideology out-of-date even in Hungary. They emigrated because it is impossible to live in this land without the threat of famine and pestilence unless every year a few hundred thousand human beings are exported. The Cunard Line carries more and more of them. And there they are isolated and besieged by the ideas of America, and by her great life which is terrifying, unknown and difficult: so they daydream. Their souls fly across the ocean with ever-painful nostalgia." Endre Ady, *The Explosive Country: A Selection of Articles and Studies, 1898–1916* (Budapest, 1977), 104–5.

4. Ibid., 242.

5. Ibid., 106.

6. John O'Hara, *Collected Stories of John O'Hara* (New York, 1984), 11.

7. Ibid.

8. Ibid., 14.

9. Ibid., 26.

10. John Marlyn, *Under the Ribs of Death* (Toronto, 1990), 13.

11. Ibid., 13–14.

12. Ibid., 15.

13. John Marlyn's Hungarian surname, Mihaelovitcz, was changed to Marlyn by his father. I am grateful to Marlene Kadar, who traced this fact through Marlyn's brother Frank and cited it in her paper "Reading Ethnicity."

14. Marlyn, *Under the Ribs of Death*, 17.

15. Ibid., 18–19.

16. Hortense Calisher, *The New Yorkers* (New York, 1988), 79.

17. Ibid., 86.

18. Ibid., 90.

19. Ibid., 107.

20. Ibid., 350.

21. John Marlyn, *Putzi, I Love You, You Little Square* (Toronto, 1981), 24.

22. Ibid., 29.

23. Ibid., 61.

24. Ibid., 83.

25. This is not to say that it is impossible to write without a tradition. In Britain, for example, Tibor Fischer's much-praised novel *Under the Frog* (1992) was shortlisted for the 1993 Booker Prize. Fischer was born of Hungarian parents in England, in 1959, and educated at Cambridge. As a journalist he often traveled in Hungary, where he married a Hungarian woman. His novel, about a Hungarian basketball team in the years preceding the 1956 uprising, is a dark comic evocation of a time he knew only through stories of family and friends.

26. George Bisztray, *Hungarian-Canadian Literature* (Toronto, 1987), 68.

27. Ibid., 54–55.

28. Stephen Vizinczey, *In Praise of Older Women* (Chicago, 1990), 1.

29. Ibid., 162, 161, 164.

30. Ibid., 175–76, 161.

31. Frank Rich, "How Far Good Sports Will Go," *New York Times*, March 5, 1993, 32.

32. Linda Hutcheon and Marion Richmond, eds., *Other Solitudes: Canadian Multicultural Fictions* (Toronto, 1990), 368.

33. Margaret Atwood, *Wilderness Tips* (New York, 1991), 181.

34. Ibid., 181–84.

35. Ibid., 187–90.

36. Ibid., 195.

37. In an interview with Eleanor Wachtel, Ondaatje spoke of his fascination with "minor" historical figures who are seldom written about: "In *The English Patient* I drew on Count Almasy the spy, but mostly on the explorer, a really respected explorer. I used the first part of his life and then moved on into fiction." Eleanor Wachtel, *Writers & Company* (Toronto, 1993), 58.

38. Michael Ondaatje, *The English Patient* (New York, 1992), 121.
39. Ibid., 253.
40. Ibid., 283.
41. Ibid., 286.

The Empty Box: Hollywood Ethnicity and Joe Eszterhas

1. Susan M. Papp, *Hungarian Americans and Their Communities of Cleveland* (Cleveland, 1981), 2.
2. Ibid., 3.
3. Quotations from *The Music Box* are transcribed from the film, which is available on videocassette from Carolco Home Video.
4. Paul Chutkow, "From the 'Music Box' Emerges the Nazi Demon," *New York Times*, December 24, 1989, H-25.
5. Kathy Holub, "Ballistic Instinct," *Premiere*, August 1991, 81–82.
6. Transcribed from *Stranger Than Paradise*, which is available on videocassette from Vestron Video.

A Short Dictionary of Hungarian Stereotypes and Kitsch

1. Claudio Magris, *Danube: A Sentimental Journey from the Source to the Black Sea* (London, 1990), 29.
2. Hugh Fordin, *Getting to Know Him: A Biography of Oscar Hammerstein II* (New York, 1977), 232. Molnár does not include this story in his memoir, *Companion in Exile* (New York, 1950). It does tell, however, that his favorite music was the *Pavane pour une infante défunte* by Maurice Ravel, his favorite composer, until he heard the score of *Carousel*, which quickly supplanted it (215).
3. Oscar Wilde and others, *Teleny* (London, 1986), 29.
4. Ibid., 36, 110, 31, 116, 122. Wilde wouldn't have known that it was a Hungarian writer and sex researcher — Karl Maria Kertbeny — who coined the terms "heterosexual" and "homosexual" in a personal letter of May 6, 1868, and publicly in an anonymous leaflet in the fall of 1869 (Katz, *The Invention of Heterosexuality*, 53, 215). For an account of his work see Jean-Claude Féray and Manfred Herzer, "Homosexual Studies and Politics in the 19th Century: Karl Maria Kertbeny," *Journal of Homosexuality* 19, no. 1 (1990): 23–47.
5. Anaïs Nin, *Delta of Venus* (New York, 1990), 1.
6. Ibid., 9.
7. Eleanor Perényi, *More Was Lost* (Boston, 1946), 4.
8. Ibid., 249.
9. Jessica Steele, *Hungarian Rhapsody* (Toronto, 1992), 37, 39, 57, 81.

10. Richard Traubner, *Operetta: A Theatrical History* (New York, 1983), 265.

11. Edmund Wilson, *Letters on Literature and Politics: 1912–1972* (New York, 1977), 603.

12. László Dobszay, *A History of Hungarian Music* (Budapest, 1993), 167.

13. Quotations from *Christmas in Connecticut* are transcribed from the film, which is available on videocassette from MGM/UA Home Video.

14. Transcribed from *Midnight*, which is available from MCA Universal Home Video.

15. Transcribed from *The Shop Around the Corner*, which is available from MGM/UA Home Video.

16. William Lanouette, *Genius in the Shadows: A Biography of Leo Szilard* (New York, 1992), 257.

17. Eleanor Perényi, *Liszt: The Artist as Romantic Hero* (New York, 1974), 10.

18. Alan Walker, *Franz Liszt: The Weimar Years, 1848–1861* (Ithaca, 1989), 380.

19. Ibid., 381.

20. Alfred Brendel, *The Alfred Brendel Collection/Franz Liszt: The Hungarian Rhapsodies*, Vanguard Classics, OVC 4024 (1991).

21. J. D. Salinger, *Franny and Zooey* (Boston, 1961), 106.

22. Stephen R. Burant, *Hungary: A Country Study* (Washington, D.C., 1990), 1010.

23. John Lukacs, *Budapest 1900: A Historical Portrait of a City and Its Culture* (New York, 1988), 24.

24. Christopher Condon, "When Only Despair Makes Sense," *Budapest Week*, August 19–25, 1993, 5.

25. Laurie Lisle, *Portrait of an Artist: A Biography of Georgia O'Keeffe* (New York, 1981), 5.

26. George Lang, *The Cuisine of Hungary* (New York, 1971), 126.

27. Edmund Wilson, *The Sixties: The Last Journal, 1960–1972* (New York, 1993), 510.

28. Camille Paglia, *Sexual Personae: Art and Decadence from Nefertiti to Emily Dickinson* (New York, 1991), 247.

29. Bram Stoker, *Dracula* (Oxford, 1983), xvii.

30. Ibid., 1.

31. Zsa Zsa Gabor, *One Lifetime Is Not Enough* (New York, 1993), 2–4.

32. Seth Mydans, "Confessions of a Star-Struck Looter," *New York Times*, May 6, 1992, A-13.

Visiting Pannonia

1. Pannonia Books has moved again. It is currently located at 344 Bloor Street West, Suite 509, Toronto, Ontario M5S 1W9.

Toward a Course on Central European Literature in Translation

1. Several years after writing this essay I'm pleased to note that an English translation of Margit Kaffka's last novel, *The Ant Heap*, has just been published (1995).

2. Hannah Arendt, *Hannah Arendt–Karl Jaspers Correspondence, 1926–1969* (New York, 1992), 375.

3. "University of Toronto Ethnic Origins," *Globe and Mail*, December 3, 1992, C-6.

4. William Found and Sheila De Cupyer, "Women and Men at York," figure 8 (North York, Ont., n.d.).

5. Since the end of the Second World War, the term "Central Europe" has largely been replaced in Western writing by the more contemporary and political term "Eastern Europe." Timothy Garton Ash's excellent essay "Does Central Europe Exist?" In *The Uses of Adversity: Essays on the Fate of Central Europe* (New York, 1989, 179–213) suggests the complexities involved in these terminologies and relates their historical, geographical, and political factors. Following Garton Ash, I use the term "Central Europe" (which has reappeared in discussions of the region since the breakup of Soviet power over it) to suggest the historical connection of the region to the Habsburg empire and its ethos. This usage is also common with Central European writers such as Milan Kundera, whose essay "The Tragedy of Central Europe" (*New York Review of Books*, April 26, 1984) reminds readers of the importance of the region's history. I want to thank Steven Tötösy de Zepetnek for directing me to Virgil Nemoianu's provocative essay "Learning over Class: The Case of the Central European Ethos," which examines Central European attitudes toward learning as a key aspect of the region's social and cultural ethos.

6. Novelist Mordecai Richler's *Oh Canada, Oh Quebec: Requiem for a Divided Country* (Toronto, 1992) explores these language laws in depth.

7. Inevitably, political pundits began to make connections between events in Central Europe and those in North America. For example, see Jeffrey Simpson's op-ed piece "Four Lessons Canada Can Learn from What Used To Be Czechoslovakia," *Globe and Mail*, January 12, 1993. My students, who had come up with more "lessons" of their own, were not impressed.

8. Garton Ash, *The Uses of Adversity*, 189.

The Poet as Translator:
Margaret Avison's "Hungarian Snap"

1. Avison's comments were made during a taped interview on July 3, 1991. We had had several previous discussions about her translations while I edited her *Selected Poems*, and Avison knew of my studies of the Hungarian language. All further comments by Avison are from this interview.

2. Along with Avison, Duczyńska was able to gather around her a number of Canadian poets who contributed translations, including Earle Birney (2), John Robert Colombo (1), Louis Dudek (2), Eustace Ross (1, with Avison), A. J. M. Smith (3), and Raymond Souster (2), as well as Kenneth McRobbie, a coeditor of *Mosaic* and a professor of history at the University of Manitoba, whose wife was Hungarian. However, Avison's eight translations included the longest poems (apart from McRobbie's translation of Juhász's "The Boy Changed into a Stag Cries Out at the Gate of Secrets") and totaled eighteen pages, making them the most significant contribution to the anthology and the most sustained effort at translation.

3. In his article "The Only Political Duty: Margaret Avison's Translations of Hungarian Poems," Ernest Redekop wrote: "Without knowledge of Hungarian or even of the literal translations, it is difficult to sort out Avison's particular contributions to the original [*sic*] poems. Nevertheless, certain familiar images do appear, and some of the diction is recognizably hers" (*The Literary Half-Yearly* 13, no. 2 (July 1972): 159. Redekop's main interest is in noting similar concepts ("the nature of the individual human being") and images ("the Milky Way") in Avison's translations and in her own poetry. His title is a phrase from the foreword to *The Plough and the Pen*, where Auden suggested that a writer's "only political duty" is to translate the fiction and poetry of other countries.

4. Robert Lowell, *Imitations* (New York, 1958), xi–xiii. All quotations from Lowell come from this edition.

5. Hungary is still a culture of the word, not the image. As recently as June 1990, when the distinguished émigré poet George Faludy returned to Budapest, his publisher brought out a new collection of his sonnets with a first printing of 80,000 copies. In North America, where the print run of books by established poets is rarely more than several thousand, this figure seems astronomical.

6. Ilona Duczyńska and Karl Polanyi, eds., *The Plough and the Pen: Writings from Hungary, 1930–1956* (Toronto, 1963), 15. In their preface to the anthology the Polanyis describe the bilingual "work sheets" they gave their translators.

7. Adding further strain, during this time Karl Polanyi, who had origi-

nally been teaching at Columbia and flying back and forth between New York and Toronto, was slowly dying of cancer.

8. Duczyńska and Polanyi, eds., *The Plough and the Pen*, 200.
9. Ferenc Juhász, *A Mindenség Szerelme: A Szarvassá változott fiú* (Budapest, 1971), 576.
10. Avison's translation of "Farm, at Dark, on the Great Plain" was included in Ferenc Juhász, *The Boy Changed into a Stag: Selected Poems, 1949–1967*, translated by McRobbie and Duczyńska (Toronto and New York, 1970).
11. Duczyńska and Polanyi, eds., *The Plough and the Pen*, 169.
12. Attila József, *Összes versei 2/1928–1937*, 343.
13. Margaret Avison, *No Time* (Hantsport, N.S., 1989), 107.
14. Ibid.
15. Gyula Illyés, *Összegyűjtött versi/Második kötet* (Budapest, 1977), 240.
16. Duczyńska and Polanyi, eds., *The Plough and the Pen*, 173.
17. Gyula Illyés, *Összegyűjtött versei/Első kötet* (Budapest, 1977), 556.
18. Margaret Avison, *The Dumbfounding* (New York, 1966), 71.
19. Redekop, "The Only Political Duty," 159.

Introducting Péter Esterházy

1. I will mention several of Esterházy's books, but my detailed comments will be reserved for texts that have been translated into English, in the hope that readers will want to discover them for themselves. While several of Esterházy's novels are now available from Western publishers, *The Transporters* and his short story "No Title: This Isn't It Either" appear in English in anthologies published by Corvina, in Budapest. They will be found only in Hungarian-language bookstores such as Manhattan's Püski-Corvin (251 East 82nd Street, New York, New York 10028) and Toronto's Pannonia Books (344 Bloor Street West, Suite 509, Toronto, Ontario M5S 1W9). Both booksellers publish extensive catalogues. One can only hope that recent economic changes in Hungary will permit a fine publisher like Corvina to continue its wide range of literary and scholarly publishing in English.
2. Richard Aczel, "'Modernism' and 'Postmodernism' in Contemporary Hungarian Fiction," *Studies in Cultural Interaction in Europe, East and West* (University of Amsterdam), no. 3 (1993) 38.
3. Aczel, "The Pillaged Archive: Attitudes to History in the Fiction of Péter Nádas, Lajos Grendel and Miklós Mészöly," ibid., 53.
4. Ibid., 54.
5. Surveys of Hungarian literature in English generally refer to Kosztolányi as a *Homo aestheticus*. The term appeared in Joseph Reményi's *Hungarian Writers and Literature* in 1964 and again, in 1983, in *A History of Hungarian Literature*, edited by Tibor Klaniczay for Corvina, as well as in Lóránt Czigány's *The Oxford History of Hungarian*

Literature (1984). An interesting term, it might also be used to describe postmodernists like Esterházy.

6. Dezső Kosztolányi, *Skylark* (London, 1993), ix.
7. Ibid., x.
8. Péter Esterházy, *The Transporters*, in *Hungarian Quartet* (Budapest, 1991), 152.
9. Ibid., 150.
10. Ibid., 159.
11. Ibid., 155.
12. Ibid., 165–66.
13. Péter Esterházy, "On Laziness," *Partisan Review* 56, no. 2 (Spring 1989): 247–49.
14. Ibid., 251.
15. Banville, "Laughter in the Dark," *New York Review of Books*, February 14, 1991, 16–17.
16. Péter Esterházy, *Helping Verbs of the Heart* (New York, 1991), 2, 4.
17. Ibid., 14.
18. Ibid., 12.
19. Ibid., 26.
20. Ibid., 44.
21. Ibid., 47.
22. Ibid., 47, 55, 76.
23. Ibid., 110–11.
24. Ibid., 50.
25. Péter Esterházy, *The Book of Hrabal* (London, 1993), 13.
26. Ibid., 167–68.
27. Ibid., 146–47.
28. Péter Esterházy, *The Glance of Countess Hahn-Hahn: Down the Danube* (London, 1994), 33.
29. Ibid., 50.
30. Ibid., 24.
31. Ibid., 139.
32. Ibid., 128.
33. Ibid., 57.
34. Ibid., 45.
35. Aczel, "The Pillaged Archive," 54.
36. Philip Marsden, "Deep as a River," *Times Literary Supplement*, April 15, 1994, 24.
37. Péter Esterházy, "God's Hat," *Partisan Review* 57, no. 3 (Summer 1990): 423.
38. Ibid., 424.

The Third Generation and the
"Problem" of Ethnicity

1. James Frazer, *The Golden Bough: A Study in Magic and Religion* (London, 1966), 12: 312.
2. David Remnick, "News in a Dying Language," *New Yorker,* January 10, 1994, 41.
3. John de Vries, "Language and Ethnicity: Canadian Aspects," in Peter S. Li, ed., *Race and Ethnic Relations in Canada* (Toronto, 1990), 235.
4. Mary Gordon, *Good Boys and Dead Girls and Other Essays* (New York, 1991), 124.

Bibliography

The following list includes titles of books, articles, films, and recordings cited in English and Hungarian in this volume, as well as titles that deserve to be recorded here because they have influenced my thinking or because they are among the rare translations from Hungarian into English. When one or two translators are named, I have listed them; but for books with numerous translators, I list only the first. Publication dates of Hungarian texts are cited only for original language editions. The dates given for translations from Hungarian are for the translations and not the original language editions.

Aczel, Richard. " 'Modernism' and 'Postmodernism' in Contemporary Hungarian Fiction"; "The Pillaged Archive: Attitudes to History in the Fiction of Péter Nádas, Lajos Grendel and Miklós Mészöly"; and "Liberating Hungarian Literature: The Achievement of Péter Esterházy." In *Studies in Cultural Interaction in Europe, East and West.* No. 3. Totfalusi Series, The Journal of the Hungarian Studies Program of the University of Amsterdam (1993).

Aczel, Tamas, and Tibor Meray. *The Revolt of the Mind: A Case History of Intellectual Resistance Behind the Iron Curtain.* New York: Frederick A. Praeger, Publishers, 1959.

Ady, Endre. *The Explosive Country: A Selection of Articles and Studies, 1898–1916.* Translated by G. F. Cushing. Budapest: Corvina, 1977.

———. *Neighbours of the Night: Selected Short Stories.* Translated by Judith Sollosy. Budapest: Corvina, 1994.

———. *Összes versei.* Vols. 1 and 2. Budapest: Szépirodalmi Könyvkiadó, 1972.

———. *Poems.* Translated by Rene Bonnerjea. Budapest: Dr. Vajna and Bokor Publishers, 1941.

———. *Poems of Endre Ady.* Translated by Anton N. Nyerges. Buffalo: Hungarian Cultural Foundation, 1969.

Allen, James Paul, and Eugene James Turner. "People of Eastern European Origin—Hungarian Ancestry." In *We the People: An Atlas of American Ethnic Diversity,* 89–92. New York: Macmillan, 1988.

Anger, Per. *With Raoul Wallenberg in Budapest: Memories of the War Years in Hungary.* Translated by David Mel Paul and Margareta Paul. New York: Holocaust Library, 1981.

Arendt, Hannah. *Hannah Arendt–Karl Jaspers Correspondence, 1926–1969.* Translated by Robert Kimber and Rita Kimber. Edited by Lotte Kohler and Hans Saner. New York: Harcourt Brace Jovanovich, 1992.

Aronowitz, Stanley. *The Politics of Identity: Class, Culture, Social Movements.* New York: Routledge, 1992.

Atwood, Margaret. *Wilderness Tips.* New York: Doubleday, 1991.

Avison, Margaret. *The Dumbfounding*. New York: Norton, 1966.
———. *No Time*. Hantsport, Nova Scotia: Lancelot Press, 1989.
———. *Selected Poems*. Toronto and New York: Oxford University Press, 1991.
Banville, John. "Laughter in the Dark." *New York Review of Books*, February 14, 1991, 16–17.
Barany, George. *Stephen Széchenyi and the Awakening of Hungarian Nationalism, 1791–1841*. Princeton: Princeton University Press, 1968.
Barber, Noel. *Seven Days of Freedom: The Hungarian Uprising, 1956*. New York: Stein and Day, 1974.
Bart, István, ed. *Present Continuous: Contemporary Hungarian Writing*. Budapest: Corvina, 1985.
Barthes, Roland. *A Lover's Discourse: Fragments*. Translated by Richard Howard. New York: Hill and Wang/Farrar, Straus and Giroux, 1979.
Barton, Josef J. *Peasants and Strangers: Italians, Rumanians, and Slovaks in an American City, 1890–1950*. Cambridge: Harvard University Press, 1975.
Basa, Enikő Molnár. *Sándor Petőfi*. Boston: Twayne Publishers, 1980.
Bender, Thomas, and Carl E. Schorske, eds. *Budapest and New York: Studies in Metropolitan Transformation, 1870–1930*. New York: Russell Sage Foundation, 1994.
Bisztray, George. *Hungarian-Canadian Literature*. Toronto: University of Toronto Press, 1987.
Boehm, Charles. *Magyarországi Szent Erzsébet Amerikai Hirnöke*. Cleveland: Calumet Printing Company for St. Elizabeth Church, 1893.
Boelhower, William. *Through a Glass Darkly: Ethnic Semiosis in American Literature*. New York: Oxford University Press, 1987.
Botar, Oliver A. I., with M. Phileen Tattersall. *Tibor Polya and the Group of Seven: Hungarian Art in Toronto Collections, 1900–1949*. Toronto: Justina M. Barnicke Gallery, Hart House, University of Toronto, 1989.
Brace, Charles Loring. *Hungary in 1851; with an Experience of the Austrian Police*. New York: Charles Scribner, 1853.
Braham, Randolph L., and Bela Vago, eds. *The Holocaust in Hungary: Forty Years Later*. New York: Social Science Monographs and Columbia University Press, 1985.
Brendel, Alfred. *The Alfred Brendel Collection/Franz Liszt: The Hungarian Rhapsodies*. Vanguard Classics, OVC 4024 (1991).
Brunauer, Dalma H. "A Woman's Self-Liberation: The Story of Margit Kaffka (1880–1918)." *Canadian-American Review of Hungarian Studies* 5, no. 2 (Fall 1978): 31–42.
Burant, Stephen R., ed. *Hungary: A Country Study*. Washington, D.C.: Federal Research Division, Library of Congress, 1990.
Calisher, Hortense. *The New Yorkers*. 1966. New York: Weidenfeld and Nicolson, 1988.

Callinicos, Alex. *Against Postmodernism: A Marxist Critique*. New York: St. Martin's Press, 1990.

Carlson, Lewis H., and George A. Colburne. *In Their Place: White America Defines Her Minorities, 1850–1950*. New York: John Wiley and Sons, Inc., 1972.

Chutkow, Paul. "From the 'Music Box' Emerges the Nazi Demon." *New York Times*, December 24, 1989, H-25.

Codrescu, Andrei. *The Blood Countess*. New York: Simon and Schuster, 1995.

Condon, Christopher. "When Only Despair Makes Sense." *Budapest Week* 3, no. 24 (August 19–25, 1993): 5.

Csécsy, Madeleine. *Études de Linguistique Française et Hongroise: Description et Enseignement*. Nice: Université de Nice/Publications de la Faculté des Lettres, Arts et Sciences Humaines de Nice, 1966.

——— "La Langue Hongroise." In *Lettres Grecques Modernes, Slaves et Hongroises*, 163–81. Annales de la Faculté des Lettres et Sciences Humaines de Nice, no. 41 (1981).

Czigány, Lóránt. *The Oxford History of Hungarian Literature*. Oxford: Oxford University Press, 1984.

Davis, Keith F. *André Kertész: Vintage Photographs*. New York: Edwynn Houk Gallery, 1985.

Dawidowicz, Lucy S. *The War Against the Jews, 1933–1945*. New York: Holt, Rinehart and Winston, 1975.

de Vries, John. "Language and Ethnicity: Canadian Aspects." In Peter S. Li, ed., *Race and Ethnic Relations in Canada*. Toronto: Oxford University Press, 1990.

Deák, István. *Beyond Nationalism: A Social and Political History of the Habsburg Officer Corps, 1848–1918*. New York: Oxford University Press, 1990.

———. *The Lawful Revolution: Louis Kossuth and the Hungarians, 1848–1849*. New York: Columbia University Press, 1979.

Dobszay, László, *A History of Hungarian Music*. Translated by Maria Steiner and Paul Merrick. Budapest: Corvina, 1993.

Dolan, Jay P. *The American Catholic Parish: A History from 1850 to the Present*. Vol. 3. Mahwah, N.J.: Paulist Press, 1987.

Dreisziger, N. F., with M. L. Kovacs, Paul Bödy, and Bennett Kovrig. *Struggle and Hope: The Hungarian-Canadian Experience*. Toronto: McClelland and Stewart Inc., 1982.

Duczyńska, Ilona, and Karl Polanyi. *The Plough and the Pen: Writings from Hungary, 1930–1956*. Toronto: McClelland and Stewart Limited, 1963.

Dwork, Debórah. *Children with a Star: Jewish Youth in Nazi Europe*. New Haven: Yale University Press, 1991.

Eri, Gyongyi, Zsusza Jobbagyi, and others. *A Golden Age: Art and Society in Hungary, 1896–1914*. Budapest and London: Corvina/Barbican Art Gallery/Center for the Fine Arts, Miami, 1989.

Esterházy, Péter. *Bevezetés a szépirodalomba*. Budapest: Magvető, 1986.
——. *The Book of Hrabal*. Translated by Judith Sollosy. London: Quartet Books Limited, 1993.
——. *The Glance of Countess Hahn-Hahn: Down the Danube*. Translated by Richard Aczel. London: Weidenfeld and Nicolson, 1994.
——. *Helping Verbs of the Heart*. Translated by Michael Henry Heim. New York: Grove Weidenfeld, 1991.
——. *The Transporters*. Translated by Ferenc Takacs. In *Hungarian Quartet: Four Contemporary Short Novels*. Budapest: Corvina, 1991.
——. "God's Hat." Translated by Michael Henry Heim. *Partisan Review* 57, no. 3 (Summer 1990): 423–27.
——. "No Title: This Isn't It Either." Translated by Ivan Sanders. In *Nothing Lost: Twenty-five Hungarian Short Stories*. Budapest: Corvina, 1988.
——. "On Laziness." Translated by Zsuzsanna Ozváth and Martha Satz. *Partisan Review* 56, no. 2 (Spring 1989): 247–51.
Eszterhas, Joe, screenwriter. *The Music Box*. With Jessica Lange and Armin Mueller-Stahl. Carolco Home Video.
Faludy, George. *My Happy Days in Hell*. 1962. Translated by Kathleen Szasz. Toronto: Totem Press/Collins Publishers, 1985.
——. *Notes from the Rainforest*. Toronto: Hounslow Press, 1988.
——. *Selected Poems, 1933–80*. Translated by Robin Skelton and others. Athens: University of Georgia Press, 1985.
Fehér, Zsuzsa D., and Gábor Ö. Pogány. *Twentieth Century Hungarian Painting*. Translated by Caroline and István Bodóczky. Budapest: Corvina, 1975.
Fenyvesi, Charles. *When the World Was Whole: Three Centuries of Memories*. Toronto: Key Porter Books Limited, 1990.
Féray, Jean-Claude, and Manfred Herzer. "Homosexual Studies and Politics in the 19th Century: Karl Maria Kertbeny." Translated by Glen W. Peppel. *Journal of Homosexuality* 19, no. 1 (1990): 23–47.
Fermor, Patrick Leigh. *Between the Woods and the Water: On Foot to Constantinople from The Hook of Holland: The Middle Danube to the Iron Gates*. London: Penguin Books, 1988.
Fischer, Tibor. *Under the Frog*. 1992. London: Penguin Books, 1993.
Fishman, Joshua A. *Hungarian Language Maintenance in the United States*. Uralic and Altaic Series, vol. 62. Bloomington: Indiana University Publications, 1966.
Ford, Colin. *André Kertész: An Exhibition of Photographs from the Centre Georges Pompidou, Paris*. London: Arts Council of Great Britain, 1979.
Fordin, Hugh. *Getting to Know Him: A Biography of Oscar Hammerstein II*. New York: Random House, 1977.
Found, William, and Sheila De Cupyer. "Women and Men at York."

Figure 8. North York, Ontario: Office of the Vice President (Institutional Affairs), York University, n.d.

Frazer, Sir James George. *The Golden Bough: A Study in Magic and Religion*. Vol. 12. 1915. London: Macmillan, 1966.

Fügedi, Erik. *Castle and Society in Medieval Hungary (1000–1437)*. Budapest: Akadémiai Kiadó, 1986.

Fülöp, László. *Kaffka Margit*. Budapest: Gondolat, 1987.

Fust, Milan. *The Story of My Wife*. Translated by Ivan Sanders. New York: Vintage Books, 1989.

Gabler, Neal. *An Empire of Their Own: How the Jews Invented Hollywood*. New York: Crown Publishers, 1988.

Gabor, Zsa Zsa, with Wendy Leigh. *One Lifetime Is Not Enough*. 1991. New York: Dell Publishing, 1993.

———, with Gerold Frank. *Zsa Zsa Gabor: My Story*. 1960. Greenwich: Fawcett Publications, 1961.

Garton Ash, Timothy. *The Uses of Adversity: Essays on the Fate of Central Europe*. New York: Random House, 1989.

Gates-Coon, Rebecca. *The Landed Estates of the Esterházy Princes: Hungary during the Reforms of Maria Theresia and Joseph II*. Baltimore: Johns Hopkins University Press, 1994.

Gati, Charles. *Hungary and the Soviet Bloc*. Durham: Duke University Press, 1986.

Gelderman, Carol, ed. *Conversations with Mary McCarthy*. Jackson: University Press of Mississippi, 1991.

Gergely, Emro Joseph. *Hungarian Drama in New York: American Adaptations, 1908–1940*. Philadelphia: University of Pennsylvania Press, 1947.

Gluck, Mary. *Georg Lukács and His Generation, 1900–1918*. Cambridge: Harvard University Press, 1985.

Göncz, Árpád. *Homecoming and Other Stories*. Translated by Katharina M. and Christopher C. Wilson. Budapest: Corvina, 1991.

Gordimer, Nadine. "The Empire of Joseph Roth." *New York Review of Books*, December 5, 1991, 16–21.

Gordon, Mary. *Good Boys and Dead Girls and Other Essays*. New York: Viking Penguin, 1991.

Grosz, Joseph, and W. Arthur Boggs, trans. *Hungarian Anthology: A Collection of Poems*. Second edition. Toronto: Pannonia Books, 1966.

Gyorgyey, Clara. *Ferenc Molnar*. Boston: Twayne Publishers, 1980.

Hamilton, Albert. *The Catholic Journey through Ohio*. St. Meinrad, Ind.: Abbey Press, 1976.

Hanák, Péter, and Joseph Held. "Hungary on a Fixed Course: An Outline of Hungarian History." In *The Columbia History of Eastern Europe in the Twentieth Century*, 164–228. New York: Columbia University Press, 1992.

Handke, Peter. *Across*. Translated by Ralph Manheim. New York: Collier Books/Macmillan Publishing Company, 1987.

Handler, Andrew, ed. *The Holocaust in Hungary: An Anthology of Jewish Response.* Translated by Andrew Handler. University: University of Alabama Press, 1982.

Hankiss, Agnes. *A Hungarian Romance.* Translated by Emma Roper-Evans. London: Readers International, 1992.

Haraszti, Miklós. *The Velvet Prison: Artists under State Socialism.* New York: Basic Books, 1987.

Harmetz, Aljean. *Round Up the Usual Suspects: The Making of Casablanca—Bogart, Bergman, and World War II.* New York: Hyperion, 1992. London: Weidenfeld and Nicolson, 1993.

Havel, Václav. "A Dream for Czechoslovakia." *New York Review of Books,* June 25, 1992, 8–13.

———. *Letters to Olga: June 1979–September 1982.* 1985. Translated by Paul Wilson. New York: Henry Holt and Company, 1989.

Held, Joseph, ed. *The Columbia History of Eastern Europe in the Twentieth Century.* New York: Columbia University Press, 1992.

Herczl, Moshe Y. *Christianity and the Holocaust of Hungarian Jewry.* Translated by Joel Lerner. New York: New York University Press, 1993.

Herzer, Manfred. "Kertbeny and the Nameless Love." *Journal of Homosexuality* 12, no. 1 (Fall 1985): 1–26.

Higham, John. *Strangers in the Land: Patterns of American Nativism, 1860–1925.* New Brunswick, N.J.: Rutgers University Press, 1955.

Hoensch, Jörg K. *A History of Modern Hungary: 1867–1986.* Translated by Kim Traynor. London and New York: Longman, 1988.

Hoffman, Eva. *Lost in Translation: A Life in a New Language.* New York: E. P. Dutton, 1989.

Holub, Kathy. "Ballistic Instinct." *Premiere,* August 1991, 81–82.

Hungarian Quartet: Four Contemporary Short Novels. Géza Ottlik: *Logbook;* Iván Mándy, *Left Behind;* Miklós Mészöly, *Forgiveness;* and Péter Esterházy, *The Transporters.* Budapest: Corvina, 1991.

Hungarian Short Stories: 19th and 20th Centuries. Introduced by István Sőtér. Budapest: Corvina, 1962.

Hutcheon, Linda, and Marion Richmond, eds. *Other Solitudes: Canadian Multicultural Fictions.* Toronto: Oxford University Press, 1990.

Hynes, Michael J. *History of the Diocese of Cleveland: Origin and Growth, 1847–1952.* Cleveland: Diocese of Cleveland, 1953.

Ignotus, Paul. *Hungary.* New York: Praeger Publishers, 1972.

Illés, Lajos, ed. *Nothing's Lost: Twenty-five Hungarian Short Stories.* Budapest: Corvina, 1988.

Illyés, Gyula. *People of the Puszta.* Translated by G. F. Cushing. Budapest: Corvina, 1967.

———. *Petőfi.* Translated by G. F. Cushing. Budapest: Corvina, 1963.

———. *Összegyűjtött versi/Második kötet.* Budapest: Szépirodalmi Könyvkiadó, 1977.

————. *Összegyűjtött versei/Első kötet*. Budapest: Szépirodalmi Könyvkiadó, 1977.

————. *Selected Poems*. Translated by Thomas Kabdebo, Paul Tabori, and others. London: Chatto and Windus, 1971.

Janikovszky, Éva. *Ha én felnőtt volnék*. Budapest: Móra-Háttér Kiadó, 1965.

Janos, Andrew C. *The Politics of Backwardness in Hungary, 1825–1945*. Princeton: Princeton University Press, 1982.

————, and William B. Slottman, eds. *Revolution in Perspective: Essays on the Hungarian Soviet Republic of 1919*. Berkeley: University of California Press, 1971.

Jarmusch, Jim, director and screenwriter. *Stranger Than Paradise*. With Eszter Balint. Vestron Video.

Jászi, Oscar. *The Dissolution of the Habsburg Monarchy*. Chicago: University of Chicago Press, 1929.

Jókai, Mór. *The Golden Age in Transylvania*. Translated by S. L. and A. V. Waite. New York: R. F. Fenno and Company, 1898.

Jones, D. Mervyn. *Five Hungarian Writers: Zrínyi, Mikes, Vörösmarty, Eötvös, Petőfi*. Oxford: Clarendon Press, 1966.

József, Attila. *Összes versei 2./1928–1937*. Budapest: Akadémiai Kiadó, 1984.

————. *Selected Poems and Texts*. Translated by John Bátki. Cheshire: Carcanet Press, 1973.

Juhász, Ferenc. *The Boy Changed into a Stag: Selected Poems, 1949–1967*. Translated by Kenneth McRobbie and Ilona Duczyńska. Toronto and New York: Oxford University Press, 1970.

————. *A Mindenség Szerelme: A Szarvassá változott fiú*. Budapest: Szépirodalmi Könyvkiadó, 1971.

Kadar, Marlene. "Earle Birney's 'Translations' of Attila Jozsef: The Idea of the Midwife-Translator." *Hungarian Studies Review* 15, no. 2 (Fall 1988): 5–11.

————. "Reading Ethnicity." A paper delivered for the Division of Humanities, York University, North York, Ontario, December 15, 1992.

Kaffka, Margit. *The Ant Heap*. Translated by Charlotte Franklin. London: Marion Boyars Publishers, 1995.

————. *Regényi*. Budapest: Szépirodalmi Könyvkiadó, 1968.

Kafka, Franz. *Selected Short Stories of Franz Kafka*. Translated by Willa and Edwin Muir. New York: Random House, 1952.

Kaplan, Alice. *French Lessons: A Memoir*. Chicago: University of Chicago Press, 1993.

Karinthy, Frigyes. *A Journey Round My Skull*. Translated by Vernon Duckworth Barker, 1939. Budapest: Corvina, 1992.

————. *Please Sir!* Translated by István Farkas. Budapest: Corvina, 1968.

Katz, Jonathan. *The Invention of Heterosexuality.* New York: Dutton/Penguin, 1995.

Kertész, André. *Hungarian Memories.* A New York Graphic Society Book. Boston: Little, Brown and Company, 1982.

———. *Kertész on Kertész: A Self-Portrait.* London: British Broadcasting Corporation, 1985.

Kertész, Imre. *Fateless.* Translated by Christopher C. Wilson and Katharina M. Wilson. Evanston: Northwestern University Press, 1992.

Kessler, Jascha, trans. *The Face of Creation: Contemporary Hungarian Poetry.* Minneapolis: Coffee House Press, 1988.

Király, Béla K. *Hungary in the Late Eighteenth Century: The Decline of Enlightened Despotism.* New York: Columbia University Press, 1969.

Kirkconnell, Watson, ed. *The Magyar Muse: An Anthology of Hungarian Poetry, 1400–1932.* Translated by Watson Kirkconnell. Winnipeg: Kanadi Magyar Ujság Press, 1933.

Klaniczay, Tibor, ed. *A History of Hungarian Literature.* Budapest: Corvina, 1982.

———. *Old Hungarian Literary Reader: 11th–18th Centuries.* Translated by Keith Bosley and others. Budapest: Corvina, 1985.

Koestler, Arthur. *The Thirteenth Tribe: The Khazar Empire and Its Heritage.* New York: Random House, 1976.

Konnyu, Leslie. *A History of American Hungarian Literature.* St. Louis: Cooperative of American Hungarian Writers, 1962.

———. *Hungarians in the United States: An Immigration Study.* St. Louis: American Hungarian Review, 1967.

———. "Modern Magyar Literature: A Literary Survey and Anthology of the XXth Century Hungarian Authors." *American Hungarian Review* 2, no. 3–4 (1964): 1–124.

Konrád, George. *The Case Worker.* Translated by Paul Aston. New York: Harcourt Brace Jovanovich, 1974.

———. *A Feast in the Garden.* Translated by Imre Goldstein. New York: Harcourt Brace Jovanovich, 1992.

———. *The Loser.* Translated by Ivan Sanders. New York: Harcourt Brace Jovanovich, 1982.

Kopacsi, Sandor. *"In the Name of the Working Class": The Inside Story of the Hungarian Revolution.* Translated by Daniel and Judy Stoffman. New York: Grove Press, 1987.

Korda, Michael. *Charmed Lives: A Family Romance.* New York: Avon Books, 1981.

Kosztolányi, Dezső. *Anna Édes.* Translated by George Szirtes. Budapest: Corvina, 1991.

———. *Darker Muses: The Poet Nero.* Translated by Clifton P. Fadiman and George Szirtes. Budapest: Corvina, 1990.

———. *Skylark.* Translated by Richard Aczel. Introduction by Péter Esterházy. London: Chatto and Windus, 1993.

Kovács, Ilona, ed. *Search for American Values: Contribution of Hungarian Americans to American Values.* American-Hungarian binational symposium, Budapest, December 1983. Budapest: Országos Széchényi Könyvtár (National Széchényi Library of Hungary), 1990.

Kundera, Milan. "The Tragedy of Central Europe." *New York Review of Books,* April 26, 1984, 33–38.

———. *The Unbearable Lightness of Being.* Translated by Michael Henry Heim. New York: Harper and Row, Publishers, 1984.

Kurit, Laszlo. "Hungarians in the United States." *Hungarian Studies Review* 12, no. 1 (Spring 1985): 43–48.

Lang, George. *The Café des Artistes Cookbook.* New York: Clarkson N. Potter, Inc., 1984.

———. *The Cuisine of Hungary.* New York: Bonanza Books/Crown Publishers Inc., 1971.

Langer, Lawrence L. *Holocaust Testimonies: The Ruins of Memory.* New Haven: Yale University Press, 1991.

Lanouette, William, with Bela Silard. *Genius in the Shadows: A Biography of Leo Szilard.* New York: Charles Scribner's Sons, 1992.

Leader, Ninon A. M. *Hungarian Classical Ballads and Their Folklore.* Cambridge: Cambridge University Press, 1967.

Leith, Linda. *Birds of Passage.* Montreal: NuAge Editions, 1993.

Lengyel, Emil. *Americans from Hungary.* Westport: Greenwood Press, 1948.

Liptak, Dolores. *Immigrants and Their Church.* New York: Macmillan, 1989.

Lisle, Laurie. *Portrait of an Artist: A Biography of Georgia O'Keeffe.* 1980. New York: Washington Square Press, 1981.

Lowell, Robert. *Imitations.* New York: Farrar, Straus and Giroux, 1958.

Lubitsch, Ernst, director. *The Shop Around the Corner.* With James Stewart, Margaret Sullavan. Screenplay by Samson Raphaelson, from a play by Nikolaus Laszlo. MGM/UA Home Video.

Lukacs, John. *Budapest 1900: A Historical Portrait of a City and Its Culture.* New York: Weidenfeld and Nicolson, 1988.

———. *Confessions of an Original Sinner.* New York: Ticknor and Fields, 1990.

———. "The Sound of a Cello." *New Yorker,* December 1, 1986, 43–60.

Macartney, C. A. *Hungary: A Short History.* Edinburgh: University Press, 1962.

———. *Hungary and Her Successors: The Treaty of Trianon and Its Consequences, 1919–1937.* London: Oxford University Press, 1937.

McGilligan, Patrick. *George Cukor: A Biography of the Gentleman Director.* New York: St. Martin's Press, 1991.

Madách, Imre. *The Tragedy of Man.* Translated by Iain MacLeod. Edinburgh: Canongate Press, 1993.

Magris, Claudio. *Danube: A Sentimental Journey from the Source to the Black Sea.* London: Collins Harvill, 1990.

Malcolm, Janet. "A Reporter at Large (Czechoslovakia)/The Window Washer." *New Yorker*, November 19, 1990, 56–106.

Mansbach, S. A., and others. *Standing in the Tempest: Painters of the Hungarian Avant-Garde, 1908–1930*. Santa Barbara: Santa Barbara Museum of Art/MIT Press, 1991.

Marlyn, John. *Putzi, I Love You, You Little Square*. Toronto: Coach House Press, 1981.

———. *Under the Ribs of Death*. 1957. Toronto: McClelland and Stewart Inc., 1990.

Marsden, Philip. "Deep as a River." *Times Literary Supplement*, April 15, 1994, 24.

Meray, Tibor. *Thirteen Days That Shook the Kremlin*. Translated by Howard L. Katzander. New York: Frederick A. Praeger, Publishers, 1959.

Meyers, Jeffrey. *Edmund Wilson: A Biography*. Boston: Houghton Mifflin Company, 1995.

Michener, James A. *The Bridge at Andau*. New York: Random House, 1957.

Mikszáth, Kálmán. *St. Peter's Umbrella*. Translated by B. W. Worswick. Budapest: Corvina, 1962.

Miska, John, ed. *The Sound of Time: Anthology of Canadian-Hungarian Authors*. Lethbridge: Canadian-Hungarian Authors' Association, 1974.

Molnár, Ferenc. *Companion in Exile: Notes for an Autobiography*. Translated by Barrows Mussey. New York: Gaer Associates, 1950.

———. "Liliom." Translated by Benjamin F. Glazer, 1929. In *All the Plays of Molnár*. Garden City: Garden City Publishing Co., 1973.

———. *The Paul Street Boys*. Translated by Louis Rittenberg and George Szirtes. Budapest: Corvina, 1994.

Móricz, Zsigmond. *Seven Pennies and Other Short Stories*. Translated by G. F. Cushing. Budapest: Corvina, 1988.

Musil, Robert. *Young Törless*. Translated by Eithne Wilkins and Ernst Kaiser. New York: Pantheon Books, 1982.

Mydans, Seth. "Confessions of a Star-Struck Looter." *New York Times*, May 6, 1992, A-13.

Nagy, László. *Love of the Scorching Wind: Selected Poems, 1953–1971*. Translated by Tony Connor and Kenneth McRobbie. London: Oxford University Press, 1973.

Nemes Nagy, Ágnes. *Between: Selected Poems of Ágnes Nemes Nagy*. Translated by Hugh Maxton. Budapest: Corvina, 1988.

Nemoianu, Virgil. "Learning over Class: The Case of the Central European Ethos." In *Cultural Participation: Trends Since the Middle Ages*, edited by Ann Rigney and Douwe Fokkema, 79–107. Utrecht Publications in General and Comparative Literature 31. Amsterdam and Philadelphia: John Benjamins Publishing Company, 1993.

Nin, Anaïs. *Delta of Venus: Erotica*. 1977. New York: Pocket Books, 1990.

O'Hara, John. *Collected Stories of John O'Hara.* New York: Random House, 1984.

Ondaatje, Michael. *The English Patient.* New York: Alfred A. Knopf, 1992.

Orth, Samuel P. *Our Foreigners.* New York: United States Publishers Association Inc., for Yale University Press, 1920.

Paglia, Camille. *Sexual Personae: Art and Decadence from Nefertiti to Emily Dickinson.* 1990. New York: Vintage Books, Random House, 1991.

Papp, Susan M. *Hungarian Americans and Their Communities of Cleveland.* Introduction by Joe Eszterhas. Cleveland: Cleveland State University, 1981.

————, ed. "Hungarians in Ontario." *Polyphony: The Bulletin of the Multicultural Society of Ontario* 2, no. 2–3 (1979–80).

Patai, Joseph. *The Middle Gate: A Hungarian Jewish Boyhood.* Translated by Raphael Patai. Philadelphia: Jewish Publication Society, 1994.

Patai, Raphael. *Apprentice in Budapest: Memories of a World That Is No More.* Salt Lake City: University of Utah Press, 1988.

Pearson, Diane. *Csardas.* 1975. Greenwich: Fawcett Crest Book, 1976.

Perényi, Eleanor. *Liszt: The Artist as Romantic Hero.* Boston: Little, Brown and Company, 1974.

————. *More Was Lost.* Boston: Little, Brown and Company, 1946.

Perko, S. J., F. Michael. *Catholic and American.* Huntington, Ind.: Our Sunday Visitor Publishing Division, 1989.

Perlman, Robert. *Bridging Three Worlds: Hungarian-Jewish Americans, 1848–1914.* Amherst: University of Massachusetts Press, 1991.

Petrie, Graham. *History Must Answer to Man: The Contemporary Hungarian Cinema.* Budapest: Corvina, 1978.

Phillips, Sandra S., David Travis, and Weston J. Naef. *André Kertész of Paris and New York.* New York: Thames and Hudson, 1985.

Phillips, William, ed. *Partisan Review.* A Special Issue: Intellectuals and Social Change in Central and Eastern Europe, 59, no. 4 (1992).

Porter, Monica Hulasz. *The Paper Bridge: A Return to Budapest.* London: Quartet Books, 1981.

Puskás, Julianna. *Emigration from Hungary to the United States before 1914.* Budapest: Akadémiai Kiadó, 1975.

————. *From Hungary to the United States (1880–1914).* Budapest: Akadémiai Kiadó, 1982.

————, ed. *Overseas Migration from East-Central and Southeastern Europe, 1880–1940.* Budapest: Akadémiai Kiadó, 1990.

Racz, Barnabas. "The Hungarian Left: Opposition in the Pre-Election Campaign in 1993." *Letters and Papers in Hungarian Studies,* no. 6. Toronto: Hungarian Studies Association of Canada, 1994.

Radnóti, Miklós. *The Complete Poetry.* Translated by Emery George. Ann Arbor: Ardis, 1980.

————. *Foamy Sky: The Major Poems of Miklós Radnóti.* Translated by
 Zsuzsanna Ozsváth and Frederick Turner. Princeton: Princeton
 University Press, 1992.
————. *Under Gemini: A Prose Memoir and Selected Poetry.* Translated
 by Kenneth and Zita McRobbie and Jascha Kessler. Athens: Ohio
 University Press, 1985.
Ray, David, ed. *From the Hungarian Revolution: A Collection of Poems.*
 Ithaca: Cornell University Press, 1966.
Redekop, Ernest. "The Only Political Duty: Margaret Avison's
 Translations of Hungarian Poems." *The Literary Half-Yearly*
 (University of Mysore, India) 13, no. 2 (July 1972): 157–70.
Reményi, Joseph. *Hungarian Writers and Literature: Modern Novelists,
 Critics, and Poets.* New Brunswick: Rutgers University Press, 1964.
————. *Sándor Petőfi: Hungarian Poet (1823–1849).* Washington, D.C.:
 Hungarian Reformed Federation of America, 1953.
Remnick, David. "News in a Dying Language." *New Yorker,* January 10,
 1994, 40–47.
Rich, Frank. "How Far Good Sports Will Go." *New York Times,* March 5,
 1993, B2.
Richler, Mordecai. *Oh Canada, Oh Quebec: Requiem for a Divided
 Country.* Toronto: Penguin Books, 1992.
Rodriguez, Richard. *Days of Obligation: An Argument with My Mexican
 Father.* New York: Viking Press, 1992.
Rose, William Ganson. *Cleveland: The Making of a City.* Cleveland:
 World Publishing Company, 1950.
Roth, Joseph. *The Emperor's Tomb.* Translated by John Hoare.
 Woodstock: Overlook Press, 1984.
————. *The Radetzky March.* Translated by Eva Tucker. Woodstock:
 Overlook Press, 1983.
Saint Elizabeth of Hungary Church. Golden Jubilee Pamphlet.
 Cleveland: Wm. J. Gall Printing Company, 1942.
————. 95th Anniversary Pamphlet. Printer unspecified, 1987.
Sakall, S. Z., actor. *Christmas in Connecticut.* Directed by Peter Godfrey.
 With Barbara Stanwyck, Dennis Morgan. Screenplay by Lionel
 Houser and Adele Commandini. MGM/UA Home Video.
————. *The Story of Cuddles: My Life under the Emperor Francis
 Joseph, Adolf Hitler and the Warner Brothers.* Translated by Paul
 Tabori. London: Cassell & Co. Ltd., 1954.
Sakmyster, Thomas L. *Hungary, the Great Powers, and the Danubian
 Crisis, 1936–1939.* Athens: University of Georgia Press, 1980.
————. *Hungary's Admiral on Horseback: Miklós Horthy, 1918–1944.*
 Boulder and New York: East European Monographs and Columbia
 University Press, 1994.
Salinger, J. D. *Franny and Zooey.* Boston: Little, Brown and Company,
 1961.

Sanders, Ivan. "Budapest Letter: New Themes, New Writers." *New York Times Book Review*, April 10, 1988, 1, 40–42.

Scheer, Steven C. *Kálmán Mikszáth*. Boston: Twayne Publishers, 1977.

Schorske, Carl E. *Fin-de-Siècle Vienna: Politics and Culture*. New York: Alfred A. Knopf, 1980.

Search for American Values: Contribution of Hungarian Americans to American Values. American-Hungarian bi-national symposium, Budapest, December 1983. Budapest: Országos Széchényi Könyvtár, 1990.

Sennett, Richard. *The Frog Who Dared to Croak*. New York: Farrar, Straus and Giroux, 1982.

Simpson, Jeffrey. "Four Lessons Canada Can Learn from What Used To Be Czechoslovakia." *Globe and Mail*, January 12, 1993, A-14.

Sinclair, Jo. *Anna Teller*. 1969. New York: Feminist Press at City University of New York, 1992.

Skvorecky, Josef. *The Swell Season*. Translated by Paul Wilson. New York: Harper Perennial/Harper Collins Publishers, 1991.

Sollors, Werner. *Beyond Ethnicity: Consent and Descent in American Culture*. New York: Oxford University Press, 1986.

Sontag, Susan. *On Photography*. New York: Farrar, Straus and Giroux, 1977.

Spira, György. *The Nationality Issue in the Hungary of 1848–49*. Translated by Zsuzsa Béres and Christopher Sullivan. Budapest: Akadémiai Kiadó, 1992.

Steele, Jessica. *Hungarian Rhapsody*. Toronto: Harlequin Books, 1992.

Stoker, Bram. *Dracula*. 1897. Oxford: Oxford University Press, 1983.

Sugar, Peter F., Péter Hanák, and Tibor Frank, eds. *A History of Hungary*. Bloomington: Indiana University Press, 1990.

Szabados, Bela. *In Light of Chaos*. Saskatoon: Thistledown Press Ltd., 1990.

Szczypiorski, Andrzej. *The Beautiful Mrs. Seidenman*. Translated by Klara Glowczewska. New York: Grove Weidenfeld, 1989. Vintage/Random House, Inc., 1991.

Széplaki, Joseph, ed. *The Hungarians in America, 1583–1974: A Chronology & Fact Book*. Dobbs Ferry, N.Y.: Oceana Publications, Inc., 1975.

Talese, Gay. "Where Are the Italian-American Novelists?" *New York Times Book Review*, March 14, 1993, 1, 23–29.

Tandori, Dezső. *Birds and Other Relations: Selected Poetry of Dezső Tandori*. Translated by Bruce Berlind. Princeton: Princeton University Press, 1986.

Tezla, Albert, ed. *The Hazardous Quest: Hungarian Immigrants in the United States, 1895–1920—A Documentary*. Translated by Albert Tezla. Budapest: Corvina, 1993.

———. *Hungarian Authors: A Bibliographical Handbook*. Cambridge: Harvard University Press, 1970.

Toma, Peter A. *Socialist Authority: The Hungarian Experience.* New
     York: Praeger, 1988.
Translation: The Journal of Literary Translation. A Hungarian Issue.
     Guest editor, Miklós Vajda. Vol. 15 (Fall 1985).
Traubner, Richard. *Operetta: A Theatrical History.* New York: Oxford
     University Press, 1983.
Twenty-two Hungarian Short Stories. Introduction by A. Alvarez.
     Budapest: Corvina, 1967.
"University of Toronto Ethnic Origins." *Globe and Mail,* December 3,
     1992, C-6.
Vajda, Miklos, ed. *Modern Hungarian Poetry.* New York: Columbia
     University Press, 1977.
Van Tassel, David D., and John H. Grabowski, eds. *The Encyclopedia of
     Cleveland History.* Bloomington: Indiana University Press, 1987.
Vardy, Steven Bela. *Clio's Art in Hungary and in Hungarian-America.*
     Boulder and New York: East European Monographs and Columbia
     University Press, 1985.
———. *The Hungarian Americans.* Boston: Twayne Publishers, 1985.
———. "The Hungarian Community of Cleveland." *Hungarian Studies
     Review* 8, no. 1 (Spring 1981): 137–43.
———. "Hungarian Studies at American and Canadian Universities." In
     Canadian-American Review of Hungarian Studies 2, no. 2 (Fall
     1975): 91–121.
———. *Modern Hungarian Historiography.* Boulder and New York: East
     European Quarterly and Columbia University Press, 1976.
Varnai, Paul, ed. *Hungarian Short Stories.* Toronto: Exile Editions, 1983.
Vizinczey, Stephen. *In Praise of Older Women.* 1965. Chicago: University
     of Chicago Press, 1990.
———. *Truth and Lies in Literature: Essays and Reviews.* 1986.
     Chicago: University of Chicago Press, 1988.
von Rezzori, Gregor. *Memoirs of an Anti-Semite: A Novel in Five Stories.*
     1979. Translated by Joachim Neugroschel. New York: Penguin Books,
     1982.
Wachtel, Eleanor. *Writers & Company.* Toronto: Alfred A. Knopf Canada,
     1993.
Walker, Alan. *Franz Liszt: The Virtuoso Years, 1811–1847.* Vol. 1. Revised
     edition. Ithaca: Cornell University Press, 1987.
———. *Franz Liszt: The Weimar Years, 1848–1861.* Vol. 2. Ithaca:
     Cornell University Press, 1989.
Weöres, Sandor. *Eternal Moment: Selected Poems.* Translated by Alan
     Dixon and others. London: Anvil Press Poetry, 1988.
Wilde, Oscar, and others. *Teleny.* London: GMP Publishers, 1986.
Wilder, Billy, and Charles Brackett, screenwriters. *Midnight.* With
     Claudette Colbert, Don Ameche, and John Barrymore. MCA
     Universal Home Video.

Wilson, Edmund. *Letters on Literature and Politics: 1912–1972.* New York: Farrar, Straus and Giroux, 1977.

————. *The Sixties: The Last Journal, 1960–1972.* New York: Farrar, Straus and Giroux, 1993.

————. *Upstate: Records and Recollections of Northern New York.* New York: Farrar, Straus and Giroux, 1971.

Yahil, Leni. *The Holocaust: The Fate of European Jewry, 1932–1945.* Translated by Ina Friedman and Haya Galai. New York: Oxford University Press, 1990.

Zalan, Magda. *Stubborn People.* Toronto: Canadian Stage and Arts Publications, 1985.

Zinner, Paul E. *Revolution in Hungary.* New York: Columbia University Press, 1962.

Credits

AVISON Passages reprinted from Margaret Avison's *Selected Poems*, copyright Margaret Avison 1991, by permission of Oxford University Press Canada. ESTERHÁZY Passages from *The Glance of Countess Hahn-Hahn*, translated by Richard Aczel, are courtesy of Weidenfeld and Nicolson Ltd.; "God's Hat" by Péter Esterházy, translated by Michael Henry Heim, first appeared in *Partisan Review*, vol. 57, no. 3, 1990; passages from *Helping Verbs of the Heart*, translated by Michael Henry Heim, are used by permission of Grove/Atlantic Inc.; passages from *The Transporters*, translated by Ferenc Takacs, are used by permission of Corvina Könyvkiadó. MARLYN from *Under the Ribs of Death* by John Marlyn, used by permission of the Canadian Publishers, McClelland and Stewart. O'HARA from *Collected Stories of John O'Hara* by John O'Hara. Reprinted by permission of Random House Inc. PAPP Passages from Joe Eszterhas's introduction to Susan Papp's *Hungarian Americans and their Communities of Cleveland* are used by permission of Cleveland State University/Office of International Programs. WILSON Excerpts from *Upstate: Records and Recollections of Northern New York* by Edmund Wilson. Copyright 1971 by Edmund Wilson. Reprinted by permission of Farrar, Straus and Giroux, Inc.

Many of the essays in this book appeared in various journals, sometimes in different versions, and I wish to acknowledge these publications. "Play Time" was published in *Dalhousie Review*," vol. 71, no. 4, Winter 1991/92. "'What the Moment Told Me': The Photographs of André Kertész" appeared in *Hungarian Studies Review*, vol. 21, nos. 1–2, 1994. "The Archives of St. Elizabeth of Hungary" was published in *Ethnic Forum*, vol. 13, no. 1, 1993. "The Empty Box" was published in *Studies in Popular Culture*, vol. 15, no. 1, 1992. "Visiting Pannonia" appeared in another version in *The Idler*, no. 34, 1991. "Towards a Course on Central European Literature in Translation" appeared in *Canadian Review of Comparative Literature*, vol. 23, no. 1, 1996. "Introducing Péter Esterházy" appeared in a shorter version in *Aloud*, vol. 1, no. 1, 1991. "The Poet as Translator: Margaret Avison's 'Hungarian Snap'" was published in *Canadian Literature*, no. 135, 1992. "Hungarian Voices, Summer 1993" is forthcoming in a shorter version in the *Midwest Quarterly*. "Without Words: Hungarians in North American Fiction" appeared in *Centennial Review*, vol. 39, no. 1, Winter 1995.

Index

Library of Congress Cataloging-in-Publication Data

Teleky, Richard, 1946–

Hungarian rhapsodies : essays on ethnicity, identity, and culture / Richard Teleky.

p. cm.

Includes bibliographical references and index.

ISBN 0-295-97582-2 (alk. paper). — ISBN 0-295-97606-3 (pbk. : alk. paper)

1. Hungary—Civilization. 2. Hungarians—Foreign countries—Ethnic identity. 3. Hungarian Americans—History. I. Title.

DB920.5.T45   1997

943.9—dc21   97-6355

                                                              CIP

Canadian Cataloguing in Publication Data

Teleky, Richard, 1946–

Hungarian rhapsodies

Includes bibliographical references and index.

ISBN 0-7748-0623-0 (bound)—ISBN 0-7748-0624-9 (pbk.)

1. Hungarian Americans—Ethnic identity. 2. Hungarians—United States. 3. Ethnicity—United States. 4. Hungary—Social life and customs. I. Title.

E184.H95T44 1997   305.89'4511073   C97-910189-1